Sex

and

The Supernatural

The Paranormal, Sexuality and The Erotic Imagination

Drew Wynn

A catalogue record for this book is available from the National Library of Australia

X X X
PGR

Psychosexuality Series
Volume 1, 2009
Second Edition 2021
Ganieda Press
Perth, Australia

Third Edition
ISBN-13: 978-1-923174-33-7

Linellen Press
265 Boomerang Road
Oldbury, Western Australia
www.linellenpress.com.au

This book is not the supernatural of otherworldly ghouls, vampires, incubi and succubi, the figures that feature so strongly in fairytales, horror stories and nightmares. Rather it is the supernatural that exists on the edge of our daily reality beyond a very thin veil. It is the supernatural that of modern times we have called the paranormal and sanitised with science and rational explanation.

Yet this very same supernatural remains alive and well, living at the edge of our consciousness and accessible spontaneously in dream and fantasy; but more actively by many methods that produce what are now commonly called 'altered states of consciousness'. At this level, the vampire could be a colleague or acquaintance who psychically bleeds you or the succubus, the wife of your best friend who flirts with you at the dinner table fuelled by the vine, and then inhabits your dream.

This understanding of the supernatural connects it back to our daily reality and maybe offers metaphoric or symbolic explanations that better explain what is happening in many experiences than any rational understanding. This understanding may explain, but it rarely disarms the experience of its emotional charm—or fear.

Sexuality is a time-honoured pathway to such expanded states of consciousness and is used as the vehicle into the supernatural in the stories. In our Western culture, much of this sexual wisdom has been lost, yet it has not disappeared and can arise under the right circumstances when encouraged – though frequently both spontaneously and unbidden.

***

Drew Wynn has spent his life preoccupied with sex, for which he makes absolutely no apology.

In this book, Drew distils his ideas and feelings regarding sexuality and its relationship to varied states of consciousness in a creative and fictional manner, using an abundance of short stories embedded within comments and discussion. He anticipates this work will spawn a lineage of writing and other creative output in this exciting field.

Warning!

This book contains material of a sexually-explicit nature.
Some readers may find this offensive.

Contents

Preface

Sex and the Supernatural was written in 2009 in the manner described in the ensuing *Introduction,* which has not been revised in this 2021 Edition. Thus, it stands as a testament to my insights over a decade ago when the stories were first written.

Nor have the stories themselves been edited. What has changed is that I have removed the various commentaries of a psychological and spiritual nature that linked the various batches of stories as themes. Instead, I have allowed the stories to kind of run into each other in a progressive manner so as to provide a more psychic impact of increasing depth without recourse to explanation and interpretation. Also, I deemed that these commentaries were more appropriately written about in the accompanying Volume 2 work, *The Porn User's Guide to Enlightenment,* so they would be a little repetitive here.

Instead, I have left in the rather lengthy *Introduction* for those of a more psychological persuasion, which touches on some history and my own personal worldview. I have continued this introductory theme in the closing *Epilogue.* These two sections are to provide a more detailed context for the stories and a possible framework in which to understand them.

But both the *Introduction* and the *Epilogue* can be safely bypassed, and the stories engaged raw; which, indeed, they are. In some ways, if they are to be read at all, they can wait until the stories have been engaged. Stripped of finesse, the stories are designed to provide a more guttural response and have a more direct sexual impact; that is, dealing with the content of the tales on their own terms.

The stories do not demand to be read in any particular order. Although they are fluid and appear random there is, however, a deeper progression in theme. So, reading them in order may be the way to go … particularly if the *Introduction* and the *Epilogue* are going to be read, as well.

Drew Wynn, March 2021

Introduction

The decision to write this book was made before I immersed myself too much in the field of paranormality and its relationship to fields such as mental health and spirituality. As the whole area of psychosexuality was uppermost in my mind at the time of writing, I decided to use sexuality as the connecting theme to the paranormal, then to radiate out and include the other relevant fields. Indeed, I felt that the nexus of sex and the paranormal might help to elucidate and further define these connections and relationships through the medium of creativity. The connections and relationships will be inherently rather than explicitly explored throughout the book within the stories.

What exactly is that paranormal field, you may ask? It is the field of parapsychology, the paranormal and the supernatural; overlapping terms that add to the confusion. A little definition would help: Supernatural is literally that which is beyond the natural, which I interpret as beyond our mundane physical or material reality. Paranormal experiences parallel this apparently normal or consensus day-to-day reality and are, for all intents and purposes, synonymous with supernatural ones. Maybe this is because the term supernatural has become somewhat prejudiced and debased, so it is feasible that the word paranormal removes the emotional investment and history that the term supernatural attracts. Parapsychology is the psychological study of the supernatural or paranormal. (Please note, these are my definitions, but will serve to orientate you through this book.)

What are the characteristics of this field?

In our more immediate vicinity these include such domains as telepathy, psychokinesis (or telekinesis) and psychometry. You may care to punch these into Google and check out the definitions in Wikipedia rather than rely on any I may give, as these definitions will then be a little more precise and academic; however, I hope they will be adequately and creatively illustrated in the stories that follow. Then we move into more remote areas of personal experience such as Out of the Body and Near Death Experiences (OBE and NDE respectively). Overlapping modern psychiatry are the more ancient concepts of soul loss and spirit possession, which then create the spiritual enigmas of past-life experience, karma, and reincarnation.

This is truly a vast field. I thought my exposure to it had been quite limited, but recently I sat down and went back through my life to see how many such experiences I could recount. I was surprised – I counted seventeen and then, as a sort of tease, I had another one the very next day! I looked back at these experiences: Had I forgotten I had experienced so many, or did they lend themselves to such a forgetting? You would expect such experiences to be shocking and frightening, but, in general, that was not how I experienced them at all. Some deep questions started arising in my mind.

A few words about the evolution of this work may be useful, as well as putting into context some of the comments made immediately above.

I had recently completed a draft of a book called *The Porn User's Guide to Enlightenment,* which is an attempt to explore the modern pornographic phenomenon from a personal, cultural and spiritual perspective; leading to the conclusion that sexuality is still poorly integrated in Western culture. When I completed the book, I was quite excited about continuing the theme of sexuality and its relationship to spirituality, and how it may impact on our current medical, psychological, philosophical, psychiatric, and religious models. As a sort of pastime, I started writing some fictional short stories that had a sexual and sometimes pornographic theme, with the common feature that all had a parapsychological twist in the tale. An additional feature is that the stories often had a medical, mental health or healing orientation – hardly surprising, really, given my background – plus the inevitable bit of occult autobiography (meaning hidden, but not a bad pun) scattered throughout and embedded within, then elaborated by the creative process into fiction.

As I did this, the stories shaped themselves into a study of the field from the creative and narrative perspective. This caused me to reflect on my own paranormal experience and, as *The Porn User's Guide to Enlightenment* had been planned as the first in an anticipated series called *Psychosexuality,* I decided to make this collection of stories the second in the series and to entitle it *Sex and the Supernatural,* as a way of embracing the two major themes in the book.

At least, that was the plan when I started out! After I had written about half of the anticipated number, I thought it was about time to pull the stories into some sort of shape. The themes, sex and the paranormal, or supernatural (terms I will be using relatively synonymously, as indicated earlier), are fairly blatant and define the nature and tone of the book. By shape, I mean putting the book itself into a context that links directly to *The Porn User's Guide to Enlightenment,* as well as connecting to future anticipated works. I set time aside to write a reasonably detailed introduction to achieve this aim and as a way of providing some initial commentary on the stories.

Ultimately, I decided that *Sex and the Supernatural* would, for many varied reasons, serve as the best introduction to the anticipated Psychosexuality Series. This choice was because it contains most, if not all of the themes that the Psychosexuality Series will explore, in at least an embryonic form. In their creative expression, the stories contain the raw material of the whole series. Although sexuality and the paranormal remain the constant themes of each and every story in *Sex and the Supernatural,* many of them delve into other topics, such as healing, mental health, magic and religion, and their association with sexuality that demand further creative, imaginative and intellectual exploration, which the series as a whole will do.

In many ways I feel inadequate writing about the paranormal at all. I have a colleague, who has extensive personal and professional interest in the field; my appreciation of it pales in comparison to his. Yet, when I look back at my actual experience, it has been reasonably extensive. Although the impetus for this work is the ongoing theme of sexuality (a term that I broaden to psychosexuality to be inclusive of sexuality and other related fields) my own paranormal experiences have been directly associated with sexual ones in a minority of occasions; although the remainder has been strong with emotional and energetic states that could easily be seen as sexual, and usually occurred around intense sexual experiences or relationships. As a consequence, I have taken some of these paranormal experiences directly into my ongoing sexual encounters and have found that, directly or indirectly, the frequency of further such experiences has increased. Indeed, of late, these encounters have established that those paranormal experiences portray an ever-present reality, one that supersedes the everyday one and seems ever-present. Mystical you may think? Possibly, but if so, it is a path that has been trod before. Magical? Inasmuch as I am actively involved in the process, yes.

As, obviously, all this may lead me into more research and study of the paranormal, I felt it would be good to finish the stories and a commentary about them without too much of this further more academic influence, so that they would remain paranormal rather than parapsychological. As you will discover, I have a lot of difficulties with the term 'psychological'. Maybe this is all best illustrated by an account of my own personal experience of these fields of study.

I have spent over thirty years in the fields of mental health, psychiatry, psychoanalysis, and psychotherapy. Initially, this was from a medical background, but I found psychiatry not to my liking for reasons it took me many years to understand. Instead, I was drawn to the more psychodynamic aspects of psychiatry. In broad terms, psychiatry can be considered either organic or dynamic. Organic is the more mechanistic view that equates the brain with the mind and has pharmaceutical chemicals as a significant part of its armoury. The dynamic branch stems essentially from Freud and is more inclined to a more differentiated view of the mind and therapeutic intervention, with closer relationships to the therapeutic arm of psychology.

Whilst the dynamic aspect of psychiatry held appeal for me, it was little in evidence in my postgraduate training, so I opted to leave the field and pursue these aspects elsewhere whilst continuing a therapeutic practice. I had found a tradition, called psychoanalysis, or more broadly 'depth psychology' (not to be confused with clinical, research, or academic psychology) stemming from Freud and involving giants in the field such as Jung and Reich, both psychiatrists and originally psychoanalysts in the Freudian tradition, although each was to go his own way.

Jung had a significant footing in the supernatural. His doctorate thesis was about the paranormal abilities of a family member. One of his early works, *The Seven Sermons to the Dead*, is distinctly parapsychological. Although his approach to the developing field of psychology (and called Analytical Psychology) has a distinctly rational flavour, possibly to further its mainstream acceptance, his own background and personal experience is both mystically and paranormally informed to a great extent and is the basis of his so-called empirical psychology. This is a fact commonly minimised or ignored. I was drawn to him for obvious reasons.

At a personal level, Jung led a varied sexual existence, the details of which I will not go into here, but it certainly didn't conform to the public image of the stable Swiss family man with five children. As a consequence, in my opinion, sexuality in Jung's Analytical Psychology has suffered from the same editing that has afflicted the paranormal field and has subsequently been either excluded from his work or reinterpreted, aided and abetted by his acolytes. Jung makes little reference to sexuality in his psychology (his writings extend to well over twenty volumes), yet it deeply informed his own experiences, which were, on occasion, considered close to being psychotic. Reich, by contrast, explored sexuality in considerable detail but was dismissive of the spiritual realms in very strong terms. His latter life was increasingly marked by speculative views and also a question mark about his own sanity. His work, in my opinion, has yet to be fully appreciated beyond these facts.

Although these disciplines were to continue to maintain my attention and satisfy my professional proclivities, there remained a division within me between my public and professional persona and the experiences of myself that I would classify as paranormal, along with a full integration of my sexuality into my day-to-day reality. *The Porn User's Guide to Enlightenment* is an attempt, in many ways, to complete a reunification of the sexual within myself, but is also representative of Western culture and its position with respect to sexuality. This present work aims further at the paranormal and mystical reunification. I have found that conventional religious systems do not satisfy such explorations; this is mainly because the concept of the Soul appears to be more embedded in experiences that conventional religion would judge negatively, such as sex and the supernatural, up to them belonging in the domain of the devil. Does all this make me unstable, an incipient psychotic or devil-worshipper? I don't believe so, and I think we need to get to a deeper appreciation of these issues, and this is precisely what the Psychosexuality Series intends to do.

Over the last one hundred years this overall situation has become worse, not better, which is why we are facing a cultural and spiritual crisis at many levels. Beginning with Freud, the more emotionally driven aspects of mental experience were labelled as *hysteria* and collectively as *neurotic*, the source of which was the *unconscious*. As we will see, this is basically an acceptable model rather than a provable theory; it certainly doesn't warrant the pseudoscientific status it has attained. Yet it was more acceptable than the alternatives and has become a pillar of the psychiatric model, mainly because of its rational basis and mechanistic outlook. Science was (and still is) very scared of the dominance of religion creeping in through the back door and, I suspect, this is the main reason Freud holds such sway; whereas Jung and Reich, who both went significantly further in their spiritual and sexual explorations respectively, do not.

We will leave the analysis of the depth psychologies there and I will leave it to the interested reader to explore the subject further. (There will be an expansion of some of the issues raised in the Epilogue.) Instead, I want to highlight some of the trends that stand behind our modern disciplines and the flaws they contain. Modern psychiatry and psychology have become further mechanised, rational and academic: As apparent sciences of the soul (psyche = soul) they fall very short and effectively exclude it altogether. Are we then surprised that we are spiritually bereft when any disturbance of the mind is not related to suffering of the soul?

My understanding and conclusion is that we need to explore recent history more deeply, beginning with the negation of other models of mental disturbance. What encourages me to undertake such an exploration is that we are now moving into a post-modern era. Pure science is no longer a valid tool of inquiry when it extends beyond areas of its expertise. At the turn of the last century, a little over one hundred years ago, the scientific method was seen to be the answer to all our ills. Freud used such a model to include areas of the mind probably outside of its domain and to provide a rational, mechanistic and scientific framework for the workings of the mind that still holds sway; in spite of its culturally influenced beginnings and continuing tenuous grip on that status.

Psychiatry has continued along this scientific path, ably supported by the pharmaceutical industry and, in spite of the resurgence of the neuroscientific disciplines, has made no significant contribution to the study or nature of the mind in my time. In fact, it does the study of the mind a disfavour by contracting its existence to the brain, a position that philosophy has not held with any seriousness for a significant period. Psychology has a broader basis with the study and therapeutic application of its tenets to human behaviour, but suffers from the same difficulties as psychiatry, whilst maintaining its position as the poorer relation.

In my opinion, psychiatry is over-inclusive, and we need to embrace the post-modern spirit and acknowledge that the mind is more than the brain, as well as admit other disciplines in this examination. In the nineteenth century, such a clear demarcation of disciplines and their boundaries was not the case, and cross-fertilisation was significant. It was not uncommon to find persons of note with qualifications from several fields: scientific, artistic and even religious. The post-modern era marks the breakdown of this modern isolated position of most disciplines and explorers are once again moving across disciplines in the examination of areas that demand it, and this is certainly the case with the mind.

Beginning with Mesmer in the early nineteenth century, extending through the so-called discovery of hypnosis and ending with Charcot (before Freud hijacked his discoveries into his theory of the 'unconscious') there was a veritable hot-bed of inquiry, which included matters paranormal and supernatural in no small measure. This was at a time when religion was losing its control over the Western mind and science was gaining it. Before science excluded the notion of the soul, which Western religion had already lost touch with, paranormal experience was included, studied and validated. To some it was a matter of circumstance that the Freudian position won the day when pitted against more spiritualistic models. These models and trends becoming formalised as *Spiritualism* and seen as a religion that was trying to get into science via the back door – which it was promptly shown again – did not help their acceptance in the mainstream; no wonder Freud was accepted. We see these same forces behind the current conflict between the Theory of Evolution (Darwin) and the concept of Intelligent Design (Creationism).

Yet if you read accounts of that period of time, the amount of material and its study beggars belief. The paradox about this I have mentioned earlier; that my appreciation of such paranormal experiences does not create the sort of excitement you might anticipate. I wonder why this is. Maybe we have become so insulated in our day-to-day reality that we cannot connect emotionally with these experiences. Or, maybe they are the norm and don't inherently excite the fear, surprise or shock that we might predict or expect? Or, is that their nature ... to be simply enigmatic on the fringes of our everyday reality, taunting us with their presence in the manner of the trickster?

I am now inclined to a wider perspective. As I have come to terms with my professional past and reintegrated matters sexual and paranormal into my daily life, I have come to see that these dimensions, known and unknown, serve to define our modern concept of the soul and its – our – relationship to the world of spirit. The conclusions regarding this I will leave for the present, as the further writing of the stories may reveal still more to me in this regard. But, maybe as a teaser, I would invite you to read these stories with the possibility that time and space as we currently understand them may not be our final model of reality. Indeed, it may be that by appreciating time and space differently – and beyond Einstein's currently accepted modification – that we may be able to fully relate to and appreciate what we currently call paranormal. Talking of Einstein, we also have his elegant and enigmatic equation: $e = mc2$. This illustrates the essential relationship between energy (e) and mass (m), held together by light (c) itself, which I invite you to look at as a metaphor rather than literally and rationally. If we then see his theory of relativity not as a final model but as a step into a multidimensional model, maybe we can see the tentative beginnings of some of the world of science connecting back to the world of spirit. It is no coincidence that Einstein came to be seen as more of a mystic as he aged.

A few words about the sexual content of these stories: I have chosen – deliberately – to continue in the narrative style of the fictional component in *The Porn User's Guide to Enlightenment*. Some of the stories have an open and even flagrant description of sexuality, extending into combinations and acts that some would consider pornographic, at least, and perverted, at worst. Others will have minimal sexual expression, but it is implied or inferred within the narrative itself. In this, they are sometimes based directly or indirectly on personal experience, as earlier described, although extending into the psychosexual imagination well beyond this. In general, what I am trying to do is to continue the theme by displaying sexuality as rich and varied, though at variance with conventional standards. This is to further demonstrate that some of our restrictions to sexual expression, particularly the self-imposed ones, also restrict our contact with other realms of reality.

Maybe this is the function of the restrictions, imposed or otherwise, to protect us from these realities and the perceived threat to an ordered society; plus or minus our individual sanity. Yet this is paradoxical, because we also exclude ourselves from a full appreciation of what our individual existence may portend, what our soul might be and even up to an appreciation of fate or destiny. This may also deny us an authentic relationship to spirit that extends beyond the routine religious or merely intellectual. If that is the case, then science and culture have continued the function of religion more than adequately. It is for these reasons, as well as the enjoyment of the narrative, that I have chosen a wide, expansive and expressive style, even if a little controversial.

To take a narrative approach that, in many ways, is continuous with the pornographic phenomenon is quite deliberate. Firstly, it places the sexual content of the book very much in the modern idiom. Secondly, it is an attempt to examine modern sexuality – and pornography as an expression of it – in a context for further exploration and a more complete integration within modern society. These points set the agenda for the entire anticipated Psychosexuality Series.

Beyond this, there is one significant but important point I wish to raise and stress with respect to pornography and erotic creativity. The greatest danger of erotic art – I will take this term as broad and inclusive of pornography, even if somewhat controversially – is that it remains objective and lends itself to addiction and even perversion, if there is no avenue for internalisation and subjectivity. This more inner dimension is the path for integration and, ultimately, a creative and spiritual existence, which sexual images can either take us away from or guide us toward. Obviously, the latter is the intent here and elsewhere and this is achieved by encouraging within the narrative inner reflection and emotional connection (plus liberal humour).

As I have stated, my appreciation of the paranormal beyond the experiential is not particularly significant, except where it intersects with my own professional interests; this point of intersection is expanding however. That being the case, how much do these stories actually reflect my own personal experience? Of course, there is some material therein, but it is creatively engaged and often the trigger to a broader fictional tale. This personal material also forms the minority of content as most stories are entirely fictional and a product of my imagination, although sometimes reflecting my experience elsewhere. Maybe I should say *the* imagination because, it seems to me, that the ideas and flow of the tales often seem to come from regions beyond; in other words, they may originate from the very world that the paranormal describes and the heightened sexual seeks to access.

A comment about the actual nature of the paranormal content is relevant here. Ghosts, ghouls, incubi and succubi, as well as all manner of witches and warlocks, people the supernatural in the popular imagination. The paradoxical relationship between these beings and the Church, most particularly the satanic aspects of it, is a further significant theme. My approach is somewhat different: As with the sexual content the figures in the stories and religious themes will have a more modern relevance and for similar reasons. There is a significant reflection on matters religious, as this is almost a given for reasons that will be elaborated on in the stories. The figures will, however, be more restricted to modern images of the same and in contexts that many of us may readily relate to in a more day-to-day manner.

The various stories are a response to any inspiration, of or an idea that took my fancy, and then written in a creative manner. There is no attempt to explore the various documented paranormal categories, some of which were outlined earlier and as parapsychology might attempt to do. Sometimes, there is more than one paranormal feature in a story, and some stories repeat a particular feature, past lives being but one example. What this indicates to me and as confirmed by my personal experience, is that paranormal experience seems to resist such categorisation and may even be frightened away: It is a known feature of paranormal experience that it seemingly diminishes in the laboratory situation.

Whilst I have used sexuality as the major connecting theme, it was not difficult to link this creatively with paranormal experience. If this doesn't occur that frequently in my personal sexual experience, unless actively engaged, it is not difficult to connect them imaginatively. And, as I see the imagination to be the voice of the soul, it is maybe in this domain that these forces unite; or maybe the reverse, they are primarily united and it is only our rational minds that separate them.

This raises some interesting issues that the stories engage on occasion, which I think is somewhat inevitable, as they also come from a common source; being ritual, magic and religion, as well as birth and death. When I started to reflect on this, the creative flow dried up for a period. At first, this disappointed me as I had anticipated that the pattern and style of the initial sections would continue until I had completed the book. I was wrong; the issue of ritual, magic and religion needed a more intense exploration within the nexus of sexuality and paranormality.

As to the stories: As stated, they were not created around any particular structure, such as paranormal categorisation or sexual orientation, but inclined more toward categories such as magic, religion, medicine, etc. They are not presented in the order they were written, but mixed to make a composition rather as a musician would in assembling a compact disc; so, they flow somewhat irrationally, yet creatively through the proposed territory. There is also an interesting emotional flow that occurs as a result of this process, such that intermingling feelings of tragedy, humour, inspiration and intellectual stimulation will arise in the reader. Oh yes, of course your loins may be stirred! I didn't forget the connection of the sexual content with *The Porn User's Guide to Enlightenment,* so there is a strong – some would say flagrant – erotic component in a number of the stories, although more subtle in others.

A final word on the vexed issue of gender and its relationship to sexuality, as well as one purpose of this work, would be appropriate before you begin:

I have also mixed up first and third person as well as past and present tenses to provide differing perspectives on similar material but also to partially deflect the kind of concerns that come up with issues of gender. The gender issue is not only unavoidable; it is an inherent part of the territory we are exploring and a challenge to be faced, so here are some maps to take with you on the journey. It is important to distinguish between sexual and gender identity: the former is inevitably dualistic, the latter paradoxical.

Sexual identity I refer to as male and female, being how we are identified in our day-to-day existence, even though there may be more than a little confusion at this level on occasion! Male and female also refer to not only much of the animal kingdom but plants as well; in the human sphere, these terms can be defined as man and woman. So, all men are male, but not all males are men! Given that we are dealing exclusively with the human sphere here, they may be used synonymously.

Gender identity is a different matter and refers to the pure – archetypal – principles of masculinity and femininity. In this definition, men and women have both masculine and feminine features; try as hard as a football player might do to convince you otherwise! We will be unravelling this paradoxical conundrum to a significant extent in this work, although it is even more predominant in *The Porn User's Guide to Enlightenment*.

This whole issue is so significant I consider it to be the dominant one of our time. The degree to which we can consciously and creatively come to terms with it is the degree to which we will be able to negotiate many of the significant global issues that face us.

With these initial insights, sit back and enjoy!

Marketplace

Matt knew now it was in the eyes.

On the previous two occasions his gaze had been interrupted when his partner had become aware of what was happening. This time he didn't let it get that far.

The first time had been in a crowded market. He was waiting at a designated place for his girlfriend and she was late – she usually was. He leant against a wall and idly watched the throngs of people passing up and down the aisle in front of him, with their varied interest in the little stalls that lined the walls of this large barn-like building. He felt himself to be separate from the crowd, somehow hovering above it and the tardiness of his girlfriend did not irritate him, as it customarily would.

Then he felt a pair of eyes on him. Before he looked to the source, he considered it strange that he could actually 'feel' this without seeing the onlooker. She was the store holder immediately to his right some five yards or so distant. She had long dark hair, which matched her gypsy-like garb and general demeanour. Matt noticed this almost on the periphery of his vision because he immediately engaged her eyes: they smiled a deep smile that touched the very core of his being and he felt himself respond. There was a sexual flavour to this, yes, but it went beyond that. He knew without a doubt that if they were lovers, it would be a reflection of the intensity and passion he could already feel and maybe take it to deeper or higher levels beyond his present experience. He felt a smile cross his lips in response to hers and then a shock as he now felt another's gaze upon him. He looked to his left and saw his girlfriend's eyes watching him with contempt, even hatred. It was one of those culminating moments when he knew the relationship was over and the incident would never be discussed.

It was many years before it happened again. This time he was walking with his wife along a road outside another market. It was raining lightly, and 'she' was standing to his left, waiting for the automatic teller machine on the wall to his right. She was dark as well, but had an air of sophistication about her that radiated through the extensive clothing that warded off the inclement weather. The gaze was the same and the smile followed as they locked eyes, whilst he continued walking by and beyond. This wife also saw the interaction, but her response was of insecurity, wondering whether she was a lover, present or past. She was reassured.

Matt and his wife were in a supermarket on this third occasion. His wife walked down an aisle and asked him to retrieve another shopping basket. On his way back to the entrance she came in and passed him; she was blonde this time, but with the same eyes and challenging sexuality. Except for a brief mutual smile, he decided not to engage for any length of time and, retrieving the basket, returned to his wife without checking where the woman had gone. On the way home, Matt told his wife what had happened, and she was only mildly amused. Maybe she was feeling more secure now.

But Matt was not: he was unsettled. It was always a marketplace and always in the company of his partner ... always the instantaneousness of the eye engagement and always the intense sexual undercurrent, which amounted to a 'knowingness'. Matt guessed by the progression that he was becoming more comfortable with his – the – feminine and his own sexuality, but there were some other unsettling features. He had felt the gaze on the first occasion before he looked at her, and by the third occasion, he knew it was going to happen just before they saw each other. There was a sense in all of them, a timelessness, and entering a reality that somehow superseded the mundane one of the marketplace and relationship: maybe that was why the setting was common to all of these incidents, he thought.

Greater than all of this was the knowingness that stemmed from the sexual energy, which somehow permeated the incidents. It was associated with unusual aspects to sensation; changes in time, and a realisation of what he considered a parallel reality that permeated the mundane. Matt then surmised that this reality was ever-present and that sexual energy was a source, even a pathway into this, but one intermingled with other perspectives that any rational and sane man would dismiss.

Matt decided not to dismiss these experiences. He felt they were a doorway to a deeper understanding of himself: A connection to his soul, maybe?

Siesta

Tim was seated cross-legged on the rug when he saw the snake writhe in their direction. He felt no concern; instead, all seemed still and peaceful. He looked to his right where Jean was stretched out on her back, quite naked, with her gorgeous breasts momentarily tempting him to play with and suck them. But she was asleep and he felt the need to assess the situation before deciding whether to wake her.

They had made love with a quiet intensity under the midday sun. Although autumn, the sun was strong and warming to their naked bodies. This was a practised tryst. Both had left marriages and found each other in a romantic haze that overshadowed their previous relationships, yet left their ex-partners deeply suspicious that their union was the cause of the respective marital breakdowns. In a literal way, this had not been the case, but symbolically there was truth: Both were searching for something more than the convention of marriage each had experienced and, predictably, it had been the mutual sexual passion that awoke a sense of romance, that seemed to transcend the mundaneness of their previous existences; almost as if they were past-lives.

For a while, they surfed on the crest of the wave of passion, high above all and everything below. The sex was easy and intense. Although each brought their share of inhibitions to the table, they were able to confront and negotiate these with some ease. The lack of completion of their respective marriages at an emotional level meant they were on guard with their love and felt the need to protect their ex-spouses. Whilst rationalised, Tim knew deep down there was guilt involved, but he struggled to give it either shape or a name. Instead, they both allowed the passion to carry them, and when this seemed to falter, they would find it easy to blame those around them for their lack of understanding.

Yet Tim was starting to feel a deeper disquiet. If their relationship was so right, why didn't it flow back into their social circles and integrate with them? Why did each feel an element of insecurity when not with the other, also jealousy when a third party aroused an emotional or sexual interest in one of them? Maybe this was another reason they kept their passion encapsulated, which is why they were in the paddock on this autumn afternoon.

Tim had taken the 'kit' from the boot of his car. He had a rug and a container with some food, wine and utensils, all quite simple and directed toward the intimacy. Jean knew this; she was a willing participant, after all, and helped by carrying some of the load as they wordlessly made their way to this new spot Tim had sourced the previous week. There were many now, the climate of the region meant there was only a rare occasion they needed to use his rather dull flat and that was reserved for the occasional evenings when Jean's children responsibilities were undertaken elsewhere.

The paddock was small and parkland cleared. There were no houses within miles and most likely no people, as the only track would alert them to any approaching vehicle. Tim spread the rug, and they immediately reclined to begin the intense kissing that was a prelude. As they kissed, Tim reflected briefly that it was rare; they either kissed or made physical contact except as a prelude to a sexual encounter. His passion rose, as did his penis, and the thought was quickly dispelled. This exotic woman fascinated him with her sultry behaviour, confident sensuality and relative silence. He freed her breasts from the light dress she was wearing and started to suck the dark nipples to an erection that seemed as intense as the one housed inside his trousers, which Jean was starting to fondle.

As the clothes were dispensed, he moved between her thighs, parted her light knickers and began an oral exploration of her now juicy pussy. As his kissing moved to a deeper sucking of her cunt lips Jean began to grind her pelvis into his face; he met the challenge head-on and deepened his sucking. After some minutes, Tim felt the need to have his cock engaged, and he gently rotated around and above her so that it was poised over her mouth. Gently, ever so gently, he lowered his cock and she started to suck it. It had taken Jean a while to feel comfortable sucking him; her husband had demanded and sometimes enforced it. It took her a little longer to allow him to cum in her mouth and swallow his seed, yet this was simply one of the several hurdles each encountered and was able to overcome.

After what seemed like hours he turned again and buried his cock in her cunt, but only for a few strokes as he felt her high arousal and knew she favoured her orgasms whilst riding him. He held her, rolled over and she assumed a crouching position; his cock had not left its home. Jean closed her eyes, started to increase the depth and frequency of her pelvic movements whilst he fondled both breasts, occasionally pulling her forward a little so that he could suck them. Her moaning increased and made it easy for Tim to recognise where she was at in the inevitable progression towards her climax. The moans became small utterances, and then cries and a deep low scream announced its arrival. He had timed his progression well and shot canons of sperm into her in the ensuing moments. She felt this, opened her eyes, smiled at him and then collapsed on his body.

They shared some wine; it was not long before Jean began to slumber and turned away from him as he cuddled her, stroking her hair. Yet the deep disquiet remained; all was not well. Once he recognised the sounds of her slumber, he disengaged himself and sat up. After pouring himself another wine he started a reflection of their relationship and it was then that he saw the snake. Why was it coming toward them? Whenever he had met a snake before and it had noticed him, it then took an alternative path so as to avoid an encounter. Maybe the snake had not known of their presence? He thought this briefly then dismissed the possibility, particularly as the snake seemed to have a determination in its movement toward them.

Tim came to a conclusion. He knew that if he awoke Jean she would be shocked and probably scream, not the scream of her orgasm and one that may startle the snake. It was then he realised that they differed in a fundamental way and that the relationship was on notice. He also knew the snake would continue its path without veering. It writhed up to the rug, onto it and passed between them. Tim knew this to be a metaphor for their relationship and he felt a deep sadness. The way of romance was a step in his journey, but not his resting place. A tear came to his eye, but he felt he must give Jean the benefit of the doubt. He awoke her, pointed to the departing snake and shed a second tear as she screamed.

Travelling Nowhere

I feel like I have always been in this carriage. It feels as if I am always going to work and every day seems to drag into an eternity that is both unfathomable and frightening. Is there an outside to that door, wherein I can step and at last feel the vast freedom of emptiness? Yet I am still in this carriage with the slow hum of the wheels and the distant engine that draws me on to... where? Work. Fucking work. Fucking, fucking work. Clicketty clack, clicketty clack, clicketty fucking clack. Idle fancy, a scan around... is she there? Will she be there today, the woman who will lift me from this madness?

I never expect it though. There may be one there I can find an angle in the form of: A sleight of form, a disguised breast oozing the precious nectar that will sustain and revive... "Make it through the night". Each day there is one; a turn of an ankle, the shape of her nose, the glitter of a necklace on a neck so subtle as to make me weep. Will there be one today? One who will lift my spirit from this profanity to the heights I sometimes glimpse but never seem to have a firm footing in? I am fooled and I know it, yet still I look. None can do that; no woman can. Yet still I look.

I look out of the carriage window into the frightening back yards. Mile after mile of nowhere land, that empty void of patterned existence that offers no solace for the soul. How do they all do it? How do they all live in this nightmare? How can I complain, aren't I doing the same? I take recourse to my fancy; my imagination, I like to think. Is that an opium to endure "through the fucking night?" Am I that deluded... the question seems too big, maybe I should just get back to that tempting leg I saw yesterday and allow my vision to creep under the dress and wander into the warmth beyond? Maybe.

It is somehow ironic that I both know there is no ultimate satisfaction there, yet still I look. There must be a 'beyondness' in the seeking that I have not yet grasped, a fullness of being that I see in a breast or experience in the depths of a cunt. Maybe those misers of my upbringing, those spiritually emaciated priests were right and Eve is the ultimate symbol of all that is fatal for man. Maybe I have got it wrong after all these years. My god, what an admission! Time to go to confession and accept the cloth.

Yeah, right.

So here I am captivated, yet again. She sits opposite, neat in her office suit. Dark and demure, with glasses that any female librarian would envy. Stockings and shoes suitably underdone, breasts collapsed beneath a top that constrains, retains and controls her. Fuck! Not another goddess to assault my senses? Well, she hardly does that, but my imagination, oh god! She takes off her top and is wearing no bra, her magnificent orbs she offers to my devouring mouth as my hand creeps underneath her suited dress and experiences her coming wetness. I gently place her back in the seat and kiss her. Her mouth is all I could hope for, inviting, deep and accepting. I take my erection in one hand, whilst the other lifts her skirt, parts her legs and opens her cunt. I guide it in, past the gentle hurdle of newness and bask in the depths of her being. I flood her and she gives a soft little moan of satisfaction.

I know he's looking at me, and he's kind of cute. Keep cool girl, eyes on the folder, don't let him see that you know. Shit! I'm getting horny and my knickers are getting hot, in a minute they'll

34

be damp, but I'd better keep my legs crossed. Fuck, I'd love to take my top off and show him I haven't got a bra, just a pair of tits that men just want to devour. I'd love him to be sucking them and then I can part my legs and he can just enter me here and now! That would be gorgeous and take my mind off the fucking meeting I'm going to. He can then gently pump me and fill my cunt with his precious seed. Wouldn't that be a nice way to spend this trip!

The train pulls to a halt. She closes the folder that has preoccupied her since she sat down and leaves, with no passing glance. Another wispy ephemeral being dissipates into an ether yet to be discovered. I look out at the backyards and wonder whether this is the day that I will finally leave.

Portrait

The agency had done well this time, she was gorgeous and quite exotic, and a mulatto with mixed parentage from somewhere in East Africa, if he appreciated her dialect correctly from his experience. There was an arrogant reserve about her, almost a sense of nobility, which belied her role in Mel's studio.

"How do you want me?"

What a question, Mel thought! Well, on my couch for starters with those thick lips sucking intently on my already raging dick and we can see how it goes from there…

"Let's start with a straightforward pose on the chaise." Mel gave the considered and appropriate response instead.

"All my clothes off?" Yes. Yes!

"I think so, then maybe that blue and yellow kimono over there – though leave it invitingly open. The cultural mix may have an additional impact."

She didn't baulk at that; didn't take any cultural offence, though she gave little away as well.

"Your name is…?"

"Kira."

"Kira, I'm Mel." No reply.

Kira disrobed easily and effortlessly, leaving her clothes tidily on the chair near the door. The elegance softened the arrogance and she turned, picked up the kimono and slipped into it. Her pubes were lightly trimmed and there was no excess body hair, no tattoos or studs, which conformed to Mel's request. The only jewellery was a solitary large left earring made of silver and of some two inches diameter, plus two matching silver rings on the index and little fingers of her right hand.

All very understated, but appropriately so. Kira was quite a beauty and he wondered what circumstances had brought this creature to the modelling agency and hence to his studio for several days of portraiture. He dismissed the speculation as he looked at her perfectly formed breasts seductively and alternatively leave the containment of the kimono, as she walked over to the couch. She knew she was beautiful, but Mel was starting to see something more mysterious that stood behind this veneer. As he grasped that feeling he felt Kira's eyes on him, which he met as a shiver shot up his spine.

The initial sittings were short and frequently broken. Mel was using a pencil on the canvas, trying to capture a pose, a look, something that would make this a portrait apart from his previous ones. His recent success had surprised him, but not those who knew him. He managed to capture something a little mysterious, even magical, in his subjects. This had put him a little in demand with the rich and famous, but this rapidly lost its appeal and the money was now no longer a necessary consideration. The book had augmented his success and the television show he now hosted was well received.

Mel knew he was in a transitional state: he had achieved all he had set out to do and realised he was in danger of becoming stereotyped and staid. He knew he needed to reinvigorate his work, his style, himself. A few weeks in India helped and he came back refreshed, but with no clear idea where the next step in his work would be. This state was not new to him; he would simply follow his intuition, explore what emerged and see where the creative impulse would take him.

A few days before Kira's arrival at his studio he awoke from a dream where a dark-skinned woman with long dark hair and a generous mouth looked up to him from a kneeling position whilst engaging his cock. Her eyes changed into those of a snake and his awakening was marked by a cold sweat, but he was also erect and excited; a strange mixture his body was exhibiting and he experiencing. He was on the phone to the agency early in the day; he knew what he was looking for, not necessarily in features but in terms of an energetic perspective he felt but could barely describe.

Daphne at the agency knew him well and also knew what he was looking for, maybe better than he did. This thought unnerved him, yet also excited him even more. Mel had the sense that Daphne was 'waiting' for this to happen and his fantasy was that she unlocked Kira from a mysterious room at the back of the shop and sent her to Mel with her calling card.

So, when Kira arrived, he was partially prepared.

The kimono wasn't working; indeed, no item of clothing was. Instead, he tried more jewellery: a necklace, bracelet and anklet. Getting better, he thought. A scarf? God, that's old hat, but it works if red and loose... the picture was starting to come together. Kira took it all impassively and he found it difficult – impossible even – to read her.

Now the position: The couch didn't work, so maybe the chaise... or a chair? Armchair or straight back? The straight back does it, but she needs to sit sideways on it. Leg crossed, arm on back of chair, leg crossed loosely... inviting cunt... was he getting lost? No, it was working. She started to look demanding, yet powerful and commanding. Her beauty moved to raw sexuality that oozed from all of her being and seemed to radiate around her. Finally, Mel was settled with clothing – or the absence of it – pose and props. The sketches were done again, completed and the brushes brought out.

Kira moved through all this preparatory work and the various stages with no complaint and only speaking in response to Mel.

At one level this made his task easier, but at another it just created more of an enigma.

The first brush strokes started and he settled into a rhythm.

Kira was seated on the chair sideways with her upper right arm on the back and supporting her head with her hand. Her left leg crossed the right somewhere near her left ankle at ninety degrees to the right leg, leaving her pussy partially concealed yet exposed at the same time, so creating a further level of enigma, even paradox. Her left forearm was casually placed across her left lower leg near the knee. The jewellery was similar to the effect created earlier and, as well as the scarf loose around her neck with one end dangling between her breasts, there was a loose black cotton skirt that had ridden above her legs to her pelvis with most draped to the left of her body. She looked directly at him as he went about his work.

After a while Mel was in what he called the 'Zone'. Not unlike an athlete, he was almost in an altered state as the classical music in the background created a timeless atmosphere in the large studio and the fire occasionally crackled above the strings. The sunlight through the overhead skylights was varied, as the sparse clouds moved across with the wind in their tails.

It would be a good day.

Mel looked at the palette casually gracing his left forearm, propped by his thumb. He began to mix up a slightly lighter colour that would match Kira's skin but reflect the light on her right forearm, as it stretched toward her head and the darker hair that was cascading down and around the propped hand. Once he felt he had the right tone and texture he took a large sable brush, scooped some of the oily paint onto the tip of it and began a long, slow, straight stroke on the canvas.

Then the state he was in began to deepen beyond a point that he had ever experienced. As the fibres of the brush moved across the canvas, he could actually feel the paint going on and it started to feel like his fingertips. Then, as the state deepened, the oil stroking the canvas began to feel like Kira's skin. It was soft and warm and responded to his touch with a light prickling: it felt exquisite. Then he found himself in front of her, although he knew this to be within the state that surrounded and included her as well as him. He took his hand from her arm and stroked her cheek as she continued the impassive gaze back into his eyes, even into his soul, so deep it felt.

Kira stood and returned his touch. Mel looked deep into her eyes, which now felt like deep, deep pools. They moved together to the couch and she lay whilst he began to kiss her body, breasts and then mouth. Her response felt tempered yet profound and the mystery that engulfed him deepened simultaneously. He discarded his trousers and then moved between her thighs without losing contact with her gaze. Penetration was easy, her pussy was overflowing and warm, oh so warm! He felt his penis move slowly within and gently stroke in and out, in and out.

There was a fathomlessness to her cunt that he had never experienced before: there was little desire now to move, simply to stay deep within. Her hands gently held his buttocks and reinforced the stillness and depth. Then he felt his cock become soft, but a slight movement confirmed that it was as erect and hard as ever, even more so. This was strange; the sense was that his cock was dissolving, disappearing into the cavern of her cunt and he along with it. He silently and slowly followed.

They were together on the savannah and wearing traditional clothes. The beasts in front of them gently grazed under the heat of the noonday sun. He recalled he had met her after finishing the portrait; they had come together as partners and he stopped his work to go back to her homeland with her. There was a task he was involved in; she had known him from her vision and come to get him from his city. He was to come back with her as the vision had told both her and her people that the white man would become the leader and amalgamate the warring tribes to strengthen their people in their fight with the dictator. The dictator had been cruel and brutal with her tribe and they had lost many. The outside world had made much noise but given little support and no action. Kira's vision showed them another path and Mel understood in his heart his destiny.

The last brush stroke had graced the canvas and he placed it down, then the palette followed and he stood back to look at his work. It was his greatest, a masterpiece. Tears came to his eyes and Kira stood and joined him. Then they looked at each other and her eyes became as the snake of his dream. She turned, dressed and silently left.

What was he to do now?

There was something vaguely in his memory about her. Maybe he should contact her and pursue it?

A Tale of Two Worlds

Kranzje knew her time was near. The twin moons of Zaug were moving into alignment that informed the females of her species to prepare for the sacred ritual of Mios and the fertilisation that ensured the continuation of their species.

The ability of the Klaan to procreate had steadily declined over the aeons of their power and control of the rich resources of Zaug and her large moon Jaun. The wise folk put this decline down to the discovery of moon-spice on Halan, the lesser of the two moons. Halan had been long ignored with the richness of minerals on Jaun, the nearer and more prominent moon that had captured the imagination and strength of the Klaan in their ascendancy, and maybe even have been responsible for it.

Then the Crejan, the lesser species and subservient to the Klaan, discovered moon-spice and used it for their own means. They became strangely indifferent to the Klaan, where before the dominance of the latter had angered and frustrated them, particularly when the Klaan assimilated their culture as their own. Although the Klaan had long dismissed Halan as the poor sister of Jaun, they noticed the quiet strength that moon-spice produced in the Crejan and sought to use it as their own.

A deal was struck and the Crejan mined the moon-spice willingly for the Klaan in exchange for some restoration of their cultural heritage. A little too easily, thought some of the wise folk and questioned the wisdom of the use of moon-spice by the Klaan, who did not seem to gain the indifferent strength that it produced in the Crejan; instead, they became apathetic and their fertility declined whilst that of the Crejan increased. Nobody could explain these paradoxical effects in species seemingly so close, but present it was.

The Klaan's casual use of their sexuality continued, but became infertile. It was only at the ritual of Mios that any offspring were produced, so this became an increasing source of interest and attention; latterly it even became critical to their survival. As the moon-spice had taken hold and the Klaan seemed reluctant to make the association between its usage and the decline of their collective fertility, the wise folk paid increasing attention to the connection between Mios and reproduction. Mios had a long tradition. Yet here was another paradox: Mios was a celebration of sexuality, not fertility. It was customary for Mios to initiate the culture into the lore of sexuality, but not to be a source of fertility. Now things seemed reversed; yet another paradox engaged the wise folk.

Mios was one of the five major festivals of the Klaan. Following the visions of their cultural founder and spiritual leader, Gral, these were established to coincide with the major transitions of the moons and their giant sun, and reflect the life transitions of birth, sexual maturity, union of partnership, eldership and transition to the otherworld. These had been signposts for the Klaan in both their individual and collective development, reinforcing their maturity and differentiating them from the Crejan.

This had been reflected in their involvement with Earth, a planet some hundred light years distant, but of a similar nature to Zaug. Using their celebrated mental abilities, they had visited this nascent planet and recognised some similarities in their own past. What were to be called the Neanderthal reminded them in a symbolic fashion of the Crejan and so they placed their energetic support behind the humans. They visited them in their dream and vision and instilled Gral's way of life into their essence, naming it within them as a soul.

Humanity experienced this in vision as visitation of the gods, so welcomed and endorsed it. The Klaan particularly enjoyed the sexual union and procreation of the human, finding it more sensuous and playful than their own. So much so that oftentimes the humans found their sexual experiences difficult to differentiate from what they perceived as their gods. Children born of such experience were considered exceptional, and the Klaan reinforced this perspective, vicariously drawn to the sexuality of the humans.

The humans established their culture and based it on the vision of Gral, though little did they know this and gave their chief god multiple names. Their festivals were fourfold, to mark the major features of their experience. Eldership was incorporated in the shape of the shaman, a representative of Gral, and permeated their culture in such a way that the humans believed that such wisdom would be so embedded in their culture, which could let the festival of experience and eldership be in the shaman, with the others reflecting their fourfold nature.

The humans celebrated the festival of Mios similarly, although the name they gave to it was Beltane after Bel, whom they identified as Gral in their visions. Celebration of Beltane was more that an expression of sex, it was an orgiastic confirmation of the rich and varied expression of sexuality. As the fires died couples would engage and move to the shadows, but in the full light of the fire other gods had their way and the sex reached its full and complex expression as man united with woman, woman with woman, and men and women both. The combinations were creative and playful, and the Klaan took it upon themselves to oversee this development. Although there was also a voyeuristic aspect which, along with the use of moon-spice, came to diminish them energetically and specifically in fertility.

Yet they recognised it not. The combination of the moon-spice and their pornographic involvement with the humans of Earth seemed to sustain them as the wise folk looked on, shedding tears and with heads waving. As this happened the strange 'reversal', as it came to be called, seemed to occur, although few recognised it in the beginning. Mios, that had spawned and fostered Beltane in her beginnings, then stopped being a celebration of sexuality as the Klaan became fascinated with the behaviour of those on the Earth. Instead, it came to be recognised as one of the few times that the Klaan females were fertile, yet in ways unfamiliar to them in their past.

Kranzje accepted all this as the feelings in the core of her body drew her to Mios. First, she was to select four mates whom, with her at the centre, would comprise the core of the ritual. As she did this, she also started to feel a power, one that had been too long on Earth. The four were selected and the sacred space made. Each of the males took a place around her, then sat and waited her instruction and direction. On Earth it was Beltane, one of the very few times the festivals coincided. Kranzje opened her vision onto the Earth and saw the revelry of the free as they embraced their full expression. She honed in on one called Lena, a beauty who received sustained attention from the male humans, who knew that Beltane would be the time she may receive their favours.

Lena danced a dance, the like of which the men had never seen. It transported them into a beauty they had not recognised in the festival, so focussed were they on the activity in their loins. The courageous of the young men, four of them, watched her every movement and formed a circle around her separate from the rest. Kranzje mimicked the pattern. Lena came to the crescendo and stood still and silent for what seemed an eternity to her entranced audience. Then she opened her eyes and slowly looked around. She beckoned the four forward to separate them from the watching crowd. Some in the background began to drum as the twilight settled in behind the crackling of the great fire. Lena stood in the midst of the four and simply stripped her clothing from her gracious body.

Kranzje watched. Also entranced, she recognised this as an opportunity in the scheme of things and knew she needed to keep her wits about her, as there may be something for her people in what was happening. Her four mates were seated around her and attentive toward her essence, the sanctity of the occasion had not escaped them. She invited them closer and their tentacles responded with an arousal that pleased her being.

Lena spread herself on the carpet of grass and gently writhed to the drumming. The hands were all over her now, fingers in her cunt and arse; mouths sucked her breasts, neck and lips. At first, she simply accepted and received the attention, but as the intensity and stimulation grew, she became more active. Their cocks protruded beneath their smocks, so it was a simple task of releasing and liberating them, which she duly did. Lena circulated, giving a depth of oral succour that she was sure none of the recipients had experienced. She continued to circulate, became almost dizzy, yet relaxed as they stilled her on her knees and rotated around her offering her cocks alternatively to her mouth. The drumming increased.

On Zaug Kranzje had allowed her four male consorts to let their tentacles be exposed and start to roam around her body. They plugged into her portals giving her a small shrill each time. Then they brought their secondary and other tentacles out and followed the same ritual of engagement of her body. At this time Lena was beyond oral pleasures, she was straddling one man and continued sucking another deeply, whilst the other two sucked her breasts. Then she was on her back with one in her cunt and the others circulating her mouth. Kranzje marvelled and tried to mimic her Earthly counterpart pulling the tentacles from their singular attention to one portal only and rotating them around.

Lena was enraptured. She squatted on one as another bored into her arse and the other two vied for her mouth. She pushed back on the two cocks in her loins and they responded with an alternating thrusting rhythm that stopped any thrusting on her part, compelling her to deeply receive them. At the same time her mouth moved from side to side and swallowed all that was before her. It mattered not that they changed position; this simply gave her respite for the next act. As the drums reached a crescendo the cocks inside became tenser and then withdrew. She felt cum on her buttocks and then another came from a differing angle to overlap the white painting and pay attention to her proud cunt lips. Then the ones at her mouth released their juice over her breasts. Lena gasped and then laughed, as her hands busily worked the man-juice into her body.

Kranzje knew what she must do. She pulled the tentacles from her portals and let them spill their fluids onto her crustacean being. She smeared the clear fluids over her exoskeleton and let her breath escape. She was done.

As was Lena: yet as a seeress she had known what had happened. She knew the spirits were to take the gift of sexual pleasure from Beltane and that one of their pseudo-mystics would diminish this festival of the Great Goddess and confine such expression to accepted and legitimised unions only. She knew also that another had watched and taken her power. Lena knew that this was the final culmination of her being. In the morning sun she would go to the river and extinguish her life.

Kranzje had her way. She was empowered. The festival of Mios was re-established in its true intention and she would proceed to the next, that of Alsay, and be easily impregnated by that being with those gorgeous tentacles she had felt beyond the others. Mios had re-established its function as a celebration of sexuality and, by her actions; Alsay would accept procreation of the Klaan. All was well.

Lena's body cut a lonely path down the river to the sea. No one mourned her. Now comes the time of the one God and the exile of Beltane. Her journey into the otherworld might – might – one day restore its place.

Theatre

Where was she taking him now? Geoff was feeling nervous, but excitement was creeping into his being and his body tingled. She held his hand lightly, leading the way. He knew not where as the mask that was her play suggestion for the evening admitted little light and no clear vision. She still remained a source of surprise, this elfish woman who excited his senses and was starting to stalk his heart. Their play always added an edge to the sensuality that flowed between and through them. He wondered whether this was love.

Sophie let go of his hand and shut a door behind him. The building was vast and he was not clear where he was, except they were still on the ground floor, so it would most likely be one of the large rooms; maybe it was the study or the drawing room? It was the drawing room he discovered as she lightly, yet with a painful slowness, undid the knot of his mask. The light was dim, very dim; where the large sofas normally resided was a platform and on it a large circular piece of furniture, something like a bed. It was soft in texture, velvet-like and a dark red colour. Cushions were scattered on it and the open fire flickered in the background adding to the sensuous nature of the atmosphere with assistance from the fragrance of burning oils. Apart from the crackling of the burning wood all was quiet.

Sophie sat him in an armchair facing the theatrical bed and instructed him to watch. To his right was a small table and on it a glass of his favourite scotch, neat with no ice. He took a sip, ostensibly to confirm it as his favoured nectar, but maybe also to calm his nerves a little. He speculated: Maybe she was going to perform a solo act and then invite him to join, otherwise why seat him in the chair? Sophie moved onto the platform and ran a hand across the textured bed whilst emitting a soft purring sound, followed by a rubbing of her cheek against a pillow she gripped and held aloft. Her eyes were closed. His were not. His heart had increased its tempo below his shirt and he felt his manhood begin to strain. Yet she had done little of a sexual nature and confined her activity to the sensual only.

Sophie tossed the cushion back on the bed. She easily slipped out of the light white gown she was wearing, yet kept on her heeled shoes. Geoff gazed upon these and slowly allowed his look to rise to the dark-stockinged legs that always excited him, then to stop at her thighs, wherein the stockings did too. They were self-maintained; no garter or belt supported them. Instead, dark panties with a red rim lightly graced her pelvis and matched the bra, seemingly a little small for her well-endowed nature. She sported no jewellery apart from a single ring on her right index finger and the earrings that were a gift from him early in their relationship. The underwear contrasted her blond hair; the waves of which cascaded around her shoulders.

Geoff briefly reflected on this, his mind scanning the prior months and their obsessive intensity. This was the first time he had remained faithful to a partner for such a period and, he presumed, she too. Their time together seemed to afford little outside influence and both had come to their initial meeting relatively unencumbered, inasmuch as their previous life experience would allow. He was becoming charmed; maybe this relationship was the one that would settle into the sort of exclusivity that he felt his life now demanded.

After a short period of allowing her hands a free roam over her form Sophie lay on the bed and continued her play, with her hands slowly and progressively engaging her breasts and then her pussy. Fingers moved slowly around, sometimes in crevices and other times within the recess of her cunt. One even found a way into her arse. Geoff's erection was beginning to strain and he took another large sip from his glass. As his eyes were becoming slowly accustomed to the light, he felt a shock move through his frame. Behind the bed and against the walls each side of the fire he noticed several male forms. They were all lightly dressed, maybe in kimonos. How many? He could not easily tell and wondered whether more were concealed in the darkness away from the fire.

What was Sophie doing? This had not been part of their relationship to date. In spite of both their prior and varied experiences, which they had shared, it had not even been discussed in their present context. Was she telling him that she was dissatisfied? He thought not sexually, yet she was introducing a dimension to their relationship with no prior warning. Was she introducing it into their relationship though, or was she defining it in a way he could not as yet ascertain? Geoff wondered whether Sophie was announcing the death knoll of their time together and, although this created an anxiety in him, he thought not; she wouldn't do it that way. Or would she? Was she being cruel? Was this a retribution for a crime in their passion he had not observed? Had he pushed some of his proclivities too early? Had he provoked something in her she had not conveyed back? He was confused, yet reflected that he remained excited and this surprised him. Then he felt anger; was she setting him up? Going to fuck these men in front of him as some sort of payback such that the weight of numbers would prevent him returning any similar favour? And who the hell were these men anyway? He smiled to himself, supped further and noticed the scotch bottle was near the tray: he may need it.

Simultaneously six men came out of the shadows and approached Sophie; they were now all naked and in various states of sexual arousal. Geoff had not seen two; one was a Negro and one of Arab appearance. All were fit and athletic; all seemed to have intent of purpose, not looking at Geoff but toward Sophie. They formed a circle on the platform, seemingly cognisant of Geoff, as they left a gap for his clear view of almost the entire width of the bed. As they stood, arms akimbo, several lights came on and highlighted the bed to give it a stage-like effect with Geoff as the audience.

Sophie rose to her knees, looked directly at Geoff in the shadows and smiled. He felt a little relieved; there seemed no hint of malice, and the theatrical effect was quietly creating a state of mind within him that had a timeless quality; it seemed like she looked at him for an age and was sometimes very still. The men did not move and continued to watch Sophie as she moved on her hands and knees around the bed attending to the men's growing erections with her hands, seemingly at random. Her eyes were now for their cocks only; Geoff saw that she did not look at their faces. Her movements became quicker and moved from hand to mouth as she tackled them orally, sometimes drawing two close and engaging their cocks in her mouth together. Some she lightly licked and played with, others she took deep into her mouth and their balls did not escape her attention. Occasionally she offered an expressionless look in Geoff's direction, but without losing her tempo. At this time, it dawned on Geoff that this was a scenario she was not unfamiliar with, yet the purpose of the show, if for him, remained enigmatic.

The pace was picking up. Some of the men gave Sophie a smack on her rump as she attended to them, occasionally getting on the bed to do so. Then, if on the bed, a man would lick her pussy from behind. Now the bed started to slowly rotate, so as to give Geoff the benefit of a complete view of the proceedings. The Negro discarded Sophie's panties in Geoff's direction as another loosened her breasts from the confines of her bra. Geoff picked up her panties and smelt the now very wet crotch, which was filled with a perfume familiar to him. He was also looking at Sophie, who returned his gaze over the top of another cock engaging her mouth. Expression, even if offered, would have been impossible.

All the men were now on the bed; Sophie on her back with legs in the air and a cock stationed each side of her face whilst the Negro ate her cunt with visible and audible satisfaction. In fact, most of the men were now making guttural noises adding a strange atmosphere to the rhythm. The dark form backed off and another took his place, then the third entered her vaginally and Geoff heard an audible gasp from Sophie above the primal music issuing from the men, who were by now taking turns to engage her cunt and then her mouth. Sophie's gaze was lost from Geoff's view, although by now he was entranced and fully involved in the performance in front of him. His hand went to his groin and stroked his erection through his trousers. He wondered briefly about releasing it, masturbating and even joining in; although he sensed that was not his place and he sipped once more from his glass.

Cocks were all over her. She took turns to ride them and continued her sucking. She moved from body to body and then crouched to allow the penetrations to continue from a different angle as well as to provide a view to Geoff. Those that couldn't find a place in one of her orifices, or were gaining relief from giving attention, gave succour to her breasts, legs and feet with mouths and tongues aplenty; the bra, stockings and shoes having followed the panties in Geoff's direction. The Arab man then took his turn behind her and gently, yet firmly, worked his cock into her arse. It didn't take him long; Sophie was receptive and it seemed to Geoff her vocal squeals were theatrical. He knew them. The men took turns after the Arab and Sophie welcomed each intruder with a backward thrust of her pelvis and joined in the rhythm. Her mouth continued to be simultaneously engaged, sometimes with two of the dicks presented for her attention.

One man crawled under her body and pulled her hips down so that she squatted and engulfed his cock with her cunt in a single motion, such that it became lost to view. Another now positioned himself behind and took the anal route. The two men started to thrust, sometimes in unison and sometimes in a complementary manner. Sophie seemed to feel the rising tension and she joined the movements until they became a blur. The man in her arse, in particular, thrust like a piston and it was to his challenges that Sophie was responded. The other, in her cunt, seemed to act as an anchor.

Geoff's body felt alive and he felt transported as the men took turns in the sometimes double, sometimes triple penetrations that enveloped Sophie. Yet she seemed not to lose poise or be swamped by the intensity and power of the attention, she seemed to rise to it and, it seemed to Geoff, to almost glow. She had started a humming that continued whilst the men's primal chants continued unabated. She was the star of the show as the bed continued its turning and the men rotated around Sophie's being like stars around a sun. Geoff had lost a sense of his body and there was a time he felt he was watching the tableau from above, as well as knowing he was still in the chair.

Then something strange happened. As he felt his being move between his body and the position from above, he started to feel that he was looking through Sophie's eyes. He was not startled, but took in the scene in front of him as cocks moved around his face. He felt his breathing, enjoyed the smells of sex and heard his groaning as Sophie's; then he had a sense of his pelvis full, oh, so full! The fullness reached an intensity that enveloped his whole body and sent waves up and down his back. They were like oscillating flows that gradually moved upward toward his head and into it. And then his mind went blank.

Geoff opened his eyes and was back in his chair. In front of him the man in Sophie's arse moved it out, whilst the contrasting black one remained in her pussy. The man gently lifted her hips and with the co-operation of the others rolled her over onto her back, as she was now quite limp and breathing in a slow still manner. Geoff had time to see her roll her head to the side, open her eyes to look at him and smile before she closed them again.

They knelt around her, each holding his erection and slowly masturbating. The sounds had dropped off and the men were looking intently at Sophie's still body beneath them. Each took a turn to move forward. The Negro gently parted her legs and whilst holding her pussy lips open with the fingers of one hand shot his semen over her pink cunt and onto the brownish pubes above. Dark and white contrasted. He gently inserted his cock to its fullest and then exited. Above him one of the men sat astride her belly whilst she silently gripped her breasts so as to engulf his dick. He gently moved it along this alternate channel until he exploded onto her neck and chin. As he moved back two knelt each side of her breasts and, in succession, left the fruits of their engorgement in rivulets across them. The last men, one the Arab, presented a similar yet unified front to her face from each side. With eyes and mouth closed she accepted their offerings onto her face and hair.

As Sophie started massaging the sweet, yet pungent fluid offerings into her body, breasts and face, the men silently retired in an orderly succession and turned to return to the shadows, where each collected his kimono and put it on, resuming their original positions. All the time Sophie continued the massage in a light and gentle manner, whilst her eyes remained closed, her breathing even and a quiet smile graced her lips. Geoff also felt still, his erection was strong but not a burden. He watched

Sophie for what seemed a long time whilst she continued to toy with the sperm, and then he closed his eyes and felt a deep peace.

When he opened them again, he looked on someone he knew he now loved with a depth he had not felt before. The questionings that had marked the early part of the performance had evaporated. As her hands stopped the massage of the drying juices into her body, she became stiller. None of the men were visible now; had they left? She occasionally drew some of the thicker deposits from her body with the index finger of her left hand and sucked deeply on them with some slow audible groaning and her eyes remaining closed. Geoff was awe-struck, he had just witnessed a tableau that he found both beautiful and intense, and his own excitement was at a peak. Although her eyes had instructed him to remain in his chair during the performance, their frequent engagement with him gave him cause for solace. Where this relationship was going from here, he did not know, but he did sense it remained a relationship and Sophie had inducted him into a dimension that she presumably wanted him to join.

Geoff rose from the chair, approached and encircled the platform. He gazed at her gorgeous form, now quite still and prone, with the remaining semen cast around her body concentrated on her pussy, breasts and face, as he had witnessed. He felt a little strange, but also a power that quietly began to surge through him. He looked at her and knew Sophie to be his and that this whole scenario had been a testament to that fact. In a strange way she was being submissive; she opened her eyes and looked at him, and then slowly smiled.

He took out his cock and in two strides moved from floor to platform as she moved to the edge and let her head fall slightly off to the side and to his right. He placed his left hand on her throat and gently gripped it, whilst masturbating with his right, knowing this was not going to be a prolonged act. His body was more energised than he had ever experienced, yet he had total control of his impending orgasm and simply looked down at her whilst the stroking became yet more gentle and sensuous. The sensations concentrated in his loins and balls, and he felt the surge begin from the base of his cock. He directed the flow like an artist with paint on a canvas, as Sophie let her mouth become slightly agape and her gaze moved from his eyes to the manhood straining above her. The force in his cock surprised him and he knew the ejaculation would be strong, and it was. He directed it over her face and mouth as he used to play urinating as a child on the grass. She accepted his sacrament with eyes unwavering and soft licking of her lips around the sperm that met that mark. She was seemingly not satiated from the semen she had already savoured, or maybe this was of a different form. He may find out later, but for now he was totally engrossed in what was happening as the ejaculate continued to stream from his being onto and into the vessel before him.

Then it began to subside and he let out a gentle groan and he briefly closed his eyes. He felt whole. Sophie rolled over and sat on the edge of the bed before him and took the still firm member into her mouth. With the same low and soft groans that had commenced this performance she sucked deep on this being, yet didn't stop at what he felt may be the completion. He became hard again and her ministrations continued deeper, in a rhythm that entranced him that took his cock beyond the light constriction that marked the transition from mouth to throat. Then he felt the self-same bodily feelings as what must have been only minutes earlier and again the sperm rose, tore down his cock from within and out into the depths of her throat. Not once did her rhythm change until he was surfeit, then she slowed the tempo and depth and looked up at him through sperm surrounded eyes, let her mouth fall away and simply smiled again. He bent forward, kissed her and she responded with a warmth he had not experienced before, through the nectar that coated her lips and joined them as one.

Guardian Angel

I shouldn't have ignored my feelings, my intuition: Maybe the experience will teach me not to do so in the future, as it is something I am hardly likely ever to forget. Maybe also that was the wisdom of the experience; more like an initiation really.

It was late and I was walking home from work because I couldn't readily find a cab and that annoyed me. On the street just before my apartment I could feel eyes behind me and turned to see two men following at a discreet distance. What unnerved me a little was that they were silent and walking with intent... or so I surmised. I started to feel a little unsettled, quickened my pace and turned into my street. By the time I got to my door I thought I had 'lost' them and I let myself in quickly, bolting the door behind.

I felt safe inside. I placed my bag on the stand and made my way into the lounge feeling a relief that a drink would help confirm when I had the shock of my life; I turned on the light and they were seated in the armchairs facing me. Although they were now wearing balaclavas each had a lurid smile. Before I could turn and bolt one was out of his chair in a flash: He grabbed me, pinned my arms behind and frog-marched me into the bedroom. I heard the second a slight distance behind chuckling to himself and I then felt shit scared.

The next period in the drama was so methodical I knew they'd been in my apartment before. The second man, shorter and stockier, turned on the bedside light and made sure the curtains were adequately closed. As he went to the apartment on the other side of the bed to put on some music – although he seemed frustrated with my taste – the first one turned me around and held me against him whilst still pinning my arms to my back. His breath smelt of cigarettes and I could see that he had a dark complexion as well as being taller and skinnier than the one who had now selected some techno music, which I thought I'd ditched.

"Now be a good girl and, apart from increasing your experience, you won't come to any harm." A bit more intelligent than he appeared, this one.

Did I say anything in response? No. I looked directly in his eyes; they were brown and well dilated. Drugs I thought, better not to engage him too deeply as he might turn psycho. Anyway, I reckoned I'd be able to recognise him again with what I'd already picked up. I figured then and there that fighting would get me into deeper shit, so I decided to play along and hope all that I would get out of this was a sore cunt and a few bruises. I realised my time would be better spent picking up details for any possible future reference.

Sometimes it's strange how clear you can feel in the middle of adversity and I even thought and reflected on this whilst it was all happening. It gets kind of surreal and a bit timeless, but there's a sort of alertness that has a strange almost altered state feel about it. I also wonder why they didn't blindfold me? Maybe they wanted me to witness the whole thing, for reasons not obvious at the time… and might never become so.

Here we go I thought; the arm gripped my wrists even tighter. Nicknames will help: This one was Smoker and the other Shorty. Shorty took my wrists, pulled me back on the bed and after pulling off my jacket he started to tie each wrist to the upper bedposts with some really firm material that he pulled from his coat pocket. Strange, it was soft; maybe they were being kind! My skirt and knickers were off in a flash, my blouse undone and the front clasp of my bra loosened. Then they stepped back, looked at my body and started to take off their pants. Both were wearing trackies, but not underwear; so, they could leave their shoes on for a quick getaway if needed, I figured. I almost smiled, but realised that might be bad news, as they might have referred such an expression to their erections, which were both quite modest… and I've seen a few.

Shorty was really blond, may even be a redhead; his eyes were blue even with the subdued light. Smoker may well have been part native or foreign I reckoned. Both started to play with their erections as they moved forward and started to maul me. Token resistance only here gal, I reasoned, they probably expected it and wanted to leave you with a bruise or two; there's a fine line between giving them want they might want and expect and getting more than your fair share. No resistance at all may be as bad as too much.

Shorty was a bit of an oral man; he licked and bit my neck and breasts before pushing my legs apart and attending to my pussy. He was predictably rough and it was a bit of a chore, but as I always like a good munch I even enjoyed it – a bit only, of course. Smoker gripped my neck and turned my head towards his dick, which was uncircumcised like his mate. Couldn't see any ulcers, thank god, though I doubted if either would produce a condom: pot luck in that department really.

"Suck, no teeth, otherwise you might lose a few."

The instruction was fairly clear and, a bit smelly though it was, I got about giving him head, although I didn't display my expertise.

"I know you can do better than that, bitch!"

Did he now? Was that guesswork, inciting me to an improved performance, or had he – or they – been watching me in action?

If so that could have only been with Dave, as he'd been my partner for quite a while and these guys were unlikely to have held back on this little party trick for any length of time; delayed gratification was hardly likely to be part of their repertoire. I missed Dave, bastard leaving me like that, but I imagined it was his cock in my mouth, smaller though this one was, and went about my business with a marginally increased intensity. The blow to the side of my head between strokes made me realise I'd better not mess around too much, so I obliged a bit more, I didn't want too many of those!

Meanwhile Shorty stopped his meal and now placed himself between my legs, sticking his cock in with minimum preparation: good job I had a bit of juice running, reflexes can be a useful thing at times. To say he was unrefined would be an understatement and his accompanying grunts were a definite off-put, no wonder these guys needed to get their action this way. From there it was a question of changing positions with me as the pivot and I began to wonder where to from here. I started to get an inkling shortly.

As Shorty untied me from the bedposts Smoker started with the next set of instructions, as Shorty never spoke:

"Do as I say and you'll get through this OK." What the fuck did he mean by that?

I started to get the picture when I was flipped over, my face buried in the pillow and arse lifted in the air. It's Smoker first, of course. He was into my arse with only his spit as preparation whilst Shorty held my head, I spread my thighs a little as the height was a bit awkward and he hurt. When Shorty took his place, things got a little gentler... but only a little. I was due for a round of this, it seemed, so I spent a little time getting my breathing right and relaxing my anal muscles: imagining I'm going to have a shit helped the relaxation and sent at least a metaphoric message to these fuckers!

The intensity started to pick up. Shorty turned my head and I sucked him till he quickly withdrew and sprayed his sperm on my mouth and one cheek. It was a bit rank and he remained hard, immediately sticking it back in while Smoker continued his pounding of my arsehole. Then he also withdrew, pulled me away from Shorty, turned me over and came over my breasts and throat before putting his cock back in my cunt. Dirty inconsiderate fucker! Then they both resumed in varying positions and combinations and I now knew it was not going to be over for a while, so I started to ponder an escape rather than survival, particularly when Smoker started smacking me in considerably more than a playful manner. I knew what was coming next...

Shorty lay on his back and got me to straddle him. Once he was inside me and I was firmly planted on his dick he gripped my back and pulled me toward him exposing my arse. I knew that Smoker was behind and above me and he would soon penetrate me simultaneously: they were going to double penetrate me, something I've always wanted, but not under these circumstances. Shorty was looking past my shoulder with a smile on his face; sick fuck. I braced myself.

Suddenly things changed and very fast it seemed at the time. Shorty's smile broadened to a sickening grin looking alternatively at Smoker then me, as I felt him in my cunt and Smoker position himself at the entrance to my arse. Then Shorty's eyes darted to a point above Smoker's head and somewhat more distant. At the same time, I heard a thud above the music and Shorty's visible face went into shock mode and what I could see was distinctly white. Smoker's body collapsed against my back and rolled off to the right followed by Shorty's eyes. Then he quickly looked back up and beyond my head and his cock, now quite soft, slipped out of my pussy. I quickly looked to the right. Smoker was facing me, but his eyes were rolling and his lips moved only a little. Back to Shorty: his hands had gone out and above his head in an act of submission. I grabbed my opportunity and jumped off the bed to my left.

An incredible scene confronted me: Smoker was lying on his right side and still relatively motionless. Shorty hadn't moved, but for a different reason. Standing at the end of the bed was a full-on angel! He was tall, blond and wearing a white tunic with the suggestion of wings arising from his back. I couldn't be sure about the wings as they formed part of the general glow that surrounded his whole body and head and made even his outline indistinct. He was shimmering and appeared to be floating a little off the ground; no wonder Shorty was shocked.

Smoker stirred and looked around, finally seeing the angel, at which point his discernible facial features started to resemble Shorty's. The angel pointed at each of them and they removed their balaclavas. I was right; Shorty was a redhead and Smoker distinctly foreign; I could almost have guessed their features down to the stubble on Smoker's face but now they were crystal clear and became burnt in my memory. The angel's left hand dropped and the right beckoned Smoker toward him at the foot of the bed. There, in a wordless fashion, he made Smoker turn and crawl toward Shorty whilst the latter parted his thighs and to his astonishment started to get an erection. On a non-verbal instruction Smoker started to suck Shorty's cock and both had stunned looks on their faces, as if they couldn't believe what was happening with their bodies seemingly acting independently of their minds.

The angel then turned to face me: he smiled. He was the most beautiful man I had ever seen and I realised that he was my Guardian Angel. How I realised this I didn't know; afterwards I figured out that it is an intuitive and telepathic realisation, but at the time I knew it to be unequivocally the case. His eyes beckoned me forward and to the wall apartment on the other side of the room. I passed between him and the bed with absolutely no fear and opened the bottom drawer, where I keep my sex toys. I took out the strap-on dildo, the one given to me by that saucy Ginny who wanted me to fuck her with it. Thanks, but no thanks! Girls aren't my scene I told her. Keep it, says she, you may have use of it one day, even if it isn't me you fuck with it!

Maybe her Witchy looks confirmed her as a prophetess, because here I was strapping it on. The angel 'got' the dumbfounded duo to slide a little down the bed so I wouldn't have to get on. I gave Smoker the benefit of the doubt and put a little spit on the head of the black monster between my legs and then thought: "What the fuck!" as I then drove it into his arse up to the hilt. He recoiled more than a bit, but because of my position I could follow him and keep pounding; resistance was useless and he stopped moving after a while. I hope he wasn't enjoying it too much! Then I could see by his eyes that Shorty was coming, even though against his will... it's obvious he didn't have much of that. Equally powerless Smoker was compelled to swallow and I gave him an extra few rough stroke to augment his 'pleasure' as the whole scenario slipped over the peak and started to subside, as I had a very gentle orgasm to finish the show.

I undid the strap-on and left it in Smoker's arse. He removed it very slowly and with obvious discomfort, as Shorty pulled his dick away from Smoker's disengaged mouth. They both looked stunned and simultaneously looked up to my angel (I love saying that!) who simply nodded his head. They dressed and quietly left without even a glance toward me. For a multiplicity of reasons, which I would have ample time to disentangle later, I knew they would never trouble me again.

Nor will anyone now I have found my Guardian Angel. He

looked at me and smiled; wordlessly he communicated his ongoing presence at my command as his form slowly faded. I simply smiled, and then I cried. It was time for that overdue drink, I thought, and went to the lounge comfortable in my nakedness that was so recently abused, but now felt quite revered.

Later in the shower I took stock and decided there was really nothing I had to do. Well, I knew there will be the necessary check for any sexually transmitted diseases, but I also knew they would be all clear. I felt quiet and content; I even stopped texting Dave. If he couldn't value me as I was – am – then that was his loss and he could continue to use the excuse of "needing to sort myself out" as a justification to his heart's content.

Guess what? Dave did sort himself out and it's more than just lip service to me; well, I'm back to getting the right sort of lip service now methinks! I look down at his sleeping form and realise how much has changed over the last few months and know to whom I am grateful to for this.

I look over Dave's shoulder to the corner of the room and make out a vague resemblance of a shimmering form ...

Restraint

The computer screen was beginning to blur, although Jeannie knew it was her brain and not the machine that was faulty. She felt that she'd been chained to this screen for the last few days, desperately trying to get this management plan finished so that she concentrates on the things that really appealed to her but weren't, as yet, bringing food to the table.

It was hard being a single mother, particularly when her arsehole ex wasn't providing any maintenance for their son. He'd recently had himself admitted to one of the city's 'better' – read expensive, pampering and pandering – psychiatric clinics and now championed himself as having a 'bipolar disorder'. More likely personality disorder bordering on the psychopathic, thought Jeannie, as he was now on 'sickness benefit' and not required to financially contribute to Dean's upbringing. This did not stop him exercising his access rights to the boy and, even though Jeannie thought about turning the tables and using his 'illness' to prevent access, she knew it would be more trouble than it was worth.

What sort of masochist am I? She briefly reflected on this, as she still felt the victim with respect to her ex, and here she was 'chained' to this fucking machine whilst Dean was away for the night on access when, if she had any sense, she would be out finding someone to give her a good run-around in the bedroom. It was a while since she'd had a good fuck and she was missing one. Dean and her contract work were taking up all her time; even her last short relationship had used these as an excuse for 'moving on'. The fucking had been good, but it was a ready-made excuse for avoiding commitment. Users, most men, reflected Jeannie, but then again, she couldn't avoid the fact she allowed herself to be 'used'.

Back to the screen, the spreadsheet was beginning to wobble a bit. Then, out of the blue – she didn't recall touching the keyboard – her browser launched itself and went straight to a site called "Restraint". She'd never seen this site before and nobody had access to her computer, so where did this come from? A video started and a man with clown make-up faced her out of the screen, his smile ludicrous... Jeannie laughed; she didn't remember doing that for a while!

"Good evening, ladies and gentlemen. Tonight, for your pleasure, we are going to present Jeannie for restraint... "

Jeannie gasped and felt a shock go through her body bordering on panic, but she couldn't turn away.

The master of ceremonies was now silent and looking directly at her: "Would you like to see what happens to Jeannie? Well, come behind the curtain and we shall see."

He turned and parted the black curtain behind him, pulling it wide to reveal a woman lying on a bed with her hands and feet roped to each corner spread-eagling her. She wore panties and a bra and was facing away, her long auburn hair obscuring her face.

Jeannie leant back in her chair. She was beginning to feel aroused. A tingling was happening in her pelvis and her attention was drawn to her pussy as she started to lubricate – just a little. She even has hair like mine, thought Jeannie; this is weird. As her hand went to her crotch and started to finger her pussy lips, she saw the screen Jeannie tug her right hand at the restraint, unable to move. Then the screen figure turned to look at her restrained right hand: my God! It's me!

Now she was on the bed and restrained. How had that happened? She didn't know and couldn't even imagine how, but there was no doubt, here she was in bra and panties with her hands and feet restrained by rope to the bed corners and this clown with the smirk on his face even more exaggerated as he smiled a mocking smile.

"Why struggle, Jeannie? You know you like it."

Bastard. Fucking bastard. Fucking, fucking bastard.

"Fucking bastard, let me go!" This was about all she could manage to yell, but it seemed pathetic; even to her as she tried to spit out the words with venom.

"But why, Jeannie, you know you like it. In fact, you love it. Isn't your life like this?"

That's all I need, she thought, a sicko Sigmund fucking Freud telling me about my 'masochistic tendencies' and all due to 'sexual frustration', no doubt. Go on, bastard, throw in a bit of 'karma' too, give it an Eastern flavour; should go well in the mix.

"I have some friends for you, Jeannie."

Three men came behind the curtain; she briefly noticed that she couldn't see a camera. They were naked except for a jock strap that only barely disguised the burgeoning erection of each. God they're big, thought Jeannie; is this all for me? It was only then that she saw that each was wearing a large mask. One was a goat, another a dog and the third a pig. She laughed.

"I hope you find what these animals are going to do to you as funny, Jeannie." He was still mocking her and she sensed he knew her every feeling; that unnerved her and she felt a wave of panic pass through her.

Jeannie closed her eyes and for a while all was still. She briefly reflected on how this could be happening, but all reason was against it. The panic feeling came again, but passed when she decided to accept what was happening and see where it may lead. There was a sense of adventure here that was so lacking in her daily life. She briefly reflected on her life: it had to change, but how?

Then the hands started roaming her body. It was useless to resist, even though she made token gestures. Then they started to become intrusive, stretching her mouth and pussy, even her arse. Her nipples were pinched on the edge between pleasure and pain, and yet they responded. They hardened, became erect and ached, ached for more. As Jeannie responded she became confused; was this what she enjoyed? She had never let herself explore this experience before, as she became confused and then frightened, as the edge of pain would come in her lovemaking. She just wasn't that sort of girl, so she didn't allow herself to turn that corner. Therein lies depravity, even madness, so she closed the door.

A light went on: Is that why she was involved in these relationships where she was the victim? Was it because she didn't allow this into her sexuality that it was played out in social and family circumstances? If it were that simple all she needed to do was let herself go, fall into that perceived pit of depravity and see what happened. The panic welled up again and her nipples softened; the pig noticed and tweaked them harder. They responded. The panic softened and a passion started to arise in her, one that had an intensity, focus and clarity she had not experienced before. She made the choice then, the choice to submit, even though it hadn't fully occurred to her that in the current circumstances she had no choice.

They undid her legs and straightened them, pulling off her panties in one swift motion, roughly. Next, they bent her legs, parted them and pulled her knees outward so that her sex was fully exposed. Jeannie felt entirely exposed, beyond just her sex. She looked around, but the pig blindfolded her and kept her hands bound. Her legs did not resist their newfound position as one started to work on her pussy. At first this was easy, as she had started lubricating when her nipples became erect and ached. Fingers darted in and around, massaging and poking. Another went into her virgin arse, then another. She felt stretched, it reminded her of that overwhelming sensation when she had Dean. That had been painful, so painful, but – it was difficult to admit – she felt ecstatic and experienced what she now recognised as an orgasm different from the one she had when she massaged her clitoris. Strange thoughts were going through her head now.

"How are you feeling, Jeannie?"

Bastard, fucking clown, why don't you just fuck off!

"You've never had it like this before, have you, Jeannie? Only ever one at a time, such a good girl! Ever wondered why you can't come unless you thrash your clit? Getting an inkling are you, my dear?"

Patronising shit! But he did have a point ...

"Work her up, my men, there's not enough stuffed inside this docile rag doll yet."

One finger became two and three... many? She didn't know and chuckled as she remembered the primitive manner of counting: One, two, many... all she knew was that she was full, full as when Dean's head had been there. And she came, she came the coming of her birth, not Dean's, but her own.

As she came to, she could hear him again.

"Wake up Jeannie, there's more for you yet!"

And she wanted more, more! Her body was free of hands now, yet it ached for more, all over it ached.

"Which one do you want, Jeannie?"

Clown was removing her blindfold and she looked down to the three studs paraded before her, arms across their bare chests and erections straining at jocks. Now she realised that the masks were not disguises, but hints and signs for her, her alone.

As she pondered, she looked at the men. Were they men? The masks took on a reality that she could not distinguish as a mask anymore; they seemed to arise spontaneously from the necks of each male body. The eyes watched her impassively as she looked at each in turn. The moment seemed crucial as she first looked at pig. Yes, she could be indulgent; she felt little awkwardness about this, although she had an immediate sense of the extra couple of kilos that had crept onto her waist. Goat? Well, sex itself had never been a problem, although somewhat unfulfilled. Even this night was giving her a deeper sense of that and what she might step into. So, goat was her libertine side, yet this she already knew and it wasn't for more of the same that she was here for. Did she think that: "What she was here for"? Another light seemed to go on.

It was dog: she knew this irrevocably and unconditionally, and her groin ached for dog, as her body confirmed her choice.

"Here, Rover!"

Boy that clown had a weird sense of humour! Yet how did he know this? She had not at that point made any indication, yet she felt resigned. She knew it was dog, as did clown, but how and why?

It was all starting to go around in her head very rapidly now. It was not simply about sex; it was about power. She was a victim because she was powerless and she was a victim because she did have power, but she couldn't access it. Now she realised it was buried in her core, her sexuality, and it needed liberating from those social yokes of her upbringing. Dog was moving toward her and unleashing his erection, it was bigger than she had ever seen before and so erect. Clown undid her hand ties as Dog pulled her down the bed, raising her legs with his hands and penetrating her in one thrust, whilst Clown clamped her wrists together above her head with cuffs; she wasn't yet ready to be free she realised, but she was ready to enjoy this monster cock that was rhythmically opening her up.

Dog was sex, but he also exuded power and she could have both. She looked impassively into his eyes – dog's eyes – as her pelvis began to respond to the thrusts. She was full and the edge of pain was there again, but this time she let go into it and felt sheer pleasure. It was at that point that she felt her hands free, Clown must have released her, she thought, or had she freed herself? It didn't matter. Her hands went to Dog's chest and scratched and clawed. He threw her onto her knees and fucked her like a bitch as she buried her head in the mattress and let out a scream, not of orgasm… but of power.

Jeannie raised her head from the mattress and pulled away from him. She turned and looked at Dog, whom, it seemed, was a little startled. She faced him also on her knees and saw Pig and Goat standing behind watching. Her eyes were for Dog though, she may have them – even all of them together – another day; today was for Dog. She pushed Dog back onto his back and mounted him pulling his dick into her slushy cunt, first facing him, but then she decided to turn around to watch the others watching her performance. She gripped Dog's knees with her hands and rode him like she had never ridden a man – animal – in her life. She felt on top of the world and she came a thousand comes.

"Well done, Jeannie!" She was in her chair looking at the screen and Clown was looking at her.

"We may see you again, I take it?"

"You will." Jeannie said this with a smile as the screen image was replaced by the spreadsheet. There was no choice, she closed the file and went to bed. As she slipped into sleep, she realised she had turned a corner and a new life would begin from here.

The Pirate

With his patched eye he looks more like a pirate than a bikie, but that doesn't make me like him any the more. Tats on his muscular forearms, I'll bet he has them all over his body, probably even on his dick as some sort of trophy. I put the file down; I've read enough before I go to see him. Seven years for rape: about what he deserves, I surmise. She claimed abduction and pack rape by him and his cohorts, on his direction. He claims she was the seducer and came along for the 'ride'. She got more than she bargained for, one way or another. Judge didn't believe much of his story and I can't say I blame her; we need types like this well away from the public, so maybe seven years isn't long enough? Slow down girl, you're hardly being objective here and you are meant to be his 'therapist'!

I am really fed up with this. Time to change jobs, as all I seem to get are these losers. Apologies for men who just abuse women and feel like it's their God-given right. Fuck wits. I used to think something of – some – men before I got into this goddamned business, but times were tough when Steve dumped me. No option really, but fucking therapy for serial misogynists ... what a fucking life. Pays the bills though; home to the flat, the cat ... is this where I'm at? Seems so. Cunt on the shelf and retirement time: Maybe the cat is the only pussy I should be stroking.

Sits across from me, calm as a fucking tree in the middle of a storm. Bastard. Why the hell haven't I at least got a relationship together? I'm good-looking and I fuck well ... so I'm told. Now here I am, quietly slipping past my prime, childless and in a fucking job that I thought would help me to enquire into the "meaning of existence", and I end up a tool of the establishment trying to – supposedly – rehabilitate dead-shits. What did I do wrong? It must be karma, I must have killed some macho bastard in a past life, and now I'm getting my comeuppance treating these shits. Fuck.

He just sits there, the shit. Think he must be arrogant, but I have a strange unsettled feeling that I'm missing the point. Not easy to get much out of him; he's no Shakespeare. I press on and presume I'm going to get the usual defence of "I didn't do it" and the subsequent corrected version missed by her honour and the twelve men and women good and true. He doesn't do that; he talks about his dog and wonders who will be looking after it. He knows his brotherhood will, as there'll be hell to pay when he gets out if it dies while he's inside and he'll want the detail. Has power, this one.

But how come he accepts this all so easily?

I'm starting to have doubts. Maybe he didn't do it? Well, of course he fucking did, but maybe she wanted it? Well, I might too... did I just think that? Oh my god, maybe he's got me too! Back a step or two, lass, get some space and take a breath. I think I might have been too long without a fuck, though. He's looking very attractive and my body knows it. What's more scary is that I think he does too; he smiles. Bastard. We talk about his childhood. He answers in simple and sometimes monosyllabic phrases. He's more intelligent than that, but he's not going to show it... yet. I adjust my blouse; he notices. I shift in my seat; he sees that too. He doesn't show it, but I know he knows. Fuck. I'm feeling really unsettled. I mean really. The room is getting a bit hazy and this pirate is just smiling at me ...

I look down to my skirt, which circles gracefully around my ankles just above the dirt of the lane I am standing in. It runs next to the harbour with those graceful galleons that sit on the drifting sea making their presence known by an occasional wooden sound as they rub against the wharf. I escaped in this gown; Gilbert will be looking for me. The last beating was too much. I can't live with it any longer. I know if he gets me pregnant that he thinks he'll have me. I must get away before this, but I have nowhere to go and I'll be soiled and ruined. I can't stand the beatings any more... well I might... but not his.

I don't have much money and I'll have to think quickly. "The Shadow of the Night" creaks against the wharf. She's a light ship and probably very quick, I'd imagine. There's her master walking down the plank; arrogant man I suspect, but he has something in his swagger. Patch on his eye adds to the mystique, could be taken for a pirate anywhere I suspect, except in this sleepy little Cornwall harbour where everyone minds their own business, to the point we wouldn't know if we're at war with France... again. We always are, one way or another, so that hardly makes much difference.

He passes me, tips his hat and proceeds to the tavern at the corner. He may be my best option. I know Gilbert may have come out of his brandy haze and be setting the hounds after me, so I'd better be quick. I go into the tavern and see him, clay pipe in hand and pewter mug in the other, leaning against the fireplace. He looks at me, as if he knew I was coming.

"My Lady?"

"Captain," I respond, "I'm in a tricky situation and need to leave at the next tide in a way that can't be detected. There, I've told you. I pray Sir, please don't use my vulnerability to my disadvantage."

"Madam," he responds, "why me?"

"Well, I'm a little short of options at present, Sir, so I must take a gamble or two... but it seems to me you are a man of honour... or have I that wrong?"

"My lady, I am the soul of discretion. But you must be awares that my ship is a mixed bag and that you may need to be more active than passive should I be receptive to your company?"

"Sir, that I realise." I can guess what he means.

We left on the next tide. I felt a relief beyond what I could have imagined. Gilbert's cane would have cut deep and raised more blood than hitherto. The Captain gave his orders and the sloop made its way from the harbour effortlessly. He showed me to a small cabin and I slept a relieved sleep, dreamless.

He awoke me at dusk. He told me that I have some initial duties to perform and I should meet the crew. I asked of my attire, which was the silken petticoats below my gown and for which I had no replacement. No matter, says he, we are a basic sort; it is your presence that is desired. With that he leads me across the deck and into the recesses at the rear of the ship. We go down and enter a large cabin where the crew are already drinking ale and singing; I find this strangely settling and I am welcomed by them all with a toast.

I turn to my Captain with his patched eye. He smiles and with a sweep of his hand invites me in. A mug of ale is presented to me and I drink deeply. The singing has ceased but the bawdy humour now commences. The ale is strong, but I thirst; I thirst for what I have missed, lost and may never have again. The ship rolls and they bounce against me shoulder to shoulder; I like it. As with the sea the evening rolls on and I look back to the Captain in his grand chair, pipe in hand and his pewter in the other. He smiles toward me, raises his tankard and takes a draught.

There's a hand on my knee and a look in my eye. I look at the Captain, who smiles again; I know this is my choice. I also know this is the exchange and I still have the option. Was I to ask him, I would be put off at the next port to find my own way? I would not be violated. My choice is clear; it is time to spread my less than angelic wings and maybe more than that.

The hands increase their pawing. The ale has had its effect and I am so mellow. There are more hands and I look back to the Captain. He is facing me in his grand seat and from the side two wenches come out toward him, one a buxom Negress the other a mulatto of origins mixed. They drop to their knees between his spread legs, pull down his trouser and engage his already flagrant manhood with their mouths. Am I shocked? Oh Sir, yes! Yet as he engages my glance and smiles, I know he knows that I am not, so I turn to his men.

They know it too. The table is pushed back and rugs are strewn on the floor. My clothing is almost torn from me and I respond to the various mouths that engage my body at all levels of my being. I am reclined and take my place on a fur. The mouths continue and my open bodice leaves breasts for two mouths to suckle as another finds a way into my cunt. My god! Gilbert never did that; he just wanted his maidservant to do it. That was all right, but I also wanted the aggressiveness of a man's tongue and hungry mouth. That maid was too soft, frightened of Gilbert perhaps?

There's one in me. Two others vie for my mouth, I take them in turns and they oblige. The one in my cunt is hungry and I don't mind. In between I look to the Captain with his two dark wenches providing his welfare. He is looking at me and has a smile. Bastard! But I smile and turn to the cock that is insistent for my mouth. They turn me, fuck me, sodomise and smack me: I love it all. I am the whore of all whores, 'twas just a forum I needed. Every hole is now fulfilled; I can take no more into me, but if I could I would. They come on me and in me and still they fuck me. My arse overflows, and my cunt is a quagmire of man-juice. The last leave their calling cards on my face, body and breasts and I search for it with my hands and lick the remembrance with my mouth. I am full, heavenly full. They get up and recline, their mugs replenished. I let my hand go to my sodden pussy and perform; I come to my end in front of their entranced eyes. The Captain still watches on and sprays his seed onto the proffered breasts of his dark attendants. I wish they were mine.

He gives me a choice, though really there is no doubt in my mind. We are back near to harbour in Devon. Gilbert's spies will be around; we both know it. I can leave, Gilbert would accept me back, maybe a little contrite; but the beatings would resume, I know. I can implicate the Captain as 'defence' and he will be gaoled and even hung; he will certainly suffer the beating of a lifetime. He looks at me and for the first time I see his vulnerability. How could I betray him? It was my choice, and we have so many more adventures in front of us. I smile and leave the deck to go to his quarters. He has left instruction: 'The Shadow of the Night' does not dock and continues along the coast.

I look at him still sitting there looking back at me in exactly the same position as when we began. He still hasn't said much, but he now has a slight smile on his face. I feel like I now recognise him for who he truly is. I open his file and write, then show it to him. It is my recommendation for his early release and parole as I assess him to have been adequately rehabilitated and that further incarceration would not be to his or the community's benefit.

Exorcism

It had taken Karen a while to go to the police. At first, they dismissed her story and she was resigned to integrating the experience on her own without recourse to justice and move on with her life. She even lacked the support of her friends, as they found her story incomprehensible in the light of the obvious regard Pete held for her and that she reciprocated. She had confessed to them prior to that night about the passion, excitement and experimentation of their sex life. Karen was alone with her story; Pete had disappeared into the woodwork and she was left to pick up the pieces.

Then a year later a new detective picked up her file in a cold case review and it challenged him. Why would someone approach the police with such a story of violation against the background of a stable relationship and supportive social structure, unless there was more to it than met the eye? Karen had also been submitted to appreciable psychological and psychiatric examination with little to be found. Pete was put through the wringer at the time, but Mal was suspicious that the interviewing detectives were inclined to support his position, even though his story had some obvious holes in it. Mal wouldn't go so far as to say his colleagues were misogynists, but it did fit the account that was filed... and buried.

Mal felt nervous as he picked up the phone and dialled Karen's mobile.

"Karen? I hope you don't mind me referring to you as Karen: we've never met; I'm Mal Cousins of the police force. I'm doing a review of your case and there are some questions I'd like to ask, if you'd be agreeable?"

Silence, but she didn't hang up either.

"Karen, I'm suspicious of some of the conclusions that have been drawn from the evidence and I would like a little clarification."

"You want me to go through this again? Don't you think I had enough the first time?"

"If I read between the lines correctly, I can understand how you might feel."

Silence again.

This time Mal decided not to break it.

"OK, I'll meet you."

The next day in a local park these two figures cut an interesting tableau, idly feeding the ducks in the lake from their position on a nearby bench, whilst simultaneously entering into deep and sometimes animated discussion.

"What makes you think I might be telling the truth when those dick-head mates of yours didn't?"

"They're not my mates, colleagues maybe, but not mates. I think you may have hit a sort of cultural divide in the force and come down the wrong side."

Karen looked at him and her face softened for the first time giving Mal an opportunity to examine it in more detail. Her walk toward him had been a little stiff but had a distinguished feel to it. Her face indicated she was a strong personality, as her eyes flickered around his face, taking it all in. She was very attractive, even beautiful, long dark hair graced her finely featured face and full lips bordered her generous mouth. In other circumstances this would be a woman I would show an interest in, he thought.

Karen told her story again. It was largely as recounted in the file. She had met Pete at a work conference on human relations.

She described him as quiet and intelligent, but with a determined personality that shone through in the conference breakout sessions. At the conclusion of the weekend, she was preparing to go straight home and not join the others for a drink, until he made his personal invitation for her to join them – him. The evening had been brief and light, telephone numbers were exchanged and it simply started from there. Nothing untoward so far and Mal was struggling to see anything that could foreshadow what was to come.

Karen described their sex life as "open and adventurous" and volunteered this without reservation. Mal surmised that she was sexually accomplished and it seemed they were well matched in that department.

"We started to discuss living together." Karen explained. "We'd both had domestic arrangements before, but this time there was a committed edge on my part. I also thought there was for Pete too, although I now wonder."

"And the night in question?"

"Completely and utterly out of the blue."

"Can you run me through it?"

She looked away and down, stopped throwing bread out onto the lake and took a deep breath. Her voice dropped, became a monotone and lacked its previous vibrancy and self-assurance.

"It was all normal enough and we went back to his place... and bed. There were the usual preliminaries, and then he asked me if he could tie me up."

"Had you ever done this before?"

"A couple of times before, and once I returned the favour. It had been a turn on, but on this occasion, there was an edge to his voice I hadn't heard before it. I thought I was imagining it, so I dismissed any concerns and got into the action. He tied my wrists and ankles to the bed corners with his business ties and then we got into the sex like we had before. I don't think I need to go into any detail at this point?"

"No." Mal responded, even though the question was rhetorical.

"Then he wanted to turn me over. That was new, but I agreed. Then things started to change."

"How?"

"He started to spank me."

"You'd never done that before?"

"Well, yes, but this was different."

"How so?"

"Well, it was harder. Then he just stopped and walked away to a dark corner of the room. From there his voice changed even further. It was deep... and dark, cold... I started to get frightened, but I couldn't see him very clearly. Then he emerged from the shadows wearing a dark cape and carrying two large dildos."

"Is this different?"

"Yes and no. The voice was and the cape I'd never seen before, nor the dildos. We'd played with toys, but these were much bigger."

"What happened next?"

"He kept talking in this voice I'd never heard before and he blindfolded me. Anywhere else and I would have sworn it wasn't Pete. In fact, nothing that happened after this seemed like the Pete I'd grown to know... and love. The voice kept coming, denigrating me, calling me a slut, a whore. I said that I'd had enough and wanted to stop. The voice replied that we had only just begun the punishment. Now I was shit scared.

"He started the smacking again and all the time talking; Pete usually says very little when we have sex and the smacking got harder and harder. At first, I yelled and then when he didn't stop, I started to cry. Then he took one of the dildos and rammed into my vagina, literally. It hurt a bit, but was OK after a while, though I wasn't lubricating much. Whilst he did this he just kept talking and talking.

"Then he arse fucked me. He didn't wait for any relaxation like he usually did and I could feel pain and tearing. After a while he pulled out and pushed the other dildo in and pumped away with both of them. I could feel what I presumed was blood trickle down and out. I was on the edge; tears had stopped and all I could do was give this moan. There was a level of excitement to it, I admit that and did in the past. I think that's what your mates ... "

"Colleagues ..."

"Sorry, colleagues jumped on and presumed I'd not been coerced because I admitted this. A bit naïve and gullible I realise in hindsight."

"So, you'd never experienced it with him – Pete – before?"

"No, not like this. All the time I kept thinking: "This is not Pete". If he asked me and we'd had this as a part of sex play, I might have taken it – some of it – on board. But it was because it didn't really feel like him; he was so cold and the words kept coming from that awful voice. Then I passed out.

"When I came to, he was lying next to me, naked and sweating, he seemed almost delirious and was talking to himself, although I couldn't work out what he was saying. Anyway, I wasn't going to hang around. My bonds had become loose with all the activity and I was able to get out of them. I grabbed my clothes and dressed on the run.

"He called the next day. It was strange, he didn't apologise or anything. He asked me what had happened, why had I left. I was silent at first, but he disbelieved me when I said he had violated me. Violated, he said, no way! He loved me. Sure, I thought, and you do that to me? But it was odd, particularly when he asked if his drink could have been spiked, as he had an awful headache and felt sick.

"Over the next few days, I ran it all in my head many, many

times, as my pussy and arse recovered. I took a couple of days off, turned my mobile off and booked in at a motel. I needed to sort it out. When I got back, he called, desperate, but his story was the same: he didn't recall anything that happened, he denied my story entirely and went back to the "spiked drink" excuse. I was now starting to see it as an excuse, even with his apologies of anything he might have done that sounded almost incidental."

"Did you meet?"

"Once. He looked awful, but I was now numb and said I wanted time. It was brief and I asked him not to ring."

"What made you contact the police?"

"Beyond the confusion and elements of doubt I felt that I had been violated, raped, and even with our history I couldn't leave that at peace. Also, if he was right with his "spiked drink" story I thought the police might get to the bottom of it. Instead, they just took it at face value and claimed they had insufficient evidence. Pete didn't deny it; he just stuck to his "I don't know" line and they started to question my imagination... and sanity. The psychs cleared me on that count, but by then it was obvious that the detectives wanted to believe him and were going to let it drift, so I backed off."

"Not very happily, I suspect."

"Dead right! But what else could I do?"

Well now there is something, thought Mal, I'm not going to let this drift. As Mal pondered the case over the next few days he had little doubt that Karen had been violated the way she had described, but Pete's response nagged at him.

As did some other features. Mal was an unusual detective in many ways. He had been the butt of many a joke when he used psychics in unsolved crimes, and some of Karen's story sounded almost like what he knew as "spirit possession". But there were priorities before this: If he considered this could be a crime of rape then he needed to interview Pete first.

It took time to find him. Pete had quit his job shortly afterwards and gone up the coast. He was now living in a caravan park and worked casually in any local jobs that came up, like grape picking. This in itself was quite a difference from his prior life and Karen had no idea about what was happening to him; she had determined to erase him from her life. When Pete was brought in Mal was surprised at his appearance, which was quite different to the photographs on file. He had lost weight, grown his hair, added a beard and his eyes had a wild appearance. Pete's story had not changed, however, so Mal was in a difficult situation. He decided to arrest Pete, who, surprisingly, seemed almost relieved. The first query he had was for Karen's welfare, which caused Mal to raise his eyebrows somewhat.

The hearing was set down for a fortnight hence. Karen seemed ambivalent about proceeding, but responded to Mal's suggestion that all parties needed resolution to the situation and if that meant gaol for Pete's guilt of a major crime, then this would be appropriate. He tempered this by telling Karen he had some more investigative leads to pursue, although he was relieved that she didn't ask what these specifically were.

Gray was an old hippy and school-friend from way back; that was how Mal initially perceived him, at least. His opinion had changed when Gray offered his services to help solve a bush-fire that destroyed several homes and was thought to have been the result of arson. Gray was able to educate Mal a little into his spiritual beliefs and psychic abilities. Mal was to make regular use of him after this time and remained astounded by his success rate.

The first thing that Gray requested was that Karen not see or visit Pete for the time being. As Karen was still very unsure about the whole process, this was an easy request to satisfy. Next, he asked to be taken to the house that Pete was leasing at the time of the alleged crime. It was an older building in a quiet and reasonably affluent suburb. The owners had since re-leased the property but had no difficulty with Mal's request, although it did require a little delicate explaining to the current tenants. That afternoon Mal and Gray went into the unoccupied house with a spare key and stood in the hallway. It was an attractive old building, reeking character and history. Gray closed his eyes for about a minute as Mal responded to the unverbalised cue, staying still and silent. Gray opened them again and they made their way upstairs to the main bedroom where Gray repeated the procedure and spent several minutes silently walking around the room. Then they quietly left.

In the car Gray asked to be taken to somewhere quiet, Mal took him to the park where he had first spoken with Karen.

"You brought Karen here to talk as well, heh?" Gray's comment was more a statement than a question, so Mal felt no compulsion to reply.

"There has been a murder in that house, probably in that bedroom and many years ago; thirty or forty I'd say. The wife, as she would have been a wife all those years ago, had been unfaithful and her husband had found out. He didn't confront her, though. He went to bed one night and asked for his marital rights and, I suppose, she didn't feel she could refuse his request. During the sexual act he started to beat her and then turned her over to invade her anally, something that had never happened before. He abused her with instruments, maybe bottles… then as she lay bleeding and sobbing, he throttled her. The body was taken by cover of night in his car boot and disposed of in bush-land north of here. He was able to explain her absence as desertion based on infidelity and attracted sympathy rather than question. It wasn't until the body was discovered that he attracted any further attention. By then he had travelled north up the coast and was never seen again. He is still here, even though he drowned many years ago. He remains burnt up with anger, the killing of his wife only excited his thirst for the judgement of women as a class."

It didn't take Mal long to check the records and find the story of the woman's body discovered in the bush thirty-eight years before, who had lived at the very address that Pete had occupied. The hair on his back stood up. It did more so with Gray's next request:

"I'd like to meet Pete and heal him."

It was simple, straightforward and more like a polite command, so Mal arranged the meeting without any questions; these could wait till after the event. All he asked was that he could, and should in his capacity as a police officer, witness such an event.

When Gray met Pete, he was mildly shocked although not surprised at his appearance: He was a lost soul, literally.

As Gray explained to Mal later the shock of what he had experienced on the night in question had disrupted his connection with his soul and he was now operating in the world without its influence, which made him exceedingly vulnerable and appear somewhat as a zombie. What Gray also noted was that whatever the influence of the shock or trauma had been, it had not taken hold and Pete must have displayed considerable psychic strength to prevent its ongoing influence from acting through him. In doing so Pete may have saved Karen's life.

Gray explained to Pete that he would like to conduct a hypnosis session so that Pete may re-experience the evening and put it to rest. At least, that was what Gray explained to Pete as he began to "see" a hostile presence above Pete's right shoulder. Gray also confirmed that Mal and Mal only would be watching the interaction and was given permission to intervene on Pete's behalf should he consider that be appropriate, but only if really necessary. Gray also asked to be allowed to do anything psychically from a healing perspective that he may see fit; Pete nodded his approval, but the presence became agitated and darkened considerably.

Gray put Pete in a light trance and took him back to that fateful night. Pete recounted the evening to the point of the bondage and then became vague, finally stopping talking altogether as his head slumped. Gray knew the presence had re-entered Pete's body.

"What do you want with me, Magician?"

"I want you to leave this man; he is not the one responsible."

"Oh, he is," countered the male presence, "or at least he should be. It is the right of all men to deal with faithless women!"

"And you know his woman was that?"

"All women are, Magician, they are all sluts and whores. They are faithless liars who would drain a man of his goodness and intent!"

"Is that sufficient reason to take this man?"

"He put himself in my path with his act; no-one has done that in that room since I dealt with that whore of a wife of mine!"

The presence was now speaking through Pete's mouth and Mal was shocked. He could imagine what Karen must have experienced that night, although, unlike Gray, he could not "see" the presence intuitively he knew it to be there, of that he was sure, as he started to see the full picture.

What was going on beyond the one-way mirror was an exorcism, he now realised that and would not have allowed such an event to occur should he have known. Now it was too late, although he was secretly pleased at Gray's deceit. Gray closed his eyes and stepped forward toward Pete, or his possessor. He passed hands over and around Pete's head as his face became ashen and tortured. The voice became a scream as Gray persisted, with many expletives and vitriol directed at him. In spite of this Gray persisted as sweat poured from him. Pete's head started to rock and shake, as he then left his seat and started writhing on the floor in waves of convulsions. Froth came from his mouth as his face reddened in intensity and Gray joined him on the ground, holding him tight and speaking inaudibly into his left ear. The noise of Gray's speech increased above the screams as Mal realised he was speaking in no language he could recognise. Pete convulsed again and became quite rigid as Gray disengaged and knelt above him.

As Mal's hand went to the button that would end the proceedings he thought he saw a plume of dark smoke come out of Pete's body and disperse in the surrounding air. Pete visibly relaxed and his colour returned, although his eyes remained closed. After several minutes of silence Gray gently aroused Pete, took his hand and led him back to his seat, then resumed his own. Pete opened his eyes and smiled.

"I think you can come in now, detective!" Gray announced.

Gray and Mal had nearly finished the de-briefing:

"So, the murderer has gone?"

"Yes, he won't be back."

"How do you know?" Mal asked.

"Sixth sense," was all the reply he got.

"What about Karen?"

"Well, I think it's about time she paid her boyfriend a visit."

"Gray, aren't you being a little premature?"

"Maybe, but I think not."

He was right. Karen was nothing if not forgiving. Although the conveyed explanation of the events was a little "far out" for her liking, it certainly matched her experience and made sense in a way that all her musings had not. It was a small matter to drop the charges, which Mal's colleagues would interpret as a justification of their position, which was something of an irony: small matter, he felt genuine justice had been served.

Their reconnection didn't take long. There was too much love to let unnecessary impediments get in the way, but as he started to undress her, she couldn't resist one parting comment before passion consumed them:

"No ties tonight, lover boy!"

The Training Group

Mike's training had been a mixed blessing. Clinical psychology had proven dry, even boring and did neither challenge nor stimulate him intellectually, although it gave him a qualification and attendant professional status. By contrast, other psychological and therapeutic movements outside of the conventional and academic mainstream seemed to open doors of inquiry to the mind that were creative and mysterious, even spiritual in nature. Maybe he should have been a priest rather than a therapist, but sex had raised its head and the cloisters seemed a lesser quarry than the nurse-ridden hospital wards of the psychiatric hospitals. He came to understand a different perspective to "making a hospital bed"!

Mike was now separated, with a divorce immanent and back in the social (and sexual) marketplace. That, along with what alternative therapies revealed to him about his own sexual nature, was a potent and even dangerous combination. He wanted that combination to continue, as his sexual exploits were seen to be part inner discovery, part realisation, part "becoming more conscious" and so giving them plausibility, justification and even reinforcement. He was on a roll; sexual activity fuelled his creativity, self-discovery and challenged him in ways that confirmed his decision to leave his conventional marriage.

Then they suggested he undergo training in one such tradition and a dilemma opened up. He had had enough of the hospital wards and pretty nurses, now the clinical psychological option was revealing its sterility. So, he agreed and decided to quit hospital practice, continue as a therapist and train in one discipline that seemed more mysterious, even mystical. It put him out of the mainstream, but he had always been a rebel and this seem to satisfy those aspects of his personality that bespoke excitement, passion and life in the fullest sense of the word. It reached well beyond the restrictive and rational perspectives he had experienced to date exploring the feminine as well as the mysterious and creative dimensions of the mind and soul.

He was wrong. Once they had snared him, he was encouraged to mature from the path of self-discovery he had adopted, which now became defined as self-indulgent and as a future therapist he should present a picture of stability to both his clients and the public at large. Although this was at variance with the inner content of this discipline, this attitude bespoke the desire for mainstream academic and intellectual acceptance, so was fundamentally hypocritical. A division occurred at that time, one that reinforced the primal one that had caused his therapeutic search within therapy in the first place. It was not a healing in the sense that he had presumed, it became instead concealed. He learnt to conform, as he was both an intellectual asset and a good figurehead for the tradition's needs.

This was a different conformity, though. Psychology, in general, and psychiatry, in particular, were male-dominated professions. The rules of engagement were clear; they were a continuation of his schooling, ordered and linear with a defined momentum and outcome. So why had Mike chosen to leave the familiar? This much he understood: The world of the feminine had opened up for him. More than the ravaging of idle female mouths, cunts and arses, he was experiencing a strange and mysterious world of which he wanted more, and yet more. The love affair of his life had not provided it and he knew he must turn inward, not as the imperative of his training, but in response to a deep demand. His training demanded a singular loyalty that was incommensurate with his nature, although at that time he presumed it to be an unhealed split rather than a division within the motives of the organisation itself. He opted for concealment and remained psychically divided.

Women ran this organisation and maintained its conformity: these women who were acolytes of the founder and adopted his ways on his death. They did not, however, acknowledge the way he conducted his life, with his numerous affairs. Yet they were in awe of him in a manner that seemed sexual to Mike. There was a veneer that was male, familiar and which, for example, governed the imperative of his further training. But beneath this veneer, coming as it did through female guise, was an ambiguity that both suited Mike's nature and was one he felt he could explore with relative impunity. He still had the devil-may-care indestructibility that characterised one drawn to these opposing poles, yet unawares of the danger in the depths. His inherent narcissism was being exploited and he hadn't recognised it as his sense of importance was simultaneously flattered.

Mike was in a training group with three women, one of his age, Kathy, and two younger. None were medically trained, nor was the training therapist, a woman in her late forties. Kathy had a similar life experience to Mike and they struck a ready friendship. The sexual element was there, but not as strongly as with the two younger participants, Jayne and Betty. Adele was the trainer and encouraged a close relationship amongst the group members; she had also conducted Mike's earlier therapeutic training, so was aware of his proclivities. Her encouragement felt to him a bit ambiguous, to say the least.

It didn't take long for Mike to get Kathy into bed. She wasn't a bad fuck, but nothing special, although it consolidated the relationship. They both knew it was something they had to do, almost to 'get it out of the way'. The sex itself did not take them anywhere they had not been before. Mike pulled out his

94

repertoire, performed and Kathy responded, but there was no particular magic, although it didn't stop them casually repeating the exercise on a regular basis. Kathy indicated that Jayne and Betty were having a lesbian relationship, which conformed to Mike's prior assessment, but what he became increasingly aware of was that Adele had both knowledge and some sort of control over everything that was going on.

Mike started to appreciate this knowledge of Adele's first with Kathy, just in the way she expressed things and other offhand comments, so he started to be a little wary. He also began to appreciate that his sexual activities with Kathy were the subject of reportage and that Adele's interest could be at the least vicarious and at the most informative.... for reasons he did not know. He started to become weary of Kathy's holes. Her pussy was obvious; cunt lips that were almost exaggerated and an odour that made it difficult for Mike to eat it. Her mouth admitted a standard penile dose but no more and her arse ran away when his cock begged deeper and harder things. It felt as if all her apertures accepted him, yet did not fully welcome him. She was accommodating yet not so; this would not be a relationship of any substance. Yet it kept Mike away from anything and anywhere else and, after a while, he wondered whether that was what Kathy was there for, to keep him in line. His attention began to turn.

Yet this did not seem to surprise Kathy. Mike's pursuit of Jayne was like the habitual predator when both they and their prey know exactly what is on offer. Yet the games were played: a discussion of the nineteenth century philosophers and their seminal influence on the psychoanalytic movement. Yes, said Mike, but what of the Spiritualist influence in America and how that had almost turned psychiatry around? Their discussions, of course, led to a casual drink and then more, but it seemed that

Betty was never far away. Jayne's cunt was ravenous; she would have let him eat her all night. So consuming was it and receptive of his sperm that it took him three encounters to even countenance his cock in her mouth. When that happened, it was also engaging in a manner that drew his emotion into this quiet yet intense woman. He wondered whether he was starting to love her, but never felt Kathy's eyes off him, or Betty's hovering presence.

The obvious solution did not take Mike long to decipher. He spent a tranquil evening with a whiskey in hand watching Betty draw Jayne away from him to the rug-laden floor. There she quickly disposed of Jayne's underwear and immediately commenced a pussy eating that impressed Mike with its endeavour and intensity. From nowhere Betty produced a dildo and mercilessly rammed it into Jayne's arse whilst she continued to devour her cunt. Mike could sense and almost taste the familiar juice, but he was entranced, sipped his scotch and savoured the performance in front of him. Betty drew back and continued her plummeting of Jayne's arse with the dildo, then looked at Mike and invited him in. Did he need a second offer?

Betty held his cock and guided it into Jayne's cunt. He knew this receptacle and relaxed into the slow steady strokes that were his forte. Jayne responded and Betty stroked his back to then put her face in front of him and engage him with a kiss that took his awareness entirely to his mouth. He almost forgot his attention to Jayne's cunt whilst Betty's tongue dived into and around his mouth, exploring all it could find. The little wiggle of Jayne's arse reminded him and Mike continued the deep strokes of her cunt whilst his mouth explored Betty. This twofold sensation was ecstatic, yet difficult to sustain. Betty, ever the organiser, took a step back and removed Mike's cock from her lover's pit. She sucked on it deeply before placing herself on the rug and inviting the self-same treatment he had given Jayne. He obliged.

Jayne took a position between them, stroking the body of each hand-by-hand. Mike enjoyed Betty's cunt. It was tight and inviting, matching her mouth, but also had a demand that he couldn't fathom. He plundered it though, and she responded. In return Jayne dropped her head and gave Betty a deep kiss and Mike felt Betty's cunt open deeper in response. No matter, he may be the instrument in this, but he was willing and able. Jayne moved away from her lover's face, pulled his cock from her cunt and ate it like she never had when they fucked singularly. Mike was both in heaven but also deeply confused.

As he alternatively fucked each of them, and was sucked into the bargain, he felt an intensity that was both novel and confusing. He decided to deal with this by diving deeper. He placed Jayne above Betty so that they could kiss, whilst he positioned his cock at the entrance to her arse. Jayne became quite still and Betty disengaged herself so that she could see what was about to take place. Mike rubbed some saliva on his penis, thinking that it was a bit strange that he hadn't fucked Jayne's arse to this point of time. No matter, she was still, receptive, and her lover was watching, so he slowly edged it in. A little whimper and he was deeper still. Betty was watching every move as he worked up a rhythm and moved ever deeper. On one of his 'out strokes' Betty took his cock and sucked deeply on it, then to position it for return to her lover's arse.

Of course, gentleman that he was, he had to return the favour. He placed Betty on her back, raised her legs to a height and penetrated her arse, as her eyes didn't miss a beat. Jayne hovered over them and there was enough room for her to suck Betty's cunt as he stroked her arse, occasionally to pull out and let Jayne suck him deeply before the cycle was repeated. Mike was in seventh heaven, yet a deep doubt remained. No matter, he pulled his cock from Betty's arse to spray Jayne's face and mouth. What was surprising is that when he collapsed back on the carpet, he remembered nothing else.

Now he was on the carpet. Here he was with Adele, who seemed to know about everything that had taken place, giving him a hard line about the 'appropriateness of his behaviour'. What about the bitches I fucked, thought Mike, I bet they don't get the same dressing down? Or, he humoured himself; if they do get a dressing down, I'll bet they enjoy the fucking! A brief thought though; this is serious shit; my career is on the line here. What a turnaround, in my earlier worlds, guys could fuck with impunity and girls cop the shit. The rules are different here, he thought. Adele was an imposing and commanding figure; he felt he had no choice but to follow her direction. It was time the group got together and looked at the "murky undercurrents" that had emerged in their collective relationship to sort them out. Make them "conscious" or whatever. Mike didn't feel he had much choice.

It wasn't what he expected. The girls were all dressed in fetish gear; latex clothes, stockings, big heels, the works. They had whips and a variety of dildos and other toys. When Mike came into the room Betty had already begun with a black vibrator up her lover's arse whilst she sucked Jayne's pussy as Kathy simultaneously kissed her. Well, thought Mike, this wasn't the sort of "review" I expected, but it could be interesting! Then he noticed Adele in an armchair at the edge of the scenario, intensely watching the proceedings in front of her.

The evening started predictably enough. Mike accepted the circumstances before him and, with a few variations – all three women together and Adele's presence – it was almost like business as usual. He started fucking them all, serially and collectively, and felt quite comfortable with the experience as they moved around each other as well as engaging him in the dance. They took time out for a drink and it was after this that Mike passed out; he didn't know it then, but his drink had been drugged.

Mike awoke with a headache, but as a reflex when he tried to move his hand to massage his brow, he found it restrained. A quick tug, yes it was, at the wrist. The room was darker, but it was the same one where they had had the earlier orgy and lit by candles only. The women were seated on cushions in front of Adele, who was talking intently. Their eyes were fixed and there was a strong smell of incense and some drumming music coming from behind Adele.

Mike's head was thudding and he felt sick; not only due to the poison in his system, but also in response to the anxiety that was increasingly gripping him. He noticed that not only were his hands bound, but also his legs at the ankle and he was laid out as if on a cross. It made little use to try and free them, as the clasps were metal and any movement induced discomfort, then pain and bleeding. He lay still on the raised platform-cross that felt now more like a bier.

He could raise his head for a few seconds only. Beyond his feet the women were now standing in a circle, all dressed in robes now and holding hands. They were chanting with closed eyes and paid no attention to him. Was he imagining all this, was the drug a psychedelic? These thoughts crossed his mind, but he found no ready answers. Each time he looked at the group he seemed to recognise them less as the robes appeared darker. This change of recognition was not of their features, but a change in the sense of time; something told him they were moving to an ancient drumbeat.

This feeling was reinforced when the room seemed to become a cavern with granite walls and the candleholders appeared of wrought iron. He looked at them again and had the indisputable knowledge that he was in a witch's coven and that he was a captive priest. This knowledge extended to visions of himself as a champion of the God of the New Testament and a scourge of those of the old ways; he even condoned their death when they came into direct conflict with the ways of the Lord, or used rudimental magic in the healing arts.

It didn't take long for this to become evident that this was why he was in this position, laid out in a mockery of his Teacher. The women all disrobed and continued chanting as they danced a frenzy. Behind Adele's chair Mike could make out an idol on the wall with his horned human head. In his mind this confirmed them to be witches and him in a satanic cult: small matter that they saw it as representative of the old ways, which it was their duty as women to keep alive.

First Jayne (or was it Betty?) came to his side and began to masturbate him: It was Jayne. He responded quickly, which added to his anxiety and embarrassment. His cock swelled and he could feel the fluid urges move to his loins. As this happened Jayne bent her head and masturbated his semen into her mouth. She then moved away, seemed to swallow a little and then spat the remainder into a large, flat cauldron that stood on a pedestal below the idol. Then she turned, kissed Betty and Kathy and then dropped between the legs of the now seated – enthroned – Adele and began to lick her cunt with her semen coated tongue.

Next it was the turn of Betty, who undertook the same ritual. His cock was a little sore, but it responded none the less and his cum was similarly distributed. By the time Kathy had his cock hard and in her mouth, he was frightened of his response; it was so against his beliefs and teachings as a priest: How could he respond that way? But respond he did and he came in Kathy's mouth for her to distribute her offerings. Surely that was enough? For a while it was as the women returned to their dancing, with their forms silhouetted by the fire that ranged behind his head and vision.

They would not leave him alone. As long as his cock responded they kept up the performance. Although it ached it did so respond, even as Mike's body was racked with palpitations and fear. Eventually, after many rounds, he seemed to collapse both physically and mentally and was spent. Yet before he passed into a now welcome oblivion, he saw the woman make a mixture with additions to their cauldron and then share the drinking of it. He knew they had taken not only his power, but also that of the institution he represented.

Mike came to. It was his own time and place and he was in Adele's summoning room. The room was now bare and vacant with the door open. He rose from the couch feeling exhausted and felt pain in his wrists and ankles. The blood stains there seemed a further mockery of what he had experienced and inversion of the beauty of the crucifixion that in that prior time he had held with reverence, awe and majesty.

Mike now knew with a certainty that surprised him that the movement's founder had been through similar experiences, integrated them, and championed them beneath the facade of his psychology. That his private life reflected an ongoing involvement in the feminine mysteries that informed the body of knowledge he bequeathed to the world and which his acolytes – mainly women – maintained after his death. Mike knew he had been through something similar and that not only had he been stripped of his power, that he had also been stripped of the vestiges of his sexism that stood behind his involvement.

But now he was alone. He made his way to the door knowing he would never see these women again. He knew that he must recover, recuperate and rehabilitate and, further, that this would take many years. Somehow, he had to make a deeper sense of this experience and not reject it and his destiny was not to follow the path of the founder of this therapy movement, but to forge his own, whilst retaining the wisdom he had attained from the founder's explorations. In the future he knew that this destiny may well depend on this understanding and wisdom in ways that he could not presently foresee.

Stan the Man

"You have anaemia," said my doctor, "I'm fairly certain it must be your heavy periods."

"They've been slightly heavier lately, but there are no clots." I replied.

"But you don't have any other symptoms of note that could explain it and I presume you don't want to do an exhaustive investigative process?"

He was right, I didn't, but I remained a little troubled.

I had met Stan some six months earlier and we had begun a whirlwind of a relationship, so I had put my fatigue down to the late nights of love and the proverbial 'burning the candle at both ends'. Yet I was a little bemused; although the quality of the passion was the most intense I had experienced, there were times previously when I had been in such spaces, they had invigorated not depleted me. I was confused, hence the visit to my doctor. So, it was anaemia and not an emotional problem; at least that was a relief, as I obviously didn't want it to be something amiss in the relationship. My periods had been a little heavier and I had assumed that was because of the hormonal changes driven by my emotional state. I explained this to my doctor, who considered it a plausible explanation, although I did notice a quizzical look pass his brow with that tentative acceptance of my 'diagnosis'.

Stan was Hungarian by birth. He was a broody, intense man with deep-set eyes and teeth that became prominent, even a little sinister, when he smiled, which he did a lot of. I had not been attracted to him initially, although this may have been due to coming out of the grief and trauma of the relationship with Anton. I did seem to be drawn to these foreign types, something my pet astrologer had predicted! The time with Anton had been somewhat chaotic, which was fine by me being an artist, but it was the increasing violence that eventually got to me. It had started as the occasional slap on the bum when we fucked, but then he had introduced the slap and tickle prior to the bedroom, except that the tickle became less and the slaps got harder. Then there was the viciousness that accompanied them and when the fingers started to close to a fist and I had to explain a black eye to my friends, I knew it was time to leave.

That wasn't the end of it, of course. The stalking started almost straightaway and took on a threatening quality. One car chase culminated in a restraining order, but that didn't stop him, he just became more subtle. In the meantime, I went to counselling as I was convinced there was something about me that had attracted this violence, but the therapist seemed only too willing to put all the blame at Anton's door. While this was quite rational and explicable, I didn't feel entirely settled about this conclusion and went to see a psychic woman recommended to me by my closest girlfriend.

Clara was the classic New Age psychic. Her room was adorned with all the paraphernalia: crystals, candles, goddess statues and incense. I'm kind of comfortable with some of that as philosophically I incline in that direction, but sometimes it can be too blatant and Clara's room was on the edge of this. I sat down opposite her chair across a table that would have been better in a bridge card room and looked at the pack of Tarot cards in the middle, as she gave a flick of her copious gown and sat down.

The reading shocked even me. At the centre was the 'Hanged

Man' and underneath was 'The Devil'. I had sort of expected 'Death' as a major feature as I had come to the conclusion that the anaemia was an as yet undiagnosed – or undiagnosable – disease. The reading, supported by the other cards, seemed to indicate that something hidden and untoward was happening. Clara reinforced this; she knew nothing of my anaemia; she concluded that I would have to take a different attitude to 'my question' – her words, not mine, as she did not know what my 'question' was – and look to the malevolent influence in my life.

I immediately thought of Anton. But the more I considered this, the less likely it seemed. Stan had effectively dealt with that. One night he went out and stared at the car parked opposite whilst registering his number plate. The next day, unbeknownst to me, he arranged for the tyres to be let down when Anton was at work, then he left a note on his desk to gently ask him to desist from his current 'activities'. I did not know this at the time, but was pleasantly relieved to have no more of Anton's unwelcome attention. When Stan told me over dinner one night what he had done I felt an immediate thrill in my body followed by a chill. I had ignored my body, silly me! Hadn't my Guru, long since 'gone to the other shore', stressed bodily responses in issues such as this? I was confused... maybe I had thrown the baby with the bathwater in my subsequent attitudes and opinions of the New Age.

I listened to Clara; she had followed the explanation of the devil with a statement that maybe this influence was from a 'past life'. She was starting to drone on a bit; I was now somewhere else as the New Age rhetoric padded out the session. I was relieved to go and I think she knew it, although I had got good value and more than enough to ponder.

When Stan and I first fucked I was kind of surprised. We had met at a mutual friend's party and he had obviously taken an instant liking, even fixation, toward me. In the state I was in it was welcome attention, although I didn't perceive the sexual attraction as high. It was a bit of a shock when I first found myself in his bed. Sure, I'd had a shit-load to drink, but I always know where my car keys are in the morning, yet here I was in this stranger's bed and I didn't recall how I got there. Never mind, his attention toward me was singular and my battered psyche needed a bit of restoration from the outside, I figured.

His cock was big; I like them to be big. I like a cock that will fill my mouth, almost stopping my breathing in its search for my tonsils. He didn't need to worry; Linda Lovelace could have taken lessons from me! I wanted it hard. I wanted to erase the imprint of Anton from my memory and a good fuck seemed the best way to do this. That's maybe why I let him arse fuck me on the first date. Usually I wait a little, even though I love it, but on this night I wanted the intensity and even pain that it might bring to deal with what I was trying to erase. I was successful.

Stan was attentive. He didn't exploit the overt portrayal of my proclivities and held me after our intense sex; even now I hesitate to call it lovemaking. He was strong and sound, and he did deal with fucking Anton! We fell into a habit that under normal circumstances I might have questioned. And he did have a big cock, which he knew how to wield.

Then the fatigue started. It was strange... we'd have sex and I'd be satisfied, then sleep, but wake up exhausted. C'mon girl! You've done enough 'consciousness work', so how about putting some of it to use? First things first: watch. So here I am after the preliminaries and he's inside me. God, I love that big cock! Whoa, attention please! He's in me and his cock is big and satisfying. He's grinding it deep into my pelvis and I have lifted my legs to grip his hairy thighs so that he goes even deeper, which he does. It's so nice to be full. Hey, I'm so happy with being full; maybe I'm missing something?

He's kissing my face, not my lips. I don't mind usually as my focus is on my full cunt, but now I have a different level of attention. He never kisses me, or rarely, which I don't mind as that smile would impinge on my vision and conflict with the good stuff I'm getting from this. He turns me over, he usually does at this point, and so I get on my knees as a sort of reflex and start playing with my clit, knowing what will happen next. He spits on my arse and then works the fluid in with a finger; I think it's the middle one, the biggest. Sometimes he follows with two, adding his index, but usually he just puts the head of his cock there and makes the slow gentle thrust that gets beyond the restriction of my sphincter. I just have to imagine I'm having a shit in reverse, and then his cock head is in.

Of course, he's not the first man to fuck me up the arse; I like it to the point that it's almost a relationship pre-requisite. There was Mike, gorgeous man, but he wouldn't do it; thought it was 'dirty'. Maybe he really wanted a man. I never found out, because I ditched him for Anton who didn't have the same difficulty. Why does it always go back to Anton? Who the fuck is the devil in my Tarot reading? Stan is working it in now, he knows to take it a bit at a time, as the lubrication isn't as readily available as my cunt and he doesn't want to rip and tear. Well, I presume he doesn't.

He's fully in now. I push my buttocks back against his thrusts and feel him rip into my insides. It's terrific! God, am I just a filthy whore underneath this New Age bullshit? Well, if I am, just keep fucking my arse, Stan the man! Hang on. Hang on! This is where I lose it... I suddenly realise that if our sex isn't this intense then I don't wake up tired... watch it girl. He comes, a load that may give me a morning enema. No matter, I've collapsed and would normally drift, but I notice his attention to my neck still. He's kissing it as if it were my lips or, in his case, my cunt. What the fuck! It's so nice and inoffensive. Nothing untoward in all that, so I let myself drift off to sleep.

I awake. Fucked again! And I don't mean by a cock. Stan has gone already; he did say he had an early meeting. I'd better get to work too, maybe the doc is right and I should have an 'iron transfusion' whilst we look for the 'cause'. I'm reluctant, he's explained that the risks aren't like a blood transfusion, but that isn't what stops me; I want to find the cause first! I'm a mess, is that really me looking back from the mirror? You've aged gal! It's no laughing matter and my neck is so stiff.

Jesus! That's a pattern... my neck usually is a bit stiff when I feel this fucked, but the tiredness has usually over-ridden it; I'd better check this out a little further. I feel my neck and find some tenderness on the side over that big muscle that runs from the angle of the jaw to the middle of my chest. Now I think of it though, last time it was on the other side. I'd always assumed it was due to that whiplash from the car accident, but now I'm not so sure as that usually feels more in the back over my spine. I look in the mirror. My god! It's bruised! What has that fucker been doing to me? I know he's into nibbling my neck, but this is more than I'd expect from that sort of light attention, or am I deluding myself? A bit of arnica will fix that up, but how the fuck did I get it in the first place? It's got to be due to Stan, but how? I can't not let him fuck my arse, he'd suspect something if I did that, so I've just got to remain 'aware'. Now, how many workshops have I heard that in!

Here we are in this expensive restaurant and he's smiling. That smile I always had some misgivings about now seems almost offensive. I'm going off him, does he know? Don't think so, but you're here for the night, so put up with it and just enjoy the fuck if nothing else, even if it's only payment for the meal. He's talking about his work, so safe territory and not too emotionally committing. You're a good listener, even wanted to train to be a counsellor, heh? The Shiraz is good too, just remember to keep your wits about you, gal.

Here I am on my knees, face to one side on the pillow and arse in the air. Stan's big cock is filling my arse and the pumping is starting to increase. It would be easy to slip into this; orgasms from arse fucking are just my favourite! But I have a different feeling about me tonight, I want to watch as well as participate. It's like I'm hovering over my body whilst I'm still enjoying the attention. This is weird! I haven't had this sense of 'watching myself' since I was a kid, when it used to happen lots and I could somehow control it. Let's see if I can do it now.

Here I am a few feet above the bed watching me, arse in the air, getting pounded by Stan. Nothing different from a porn movie so far, except I don't have my camera! Hey, wait! Look at Stan's face... that smile is there and it's broader and more sinister than usual, even... evil. Fuck! Are you safe babe? You seem OK, but I'd better check in. Back in my body... yep, no different from a thousand arse fucks I've had before – did I say that! Pound me you motherfucker, whilst I get back above this action. That's better, now I have a ringside seat. He comes, you collapse your legs and drop into the mattress and he starts the nibbling of your neck; you smile and seem to go to sleep.

Stan is not sleeping though. He's on your right side and stroking you with his hand. This is really weird now! He smiles and then widens his lips and his teeth stand out and - my god - he's got fangs! Calm down, look a little closer. It's his incisors; they're distinctly longer than his other teeth. I hadn't noticed that before, although they've never been that long, just a little accentuated. Now he's stroking my neck and I am so asleep, then he drops down and starts to kiss my neck. I'm wriggling in a sort of contented way and he is rocking his head. Hang on a minute! I'm sure I can see blood dribbling down towards the pillow. He notices it too and lifts his head, sucks up the blood and then gets a wipe to clean my skin. When he does this, I can see two distinct marks on my neck. What the fuck! This guy is a fucking vampire!

Now I'm somewhere else. I'm in this huge room that feels almost vacant. The window is large and cathedral-like. I go to it and look out; then I see that I'm high up and it must be a castle. It's dark and stormy and I look back into the room. There's a huge bed, like something from the movies with rugs and skins over it. Candles are everywhere and there's a huge inverted crucifix over the bed. The storm has taken a turn and there's lightning and then a crack of thunder. I'm scared, but my body seems to know what to do.

Stan enters. He's dressed like some mediaeval lord. Then again, I can't complain, I look like his female counterpart with my rich velvet robes. He lifts a hand and gestures to the bed. I get on and immediately place my head in the pillow and arse in the air, pulling the robes above my waist. He does the rest; spittle on my arse, cock thrust in and then deep strokes.

He comes, I collapse and he turns my head and pulls my hair away from my neck. He then clamps his teeth into my neck and starts to groan like an animal. I smile and expose my neck even more for his convenience. I can feel him, not just sucking my blood, but him, his essence. It is almost as if I can suck it into me. I try, and when I do this, I feel strangely strong and vigorous.

I can feel him getting weaker and I stronger. I push him off me and turn his stuporous head to one side to bare his neck. Then I part my lips and recognise my incisors are long and hot. I groan and drop onto his neck and let my fangs penetrate his jugular vein. I drink my long, long fill and then scream like a hound dog. I look down at Stan, he may be asleep or dead, I know not which, but it matters not. I slap his face, he doesn't respond. I get up and go to the window, where the subsiding storm clouds reveal the full moon.

Instantaneously I'm back above my body. Stan is nowhere to be seen. I make a choice and pass back in and enjoy the warmth and invigorated feeling that now permeates my being. I know I will not see Stan again; somehow, I have absorbed him. Then I notice the car cruising up and down the road outside. It's fucking Anton! I'd thought I'd seen the last of him with Stan's dealings, but he's back.

I feel different, it's as if I feel like Stan. I go out of the front door and across to the car that's now parked a little way down the road. I tap on the window and, after a brief pause the window goes down.

"Hello Anton."

"Hi."

"Would you like to come in for a drink? It's cold out here."

Bemused, he gets out of the car, locks it and follows me inside. I pour two scotches, give one to him, which he sips while I skull mine.

"Upstairs, lover boy."

He follows.

I fuck him: fuck him real good. I even get my favourite dildo out from under the mattress, turn him over and stick it in his arse, after a bit of spit as lubricant. He doesn't resist, just moans a little and falls sound asleep as if drugged. I turn his head to one side and sink my teeth into his jugular and suck deeply, feeling the deep scream echoing in my brain.

Anton will not trouble me again.

Cockney Gin

I take a long swig from the gin bottle. Frigg! It's nearly empty
and not a ha'penny anywheres on me skirts. You're coming
unstuck luv. You only got that this morning... I think. It's getting
cold and this doorway ain't cutting off that frigging breeze. It's
getting darker and they're starting to fire up the gaslights on the
street. Better get into it, the gin's wearing off and I ain't got any
left now.

Here's a nice shop window, gaslight behind, should be able
to tart meself up reasonable, such that anys that 'ave me don't
see the wrinkles first up. You used to be something once, luv,
what the bejesus happened? 'Twas that fucking Count weren't
it? Did me well and proper, got what he wanted when I was a
looker and then took it all away... all away. What did he take
away? Straighten the skirt, fashion the bonnet, change yer
knickers and off we go! Got to be a bit careful, Jack's about still,
so they say. Gordon Bennett! Don't need shit like that; life on
these streets is 'ard enough. Swing yer 'ips, whistle a song, keep
yer chin up gal, the next gin won't be too far away!

He's getting out of a cab; he'll have a bob or two. Look
disinterested gal, keep yer eyes well in front and swing those
'ips... and for gawd's sake don't stumble. He looks... and keeps
walking. Bugger! No... he's turning, I can 'ear the tap of 'is cane.
What's the price? What do you take me for, says I, I's a nice girl!
Well, says he, and shows me what 'e 'as in 'is 'and. Shit, there's a
bottle or two there! I act coy, he's a patient one this fine lad, so
'old it gal. Another couple of coins in 'is 'and. Fair enough says

I. I's 'it hard times and it would be a welcome 'elp for me and me family. Don't know whether he swallows that shit or not, but 'is cab 'as done a circle and is now awaiting 'im or us. 'E 'ad me spotted. Shit gal! You could 'ave 'ad more en this. Never mind, there's enough to keep me warm, just got to turn the trick before the shakes come on, so let's get on with it me fine Sir!

Soft 'ands, this one. 'E even gave me a swig from his brandy flask; to keep out the cold, says 'e. Soft style too. 'Ope he ain't the Ripper. Can't be, too nice. Strokes me 'e does, 'ands roam a little and I 'elp him on. Then 'e kisses me... nobody 'as done that since the Count! Swore I'd never, never do that agin. Give yer 'eart and it gets trod on, and on, and on... But gawd this is good! 'Ope he don't get too much of me teef, they're beyond their prime, well and good. It don't stop 'im though. Aw, my fine gentleman, don't tease a young lady so, I know yer won't be 'ere in the morning, so let's get on wiv it; I know me station, the Count taught me that.

Me skirts up now, me knickers shed. Clomp, clomp, clomp goes Topsy. Rests me back in the leather does 'e and slides it in real gentle. Long time since I really felt it, you know; really, really felt it. Like the gin when it goes down, but this is up and warms yer much more. Bugger yer, yer fine gentleman, yer getting to me. Remember the Count, don't lose yerself gal! Too late. Me body wants this like it wants the gin: more than the gin, more than fucking anything! I'll melt. Frigg if 'e's the Ripper, it won't matter anymore 'cos this will be all I'll want. This second, this time, this place, this body, this 'eaven. I ain't come in years, but I'm gonna, so keep yer 'at on, me fine gentleman!

Well, it looks like the Lane, but it ain't. What's going on? Shops is big, so big, and bright. So's the wevver, naw that's a change! Keep walking luv, take it in. Then these... I dunno what. Where the carriages used to be is these tin boxes and people on funny bikes all making a whirring sound and they ain't peddling. Carnaby Street: do I remember that? All these people wearing bright stuff and wiv words on 'em. 'Free Love', well that'd stop me gin supply! But look at yerself gal, trousers yer wearing, and a gal yer is. Strange, and shoes that fit and don't 'urt yer feet. Gawd, what's going on! I'll like it for a bit, yet.

Hi Babe! Says this guy, acts like he knows me and gives me a big 'ug. Love, man! He says and walks off. Did 'e know me? I don't know 'im, do I? Start to feel a bit strange, but go wiv it gal! Then a noise above me 'ead. A 'uge big bird and now I'm really shaky. Karen! There's this gal next to me and chatting away like I's 'er long lost sister. Been away, says I, never phoned, says she. Phoned, what's phoned, I thinks? What's these machines on the road and tin birds in the air? You need a drink luv, she says, let's go to the pub. Inside she asks me what me poison is; well, I know that one, it's gin! Yeah, I know that, says she, but tonic or tomato juice? Got me, so I says tonic, could do with that. She brings it, beyond the fizz I can taste me gin. I'm settled.

He looks at her in the cab. She's mumbling something about metal cabs with no horses and great tin birds in the sky. Think she might have slipped over, hope she found herself; she's a little sweetie, this one! He thinks the push might have been just enough and he feels confident she'll be all right. He'll never know, but it doesn't stop him helping. He gives his cab driver an envelope containing the usual number of notes and a letter for the doctor, slips away telling his driver he'll be ready at the usual time tomorrow.

Another one from Mr Smith, says the orderly, must be the third this month. Wonder why he does it? Must be an angel, says the doctor. He reads the note and recognises a colleague of sorts; he'll be right about the alcoholic dementia, no doubt. He may also be right about her not having a way back and only a short time to go before the body joins her. The notes should cover this, if there's any left over just put them into the Foundation fund, says the note. The doctor goes to admit the girl and he finds Smith right on all counts.

Another sip of the gin, and... I'm back! I'm Karen! Yeah, I said to Libby, was good in France, but Darryl and me broke up so's time for 'ome, methinks. Missed yer gal! And Bob, and Mikkie, and Jake, and Suse. Let's go and paint the town, before work on Monday. Yeah, good to be back!

Immaculate Conception

"Shit!"

"Problem Bill?"

"Yeah! She's having a reaction to the anaesthetic... "

I looked at Bill and he returned my gaze with beads of sweat beginning to appear on his brow above his eyes and surgical mask, under which my guess was that his teeth were tightly clenched.

Up to this point the whole process had been fairly straightforward. I was holding a laparoscope, which I was going to insert into her inflated abdomen... sorry, forgot I'm not writing this up in a medical journal but as an account for my crazy psych mate, David, for him to use in an anthology of stories about the paranormal. Well, I can't say whether what happened is paranormal or not, I'm a fairly level-headed obstetrician and gynaecologist and all this strikes me as a bit weird at the very least. The alternative – that Kaye is a nutcase – is more plausible, although I know her well and if you set the story, she told me apart, she always struck me as sensible and level headed.

I'm getting ahead of myself. When I discussed the story that Kaye told me with David, he subsequently saw her professionally and he didn't think she had a major psych problem either. Then, after clearing it with Kaye, he asked if he could write about it – or, more correctly, gets me to write it as a 'case study' – in a compilation of medicine, mental health and the paranormal he was writing. Kaye agreed, so we went over her story again, and here it is.

Of course, all the names have been changed..., blah, blah...

Kaye came to see me for primary fertility; that is, she had been unable to get pregnant in her relationship with her husband and had never been pregnant before. I first checked out Jim, her husband, and the analysis of his sperm was normal. So, presuming he was placing it in the right spot then the problem may be with Kaye. Don't laugh about the 'placing it in the right spot', when I was a student, I came across one couple who believed the navel was the 'right spot'! There was nothing significant in Kaye's history, the examination was normal and all her tests came back clear, so we decided to do a laparoscopy; that is, for me to use a kind of telescope to have a look see at her womb and ovaries.

This was when we struck trouble. Although sometimes there is a reaction to one of the anaesthetic agents, it is usually not as severe as it was in Kaye's case. Her blood pressure dropped like a stone and we aborted the operation quick smart as she had a cardiac arrest – her heart stopped beating. There was more than one person sweating now and we quickly started resuscitation; I started to pound her chest whilst Bill continued to give her oxygen through the tube he already had in her lungs for the anaesthetic gases.

Kaye's cardiographic reading remained flat for a while and, just as we were getting to the point of bringing out the big guns, a blip crossed the scene, then another and in a short while we knew we had got out of gaol. The look Bill and I then exchanged had a mixture of relief and bemusement. Kaye was stabilised and went to the Intensive Care Unit whilst Bill and I staggered to the tearoom to debrief.

When I went up to see Kaye later, I was in for a surprise. She was sitting up in bed sipping a cup of tea looking quite serene, although surrounded by and connected to the sort of medical paraphernalia that would otherwise identify her as being a very sick bunny. Even the nurses were surprised, remarking that it seemed like she had been through a smooth and uneventful procedure and awoken to good news.

"How are you Kaye?"

"I'm fine."

"You know what happened don't you?"

"In detail, your anaesthetist explained it all to me when he came by."

Well, that made my job a little easier, so I could maybe bypass this unfortunate incident and discuss management.

"Did Bill tell you that we didn't get to do the look-see?"

"No, he didn't; but I know you didn't anyway."

That reply startled me a bit, but I thought I'd just let it pass. "Well, that leaves us where we were before we started, so we'll have to reassess management from here on."

"That might not be necessary."

Her reply was accompanied by a still and peaceful smile.

I was non-plussed. Where was the woman whose urgency had captivated me and galvanised thorough investigation? What was even more surprising is that although I had been given not one, but two uncharacteristic responses, I seemed to lose my characteristic urge to be the forensic detective and ask her what the fuck she was talking about. Instead, I simply went about my duties, arranged to see her in a month in my rooms and made my exit. It was not just her enigmatic responses that flummoxed me, but the change in the character of my mental state in a way that seemed to defy my intention; it was almost as if I was in a state beyond my will.

Equally surprising was that I seemed to forget the whole incident and its strangeness until Kaye came for her follow-up appointment a month later. Before any words were exchanged, she produced a small jar containing what I presumed was a sample of urine.

"Would you do a pregnancy test, please?" She retained the serenity I had witnessed in the hospital during her recovery.

I did as I was told and silently went through the procedure.

"It's positive." I looked directly at her, but there was no change of expression.

"Thank you."

"You're not surprised?" At least a bit of the detective was back.

"No."

"Well, I sure as hell am, so I'd be grateful if you could fill me in."

"Certainly, but I suppose you're going to have to switch hats from gynaecologist to obstetrician now!" Kaye was smiling.

Kaye then proceeded to tell me her story, whilst I buzzed my receptionist to delay the following appointments; I felt I was going to need time.

Kaye began her account with a request that what I tell be in confidence. As I spluttered out the usual medical bullshit credo about patient confidentiality, she smiled and shook her head.

"Look, I know my sanity will be in question with what I am going to share with you, and that will be understandable. If it makes it any easier, I am quite happy to have a psychiatric assessment, but I think that may be for your well-being rather than mine! I only ask that he or she be someone with a foot outside the medical camp."

That description fitted the offbeat mate of mine, Dave. I shared this with her and she nodded; they were to have more in common than I could have anticipated at that point.

Kaye began her account. "I went off to sleep OK, but then I was suddenly awake again. The weird thing was that I was looking at myself lying on the bed from the ceiling. It reminded me of a couple of experiences I had as a child, but this was as clear as a bell."

"Was this before or after you had the cardiac arrest?"

"Before, just after the anaesthetist put me under."

Interesting, I thought, as some anaesthetic agents have been known to cause a 'dissociative state', so this might explain what happened to Kaye.

"Actually, I wasn't in the room when the heart stopped beating, I was somewhere else." Her gaze was distant, but then when it returned to meet mine, she continued. "This could get a little confusing, so I'd better stick to telling the story as I saw it."

With you there gal, I thought, I was having enough trouble keeping up!

"When I woke, I realised I was looking down at myself on the table from somewhere on the ceiling. You were getting prepared and the anaesthetist was fiddling with the drip in my arm. Then he sat down and was waiting for you to get going and doing some initial observations, it was then he became startled. I continued to watch as you stopped and waited to see what was going to happen. When the panic buttons started to get pressed, I felt like I went up through the roof and then was above the hospital. The feeling was terrific at first, I also had the sense that all was not well back in the operating theatre, but I was being drawn upwards. I really had no choice and felt I had to leave my body to your collective care."

I got up and went to the window. The hospital was easily visible from my rooms and I tried to imagine what had happened to Kaye, but it was with great difficulty.

I interjected: "I get the feeling that you're going to tell me of some sort of 'journey' you went on and that this all occurred whilst we were keeping you alive?"

"Yes, I suspect so, but you may have to let go of the time and space norms otherwise it might impede you hearing me."

I got that bit, as she pressed on: "My 'journey' seemed to last quite a while, I'd say thirty minutes at least, more like an hour. As I understand it you only resuscitated me for a couple of minutes before my heart started again?"

"That's right."

"So, the time variable was certainly blown out, trying to get a grip on the spatial one won't help any insidious confusion!" Kaye was treating this so light-heartedly, so... normally. Meanwhile my reality was in tatters.

"Then I was in this beautiful countryside. All my senses were engaged with rich smells, sounds and sights. The texture of the grass was lush and soft and I simply wanted to roll in it and look up to the clear sky beyond the chattering birds and allow my body – which I now seemed to have again – to bask in the sun.

"When I sat up, I saw a figure walking toward me. He was wearing a thin, light robe. I couldn't see his face clearly with the sun behind, but I could see he had longish hair and light beard. I don't know if I've ever seen an angel, but he was the closest thing yet!

"He took my hand and raised me up, and then we walked to a small grove decked with soft undergrowth and flowers. He guided me down onto nature's bed and knelt beside me stroking my face, then my breasts."

"Didn't you want to resist such sexual advances of a complete stranger?" I asked somewhat naively, it seemed.

"I can't explain that. Rather like the time and space thing, this seemed totally right. There was no sense of 'infidelity' or something Jim should be jealous of or threatened by. In fact, I have told him the whole story, no editing, and he's totally OK with it all and happy with the outcome."

"He impregnated you, didn't he?" I blurted out.

"Yes, he did, but so much more than that. His hands moved

over my body and then he placed himself above me and entered me. I felt like I was going to melt. I couldn't really feel his penis, all I could feel was a shaft of heat that started in my vagina and then moved up and radiated through my whole body. Then it seemed to me that I totally dissolved in a kaleidoscope of colour. I felt an indescribable bliss and a love that seemed to radiate to every corner of the universe. I felt complete.

"When I came to, he had gone, in his place was a soft tingling in my womb." It was Kaye's turn to pause. She remained quite still with that serene look gazing out of the window.

"I knew I was going to come back, so I took a last look around at the wondrous setting I was in, closed my eyes and willed myself back into my physical body. Then I woke up in a very different setting!"

I had to laugh with her at that point.

"Kaye, I'm going to send you to this psych friend of mine, I think you'll find him very user-friendly. I'd also like to see you and Jim together, so we can get a plan of management together for the pregnancy?"

"I'm more than happy for you to handle the ante-natal care. However, as my time comes near, I will be going to a place in the South. I'm told there is a woman there who will help me bring my son into the world. If this embarrasses you, I can look to alternatives."

"I'm getting used to the terrain, Kaye. Humour me: we'll book you in to hospital as 'routine', then you can 'surprise' me with a change of plans later."

"Deal."

And that's how things went. Her care was kept simple, she didn't want scans or unnecessary tests, my hands were all she needed, she told me. I felt drawn into an unknown world. Then, when she was near her time, she told me a friend from the South had met a funny little old lady at the local markets who described Kaye to a tee and told — rather than ask — Kaye's friend to prepare her house for Kaye and her child. The lady arrived two days later and waited patiently, using the sleep-out in the continuing fine weather. Kaye thanked me for her help and said she would leave tomorrow, so I'd better cancel the hospital bed!

I didn't see her for two months. Then she came to see me with Michael, who was the most alert little man I had ever set eyes on at a routine post-natal check. I asked Kaye which paediatrician she would like to be referred to, but I wasn't surprised when she said none. I wasn't sure whether I would ever see Kaye again, but she staggered me by asking me for a favour:

"I would like you to be Michael's Godfather."

How could I resist being involved in the future of someone like Michael?

"I'd be honoured."

Death Throes

It took me quite a while to realise I might be dead. I watched from a respectful distance as the paramedics worked on my bloodied body next to what remained of my car. I didn't feel anything as one of them pounded my chest whilst another pumped a mask below my closed eyes. As I watched I slowly understood that I was out of my body and the connection I had with the still form that lay next to the car felt tenuous; sometimes I was connected, sometimes not.

Jane was in a wheelchair a few feet away and was watching events with a stunned look on her face. She held her ribs whilst another paramedic was checking her chest with a stethoscope. Jane was disinterested with this, her eyes fixed on my still form. I looked again at the car and saw that the impact of the utility had been on my side. I remembered little of the incident, driving home in the early evening on the highway and through a traffic light, then the memory suddenly stopped. I looked to my right and saw the utility driver still in his vehicle, which had a considerably damaged front end; I could guess the rest. He must have gone through the light when red. There were two policemen waiting for him to be removed and one was holding a breathalyser kit.

I felt a tug back to my body, but it was brief. I turned to look behind me, half wondering whether this was when the tunnel of light materialised, drawing me in to ask me whether I wanted to go or be directed back to my body. This didn't happen; so much for all that New Age stuff I had read on near death experiences!

I was certainly 'out of' my body, though, and I was increasingly feeling the disconnection. I could see tears in Jane's eyes, but she seemed otherwise all right and that was a relief. All was not good with my body though and the paramedics were looking at each other in silent concern. Then they stopped their attention, one looked at Jane and the other pulled a blanket over my head.

That was it then.

Right then it all felt so pointless. What had I been doing spending the last few days concerned about finances, when I could have enjoyed more the company of this woman whom I had latterly learnt to love? We were still relatively young... although I won't be growing old now. As I looked at Jane, I felt a lack of justice in what had happened. Here we were in a good space in our relationship, opening up to areas of intimacy with the kids growing up a bit and demanding less, and looking more creatively to where our relationship was heading, as well as to our individual directions.

This is not how it should have ended! We were through the hard times, looking forward to as yet unexplored dimensions, even if money concerns were my major nightmare and a mixed blessing of my upbringing. Shouldn't it end all nice and tidy, with a completion of your life's 'tasks'? Wasn't that 'working out your karma'? Surely it was not meant to simply get cut-off in midstream? I felt angry, ripped off, cheated... all that 'do goodness' has come to this: some drunken shit wiping out my existence jumping a red light and leaving me in limbo. And limbo is exactly what I feel. No bright lights, heavenly music or angels directing me to the 'next stage' of my 'journey'. Instead, I am this disembodied being looking down at Jane with whom I wanted to explore so much more.

During the preliminaries of courtship, the understanding and appreciation of our respective bodies deepened the intimacy. The sex with Jane became and continued to be good; it was probably what kept us together during the hard times. We were both fairly experimental, though generally faithful, particularly in the latter years. We both quietly realised if we couldn't get it – whatever it was – from each other then we were unlikely to find that quality elsewhere. Not that we hadn't tried some extra-marital experimentation to find out; particularly as we were products of the New Age and had spent a little obligatory time in a couple of Indian ashrams. This influence had moved into the background with kids and careers, and it certainly didn't seem to be helping me just at this precise moment!

He's fucking her quite aggressively, whoever he is. I can see Jane – my Jane – responding a bit, but she's finding it a bit too much. He won't last long I think, and he doesn't. Now there's a fair headed man doing just what that swarthy type was doing earlier! Is my wife some kind of whore? I was just watching her shed a tear for me and now I see her having almost mindless sex with not a guy, but a married couple. Time to get my bearings, and that is exactly it, time. My 'bearings' tell me that these aren't sequential acts, that long stretches of time have passed and that I am just tuning in when Jane is having sex.

Is this hell, or what? It certainly seems like torture! Are you telling me that my consciousness is only present when my wife is fucking? I'd better check this out a bit, but how? Well, I'm still angry so maybe the emotional angle is it, at least partly? I still seem to have my mental functions intact and that includes memory, it is just the time factor that seems a little weird. What memories do I have? More than just those above, it seems, but they do stand out. I have some of the kids, especially if they're upset or emotionally disturbed in some way. So, the emotion is definitely part of it, although the intention on my part seems a bit vicarious; for example, with the kids I seem to be wanting to help or guide them in what experiences I have, with Jane the motives are more mixed.

There are times when she's alone that I know she's thinking about me and I become present. I want to stroke her face when she's sad, but even though I reach out, nothing happens. That's frustrating, because I have the intent and her face shows me that she notices something. I wonder whether I can get 'in her mind', but know this is not fully possible. It is inasmuch as I can detect her feelings, but not in a way that I can influence them directly or exert any kind of 'mind control'. Now that's interesting; if I know mind control is 'off limits' there seem to be some rules about this state I'm in. Another feature: whilst I can create a strong presence and have Jane almost 'feel' it, I can't make my presence visible to her and I can't make anything happen physically to show to her that I'm still around; that there is life after death. I do get the impression that there are some sorts of people who may 'see' me on occasion; for example, Cindy our daughter, who is thirteen and beginning to move into womanhood.

With Jane it is most distinct when she is involved sexually with someone, which then raises all my issues of possessiveness, jealously and the like. I don't seem to be able to influence her choice of partner, but I do seem to be 'there' when she's fucking... I find it difficult to admit she may be 'making love'. And when I am there, there is some influence, although this is usually through Jane, as if she is reflecting on me at the same time and comparing. That makes her early encounters somewhat emotionally disengaged and after a while I start to get an amused voyeuristic perspective. On one occasion two guys were vying for her charms at a bar after work one evening and she cut to the chase by telling them they could both have her – at the same time. That's my gal! She certainly gave them a run for her money and left them somewhat bemused.

One time she did get close to a guy and she brought him

home for dinner 'to meet the kids'. That got to me. I was really worked up about that and found that Cindy was a good avenue; I was able to 'use' her to sabotage any likely ongoing relationship. At first, I was happy about this, but then started to feel uncomfortable when my motives were examined: was I depriving Jane? Maybe I was, because she shed a tear or two after that guy left the scene, and this time they weren't shed for me. Maybe a little emotional stock-take is in order, my friend!

After that guy left Jane felt a bit bruised and angry about the orientation of men toward her. I could sense she felt they were using her, even though that had been her motive as well as getting her sexual needs met. But the last guy had been a bit different and she really started to feel the isolation of her situation, which she first experienced as anger toward men in general – and me for leaving her.

That's where Myra stepped in. Myra was a seasoned lesbian, although she occasionally 'had' a man – or men – women were her first preference. When she met Jane, I could see how Myra was calculating how she could bed her. I suspect that is why she engineered a meeting with Jane and one of her occasional male lovers, whom she knew to be a 'player' and would help Myra in her enterprise, as long as he got at least some of the action... what a generous guy I thought!

The combination of both Myra and Dave's attention, plus a couple of cocktails, was simply too much for Jane to resist. The two simply manoeuvred Jane around a sexual landscape that she was not entirely unfamiliar with, although I knew she had not experienced any direct woman attention. Jane was also ripe for the pickings as it was only a few weeks after the disastrous 'meet the kids' dinner, and Cindy's clear and direct sabotage of any ongoing relationship. That's how she ended up back at Myra's unit with Dave. The seduction had continued with further drinks and music, even a little dancing. Dave partnered each woman in a close manner, then suggested the women partner each other whilst he went to relieve himself. I watched the two women and could feel Jane's reactivity to what was happening; she certainly wasn't going to be a passive partner in the events of the evening! When Myra started to rub Jane's cheek my wife took the initiative and started to kiss Myra with an intensity that initially surprised her, but to which she quickly responded. I was enjoying this!

By the time Dave came back the women had disappeared into the bedroom and were exploring each other's still clothed bodies with fingers and tongues. Dave smiled and followed them, simultaneously removing his jacket. Myra's bedroom was rich and luxurious, reminding me of what I imagined a high-class courtesan's place of work might look like. Dave could see that Jane was dressed for the occasion with stockings and sexy underwear, including a bra that opened from the front, which he proceeded to unclasp and liberate my wife's gorgeous tits for the attention of his mouth.

He's an artful lover, I could tell, and Jane was going to enjoy this evening. As I thought that, Myra slid down the bed and started to suck Jane's pussy by moving the panties to one side and then removing them when no resistance was forthcoming. That was a beginning of a protracted evening and there were times when I was not present, although I did not know where I was. I recall the evening ended with Dave ejaculating over Jane's parted cunt lips and Myra licking up the proceeds. He then left them to sleep. Where are the kids, I thought? I briefly tuned in to Cindy and found them with Jane's parents. My good little wife really had plans for the night, it seemed.

I was still calling her my wife, which was something that needed a bit of reflection, as did a couple of other issues. I noticed that my absences during the three-way play were at particular times. These seemed to me to be when Jane was totally immersed in the interactions: for example, there was a time when she and Myra were both sucking at Dave's cock as well as kissing each other. This was a rich dance with very rapid movements between kissing and sucking, sharing the sucking and alternating it as well. Jane felt Dave to be drawn in and allowed him to cum in her mouth, which she willingly then shared with Myra in a deep kiss, then to go back to Dave's cock and quickly revive him; not that this seemed to require a lot of attention.

I seemed to watch this in a quite distant way. This was a little strange as in my exposure to pornography this is exactly the sort of scenario I would be intensely drawn to. My description would then have been more detailed: "Jane began by running the tip of her tongue along the length of his cock, then enveloping the head whilst Myra licked the shaft and then sucked at his balls, both women muttering sighs of approval beneath Dave's deep moans of satisfaction. Jane then passed his cock to Myra who enveloped the entire length at the first attempt then stimulating him further with rapid shakes of her head, whilst Jane nibbled her ear and fingered his anal rim... "And so on.

But this was not pornography and, even with my voyeuristic attitude, I came to realise it was because Jane was intensely involved and I was not in her thoughts at all. This briefly angered me, and I was privately relieved when Myra started paying Jane solo attention. Dave was occasionally invited into the mix, as Myra was aware that Jane's predilection for the male cock was strong although she wanted more of a relationship with Jane. At first this pleased me but, attentive as Myra was, it was not Jane's orientation. Myra settled for this when Jane expressed her feelings and asked simply that Jane consider her for a little lateral play in any future relationship she became involved in. They parted good company as I started to feel the distance again...

It seemed to me that Jane and the kids settled into a pattern. My insurance policy had catered for them adequately and Jane's lecturing became an increased focus with student involvement and the kids growing up. It was at university that Jane met Al, a new lecturer in a related department. I watched their 'dating' and his presence with the kids. He liked them and they he, so I knew things would change. I needed to do some serious reflection on my emotional state, which led me to believe that it was my attachment to Jane – and hers to me – that may be depriving her of future contentment. This was painful both to admit and experience, but I also came to see that it might be limiting my 'progress', whatever that may be.

It was in this state that I decided to check in on Jane the first night that Al slept in our – now her – bed. Al paid a similar kind of attention to Jane's body as I had. I did not feel jealous or possessive, which was strange given my experience to date. After the preliminaries he gently parted her legs, knelt between and with his right hand placed the head of his penis against her pussy lips and slowly rotated it provoking a liquid reaction that I could almost smell. Then he slowly entered her and let the whole length slide into her willing cunt. He then lowered his body and looked deeply into her eyes, which met his expressionless face with one of her own. I felt strangely soft and peaceful as this happened, and this was a further surprise, yet carried little of the shadowy feelings I had experienced to date with my emotional reactions.

Then a further surprise: I was in Al's body looking at my darling wife. She stared directly back at me and her expressionless face started to smile. Then her eyes turned red and I could see the tears begin to fill and overflow as drops fell from mine onto her cheeks. I knew myself not to be Al in that moment, yet I also knew that Jane was looking at and responding to me, just me. We continued this quiet dance for several priceless and eternal moments, and I experienced a depth of love that I had never experienced when alive. It was at that moment I knew I must take my leave. From a corner of the room, I looked back at the couple, Jane and Al, who were continuing this dance. I knew Jane had said good-bye to me and that I knew it was Al for whom her tears were now.

Then I was in the tunnel. My God! Maybe all that New Age stuff wasn't bullshit after all! At the end I could see the light and was irresistibly drawn towards it. As I glided down the passage, I felt layers like gossamer fall from me and I experienced myself progressively lighter of form. Then at the end was a figure. Robed, but indistinguishable of feature with the intensity of light behind, he asked me if I was ready in a wordless fashion. I was ready and I passed effortlessly through.

Parallel Realities

I went behind the curtain to set my eyes upon a feast. Lying under a sheet on the examination couch next to the cubicle partition was the most beautiful young woman I had ever seen. Almost instantaneously the fatigue of the overnight shift lifted and I felt a glow pass through my body. I hoped it didn't continue to a facial blush, although I suspected that she would be accustomed to such a response. It didn't; the heat remained contained within the white of my doctor's coat. The nurse standing demurely in the corner was watching intently: I certainly wasn't going to give her anything to feed on and looked again at the notes.

Tanya had arrived on the interstate train earlier that night and collapsed on disembarking. She was taken by ambulance to our hospital because of this circumstance, otherwise if she had volunteered the apparent 'cause' for the collapse – heavy vaginal bleeding – she may well have gone to the neighbouring women's hospital instead of our emergency department. When she arrived, her observations were taken and she was now recovering and the bleeding had ceased. From the emergency perspective it all seemed fairly straightforward and my decision was whether to immediately transfer her for further management, or to undertake a preliminary examination to see if I could ascertain a cause for the unpredictable bleed.

I discussed these options with her, as it seemed to me that her story of a broken engagement and a last-minute decision to take the train across the continent could well explain the bleeding. In other words, it was a stress-related physical reaction and may require no further medical management at all. I discussed these options with Tanya, who explained to me that she had a job interview coming up later in the day and she did not want to spend it under the auspices of my profession, unless clinically indicated. So, we agreed that I would conduct a preliminary examination to exclude any obvious pathology, and then she could wait to see what happened with her periods subsequently.

The nurse produced the necessary tray and as I put on my gloves, I asked Tanya what the job interview was about.

"I'm a research psychologist and I've applied for a position in neuropsychology at the State University."

"A research position?"

"Yes, I'm interested in the effect of high energy states on the brain and the resulting psychological changes. There's a research position that has been vacant for some time. I was interested, but my boyfriend did not want to move here, even though he didn't have a committed working position. In some ways the position showed me that our relationship did not have a future and that I was in danger of foregoing a career move that I found exciting.

"Another reason was my age. I thought they'd want someone with more experience, but when my initial enquiries revealed that not to be the case and my academic background to be more than adequate, I had a dilemma on my hands. That culminated in a decision; well, two actually a few days ago, and here I am."

I could easily fill in the gaps from there, which pointed even further to this being a stress situation. As I was pondering this, I didn't realise I was gazing at her eyes. This did not affect her in the least and her deep green eyes held my unblinking gaze with an expressionless face that broke out into a light soft smile as I realised that I was staring at her. I briefly wondered what the nurse was picking up from this interaction so I switched into medical-mode.

"Tanya, I'm going to do a vaginal examination. First, I'll pass a speculum into your vagina and have a look to see whether there is a cause for the bleeding and then I'll do a digital examination. Oh! I'm forgetting; are you a virgin?"

"Do I look like one?"

Again, those deep green eyes engaged me. I was sure this time the heat had matured into a blush. Better get on with my job, I thought.

Her vagina was as beautiful as she. The dark hairless lips below the lightly manicured pubes were parted to reveal a rich pink, which were already moist with no evidence of blood. This should have and did alert me to what was happening between us. I found no cause for the blood when looking through the speculum, which I then withdrew.

"I'm going to pass one finger inside, then two and place my other hand on your pubes so that I can feel as deeply as possible. Please let me know if I cause any discomfort?"

"I will. Thank you for warning me, it may be a welcome change from the metal!"

The communication was deepening, I felt on the edge of a cliff. I needed to pull back. The examination was effortless, possibly assisted by the slight rocking of her pelvis as my fingers moved toward my other hand. The nurse would not notice, but my hands knew what was happening.

"I hope I am not causing any discomfort?"

"You're doing just fine, doctor."

That did it. The nurse shifted uneasily at my side. Tanya had her head slightly raised and was looking directly at me again with that slight smile.

Decision time.

"Nurse, would you please take the tray away whilst I explain the result of my examination to the patient, then you can come back and help her get dressed?"

We wouldn't have long. I took a pen out of my breast pocket and gave it to Tanya. I pulled up my left sleeve and she scribbled her number on the inside of my forearm. As she did, I memorised it, I was not going to let this chance escape.

Just in time, I returned my pen to my pocket as the door at the rear of the cubicle opened and the nurse came back in. I was right, she had delivered the tray to the sluice room in record time; she knew something was going on. I didn't miss a beat.

"My suggestion is that you wait until your next period. If this is quite normal then I think we will have concluded correctly and there will be no need to take it any further."

"Thank you, doctor. Maybe one day, if you're interested, you may want to come to the University research laboratory to see the work we're doing? That is, if I get the job!"

"I'm sure you will!"

I slipped out of the cubicle and made my way to the coffee room; I would need one. That was clever, I realised. Tanya had left open a future liaison and put it clearly on the table. I suspected that whilst I was preparing my coffee, she would be similarly softening up the nurse and closing off the whole medical scenario from her perspective. She was obviously experienced enough to know that environments such as this can be a hothouse of gossip and she would want to leave the situation unembroiled.

Of course, much of this I found out when we finally met for a drink some weeks later. From there the relationship became a whirlwind, as anticipated by that first evening. The drink led to a dinner and then to her flat for a nightcap, although we were both aware of the euphemism. The kissing on the couch was quickly interrupted as Tanya took my hand and led me to her bedroom. The room was inviting, lit with a bedside lamp that cast a soft light across the large bed that had all the trappings of a deep and rich femininity. The colours were dark, mainly deep reds. A gown and a top were suspended from the fitted wardrobe doors on hangers, giving a vague impression that this room would not be open to a visitor's eye that night. This served to provide a playful enigma to this woman who was rapidly captivating me.

Tanya lay on the bed below me and that soft smile graced her lips as I undid her blouse and then lifted one breast free of its moorings. The nipple was dark and full and responded quickly to my touch and lips. I serviced the other in a similar manner then slowly took off her blouse and undid her bra. The breasts responded further to my attention as Tanya lightly arched her back and groaned. My hand went under her skirt and found her panties. They were already wet, so I simply removed them and gazed at what was now a cunt and not a vagina. The aroma was musty as I started to lick and savour the juice that was slowly leaking out. Her pelvis gave a light rock, which I had experienced before under different circumstances, but now knew I was going beyond. She asked me to turn and whilst I continued the attention to her cunt with my lips, tongue and mouth she liberated my stiff cock from my pants and began giving it simultaneous attention.

As I drank deeply from her cunt, I could feel her lips tease my cock-head and then lick the shaft. We were on our sides by now, quite comfortable and relaxed, and my initial intensity gave way to a slow appreciation of her womanhood. I felt her mouth open around the head of my cock and then, to my surprise, in one motion she engulfed the entirety and held it deep within her mouth. She did not stop, she stayed with my cock buried there and shook her head to give a sensation I had not experienced before, and then she slowly withdrew and continued with more variation and vigour.

It had almost put me off my attention, but not for long! I resumed and we fell into a delightful rhythm for what seemed like hours. Then, from seemingly nowhere, the intensity increased for both of us. Her fluids became copious and I drank deeply. Then as she began to grind her pelvis more fervently into my mouth and face, I felt my own juices begin to rise and she came against my face whilst my sperm forced its way deep into her throat, which she swallowed effortlessly with some deep groans in response, as well as to her own orgasm. We were as one.

With a final lick I turned and looked at her and that little smile, then I kissed her slowly and deeply. My cock had barely subsided, yet it was now ready again and I parted her cunt lips and gently entered. It was as if she was sucking me in with her womanhood as her eyes never left mine. Normally, when I fucked someone, I was disinclined to look too long or deeply. Maybe this was because I was embarrassed, I thought, and I would pay attention to neck and ear nibbling with a few accompanying words. But in this moment, I realised it was because I had never been in love with the woman I was fucking. With Tanya I was, and my gaze responded.

The motion of our hips and bodies was surprisingly gentle. We both seemed to know there would be ample time for variation and phrenetic acts in the explorations of the future, so this act was to consummate the love as we moved and gently reached an edge over which we dropped together. We both knew we had arrived.

I recall asking: Where had it all gone? Sitting at my desk with my left arm rocking and twitching almost uncontrollably. In fact, if

I tried to control it then it only got worse. Bloody Parkinson's disease and I wasn't yet forty! Tanya was still in her prime and the kids were so young; what could I offer them now? Where had it all gone, what had happened?

The early years of our relationship had continued the whirlwind. Initially our passion knew no bounds and our respective careers escalated. Tanya became head of the Neuropsychology unit and managed to have kids on the way. My private psychiatric practice was successful mainly due to some innovative approaches I had introduced from overseas experience. Then things started to drift a little as the various pressures appeared to mount and take us into a kind of parallel existence. We seemed never to have time for sex and if we did it seemed more for a relief of tension, even frustration. It was then that I first noted the shaking in my left arm; initially when the stress was high and persistent, though later it became more consistent. The only thing that seemed to relieve it initially was alcohol so, of course, the consumption of it went up more than a little.

I'd had all the investigations and the diagnosis seemed fairly definite. What concerned me then was the age of onset, as that could make it potentially more serious. I knew enough about it to realise it's a 'wait and see' exercise, as the progression of the disease would be determined by the emerging pattern. In this I was a little concerned, as the onset and patterns seemed to be gaining momentum. As I poured another drink one evening Tanya looked across at me:

"Did you notice anything unusual last night?" She asked.

"No."

"C'mon big boy! What did we do?"

"We had sex... sorry, I mean we made love."

"Nice 'slip', even for a psychiatrist, but with more than a grain of truth! I agree, we have been 'having sex' for quite a while, but last night you were more vulnerable than usual. You were asking questions about our future and what you might be 'depriving' me of, then we 'made love'. And it was love-making, we haven't been that close and intimate for a while."

"What are you getting at?"

"Well, I noticed something that you probably didn't. Afterward when you held me you had no shaking at all. None. Then you fell into a peaceful sleep and I looked at your body; you were still, quite still."

We were both intrigued. Our collective heads got together and the research started. However, after a few months we seemed to be getting nowhere and I felt so frustrated. We had tried the 'love-making' formula on several occasions, but the success to date had only been partial and we both suspected we might be both trying too hard and being formulaic. In other words, we were looking for an outcome. Right at that moment we were both dispirited and I could feel that from Tanya, in particular.

Then something sprang to mind. I recalled my interest in Eastern mysticism from my student days. That one time we did make love, the one that Tanya recounted as leaving me symptomless; there had been something different. I had felt energy movement in my body and been reminded of the literature I'd read on Tantra and the notion of Kundalini energy. This is the concept of a coiled energy at the base of the spine that can be stimulated by sexuality and pass up the body, with the goal being 'enlightenment'. Maybe that's the clue, I thought? Maybe we were being too mechanical and Western in our thinking?

That had been the turning point. We reframed our knowledge and experience and entered into a sexual relationship based on Tantra. As this deepened, so did our love. Oh yes, I almost forgot! The symptoms started to abate. First this was episodic, usually after we made love. Then it became progressive and the symptoms started to lessen in a more continual manner.

The next few years were extraordinary. The symptoms progressively abated and we made the connection between Tantric practice and the release of a chemical in the brain, a neurohormone that effectively provides a cure for Parkinson's disease not caused by other disease processes, such as vascular disease. This hormone was similar to, but not the same as dopamine, which had been the cornerstone of treatment up until that time. Whilst we were basking in our success the letter of nomination for the Nobel Prize arrived in the post and we knew our lives would be irrevocably changed.

Yet in spite of this we did not fall into what we perceived as a trap. We both recognised that our spiritual practice and our sexual exploration within that context would remain the cornerstone of our relationship. We were more intrigued about the possibility of this or similar chemicals released by the Tantric process being the so-called 'elixir of life'. The possibilities in this regard seemed limitless and the world that this opened up were more eternal than temporal.

"I hope I am not causing any discomfort?"

"You're doing just fine, doctor."

That did it. The nurse shifted uneasily at my side. Tanya had her head slightly raised and was looking directly at me again with that slight smile.

Decision time.

The nurse knew what was going on; of this I was certain. I'd only just qualified and I get an ethical situation like this almost straightaway! There's no choice really, Tanya was a 'patient'. This is a line I have been 'taught' not to cross, although in later years I realised that it could easily have been negotiated with no ethical conflict. At the time, though, I didn't have that experience and it was easier to let the situation simply pass.

I recall putting my gloves in the tray and leaving it there, whilst the nurse heard me explain to Tanya about her condition and how to manage it from there. Then I asked the nurse to help Tanya dress and leave, and I went out through the curtain to have a coffee before going to see the next patient. It was to be a long night, but I wouldn't have any stares from that particular nurse to negotiate! I had done the right thing, of that I was sure at the time, although as the years ticked on, I had increasing doubts and the memory remains burned in my brain for some unknown reason.

Here I am now close to retirement. I have had a good life really. Janet has been a strong wife and the kids have all done well, even if the intimacy has gone out of the relationship and the alcohol consumption continues to climb. Then again, I have little in the way of performance to negotiate now so the twitching that has developed in my left arm and hand shouldn't prove too much of an impediment as the years gobble me up. I know it's Parkinson's disease, but there still haven't been any advances in treatment in my time in medicine, so I'll just have to accept my lot.

Alien Abduction

Where am I? This doesn't feel like a dream; it's all too real. But if I reflect... the last thing I recall is going to bed, simply that, so what the fuck is all this? I'm lying on a bed, but it's not my bed if it is a bed, it's more like one of those examination couches in a hospital and that doesn't make me feel too much better, given my previous experiences. That's it; I must have been ill and taken here. Quick check: no pain, no loss of eyesight and all limbs can move. So far so good: let's check the surroundings and get my bearings.

The room feels big; I can't see the walls although the light makes that difficult. It's bright, but I don't see any lights and it's a bit hazy. I do feel wide-awake though, so what's going on? Then there's this figure, a shape, human? Can't tell completely because of the lights and haze. He's got a long thin head and wearing a white gown, so this must be a hospital. "Hey Doc!" No reply, doesn't matter, he's coming toward me anyway. My god! This guy is freaky! His head is long and pointy and his eyes are slanted and dark, dark as deep-water pools. That doesn't look like a doctor's gown either and he has only an apology for a nose and mouth, although his ears make up for it. Now I'm scared, he has this big needle and, before I can react – or maybe I can't – it's in my leg, although it doesn't hurt.

I'm awake again, but I feel really funny, kind of disjointed and this time I can't move, although there is no pain. I'm staring at the ceiling this time and I can see the lights; they're like suns, strong and a bit hazy and you can't look directly at them. Then there are two of these faces peering down at me, looking into my eyes. It's unfair, they have no features I can connect with and their puny noses and mouths give no sign of expression. What are they looking at... or for?

I'm on a swing and getting good height. Helen is on the swing next to me, but facing the other way. She's wearing that school skirt that is starting to show her early adolescent curves, but she's still a kid at heart really. So am I. This is our game. We swing and swing until we get a rhythm going, so that we look at each other at the top of the swing and pass at the bottom. We've nearly got it in sync and it's about now that she'll loosen the skirt tucked under her bum so the air will make it billow out and I can see her knickers, whilst she watches me and smiles. The feeling is starting, there's a rush that starts deep down in my tummy and then rises with each swing. It's exciting and combined with Helen's knickers makes the whole experience something else. I wait for the moment; Helen loosens her skirt and we get to the upswing. I look at her crotch and wait for the white of her school knickers, but she isn't wearing any. I'm shocked and look at her face and she's laughing! The redness sweeps my face...

They're still looking at me, those bastards! Can they see what I see? Are they probing my mind? I haven't thought about Helen for years after her Mum caught her and forbade that game. There's something in that energy of the swinging, combined with Helen's pussy, particularly when she opened her legs. Saucy bitch! Shame her Mum caught us, never got the chance to explore that deep well any further. Hey! You guys are watching this, aren't you? What do you want to see? Don't you have peckers like us?

I am on top of Fran, although we're both still dressed. We're making a mess of the clothes piled up on the single bed whilst the party in the main room continues on; although all I can really hear is the throb of the bass. Fran's really in to it tonight, maybe I'll get lucky. Her kissing has been oiled by the vodka and lime and she's almost getting aggressive. My hand is between her legs and, after a token resistance, she parts them and I feel the warmth and wetness and a new odour that wafts to my nostrils around my smothering kiss of the creature below me. I put a finger in her, she's tight but her legs stay open, so I try a second, but she's too tight. I scramble at my zipper and my dick finds its own way out. I look at Fran, she looks back and there's no attempt to stop me. I continue to look at her eyes and direct my cock around the loose panties and place it at the head of her cunt. I can get it in a little and I feel heat in my loins and back, it'll need more so I begin a slow thrust against the vain constriction and then I'm in! God, this is wonderful! Fran gives a little shriek and closes her eyes, hugs me closer and wraps her legs around mine. I start pumping and she responds. I'm in heaven! She's moaning and shaking her head gently. The heat in my loins concentrates at the base of my dick and there's no holding back. I explode.

They're still watching me. These bastards are definitely getting off on this! There's obviously no place in their repertoire for this, but they're obviously interested in it: Why? There's more probing of my mind and the memories gush forth as do the sexual fluids that comprise the core of most of them. I still don't get what they're about with all this. Then I see only one face. My legs are being parted and these funny little fellers are holding them. Then there is this sudden, agonising feeling in my arse. I scream, but also feel that rush that makes for the core of the memories they've been perving on. The rush sweeps through in initial waves then makes a slow steady ascent up my back. I look down and the other 'face' lifts himself and holds a long syringe in his hands. He looks at the other face and nods, just as the heat gets to my head. It's agony... and ecstasy.

A Witch is Born

Karla found it strange. She had never been to this village before; how could she have; she had never even been to this country! But she knew the streets and what was around each corner. This reminded her of when she was little and she used to 'vague out', as her mother called it, often then having similar experiences that the neurologist called 'déjà vu'. He called it temporal lobe epilepsy, but she experienced it like a state of grace and sometimes she could summon it when the daily world of childhood seemed too much.

It didn't help that her stepfather seemed to take a special interest in her, particularly when her mother was absent. Karla found this uncomfortable, as he would suddenly turn up in her room or ask her to sit on his lap and idly chat. Mostly she managed to avoid these situations even though 'nothing happened', because of the emotional discomfort: although at times there was a certain intrigue in his chatting, even if she didn't recall what it was about. She could tell her mother knew, because if she caught sight of what was happening then a row between the two of them would inevitably follow. This is when Karla would 'absent' herself into an imaginary world, which seemed safer. Maybe this was why her mother decided not to take the doctor's advice about medication, as she could see the relationship and surmised that it was connected with sexual undercurrents and Karla's responses, which were before their time.

Her mother befriended her more and she was able to share

about the 'déjà vu' experiences that often happened around the same time as any 'incident' with her stepfather:

"I know this place, Mummy." She said one day in the car when she was accompanying her mother to see her grandparents in their new home.

"Honey, you can't; you've never been here before."

"But I do, I do!" Karla protested.

So, when she proceeded to describe what was around the next corner and then the next her mother stopped the car and looked quite ashen.

"Has your father done anything recently?"

Karla was a little taken aback, but she knew what her mother meant.

"No," she replied, "He never does; you know that, I've told you before. It's just the way he looks and yesterday he came in my room when you were out. He said to give me back a pen he'd borrowed, but it took a while for him to leave. It just feels creepy!"

"I know, Honey. He's a good man, really. I don't understand it and he tries to explain, but I can't get my head around it and I wonder if I should leave him because I'm concerned about you."

"Don't worry, Mummy. I know where to go. I'll tell you if anything ever happens 'cos I know what you're talking about, but it hasn't – yet."

Karla's mother was always taken aback by this quiet assuredness, although she knew Karla was troubled. She had genuinely thought of leaving the marriage out of concern for Karla, yet this option didn't seem quite right. Her husband was distressed about the apparent perception of his feelings toward Karla when confronted again and agreed to go into therapy as a 'solution' to the perceived problem.

Karla's mother actually felt a little awkward about his agreement and wondered whether this had been as a result of one rather unusual conversation they had had some months prior, seemingly out of the blue, but after the visit to the neurologist:

"Do you know Karla has psychic tendencies and that this could explain what she is experiencing?"

"No," she replied, "Why do you say that?"

"Because I do too."

He went on to explain about his own childhood experiences that bore a similarity and how his maternal grandmother, who was always considered a little 'odd' by the rest of the family, took him under her wing. The rest of the family found the intimacy between the two a little uncomfortable, particularly as his grandmother was somewhat reclusive, but accepted it even with the age difference.

"You didn't tell me about this before we married!"

"It's not an easy thing to talk about," was his response, "and I have managed to accept it as part of my life that, by and large, doesn't affect other people. That is, up till now."

"This has something to do with Karla?"

"Yes. When I could see what was happening to me, I felt I could somehow help her, like Grandma did for me. I remember she said it's often like that; a woman who 'knows' helps a man and vice versa. As this is commonly in a family and across generations it doesn't usually present a problem, particularly when outsiders feel it may be a sexual thing. So, imagine how I feel in this situation."

"Are you trying to con me? Do you have sexual feelings toward my daughter?"

"No, I don't, but the 'forces' themselves – if you want to call them that – can be misconstrued. I don't think that's happening to me."

She had watched him after her suspicions were aroused, but she saw and had seen no proclivities in that direction, so maybe he was telling the truth. He seemed to be drawn to 'mature' women; was that a 'legacy' of his grandmother? Their attraction and sexual encounters had always seemed entirely healthy and she was a couple of years older...

Karla's mother was left a little confused, but less troubled. This had made the decision about having no medical treatment somewhat easier, after her insistence that Karla see him to confirm there wasn't a medical problem. Even with the neurologist's insistence that she did have epilepsy, she was not convinced. She decided to let the situation simply continue, although she took Karla into her confidence somewhat as a backup.

Karla didn't know whether it was the decision for him to go to therapy or her blossoming adolescence that caused the events to diminish and eventually stop. What she did notice was that her absent periods and déjà vu experiences also diminished and ceased entirely with her sexual maturity. When this occurred, Karla began to look retrospectively and began to see what had driven her stepfather, as well as now beginning to appreciate the source of her prior confusion. Karla seemed relatively unscarred from the experiences; the loss of her imaginative life and déjà vu experiences were rapidly replaced by an overt sexuality that she fully enjoyed.

Now here she was on the street of this Mediterranean island village and, for the first time in years, the experience was back. She was there for a break after the ending of a long-term relationship that was also a working one, so two major pillars of her life needed a little reflection and she decided to go away — far away. The choice of the village had been a whim after a couple of glasses of wine and putting a pin in a world map with her eyes closed. Even though a 'game' at the time, the location created a strange emotional response. Normally she would have dismissed this and rationalised it away, but the mixture of fear and attraction reminded her of her relationship with her stepfather and she wondered whether there was something about this she needed to come to terms with as well.

After she settled in to her apartment Karla sought out the village square. She did not know the language and had to rely on the tourist element that meant some of the population had a rudimentary speaking knowledge of English. Once she was in the square the feelings started and she allowed herself to submit to them. There was an intensity in her stomach like a fire that radiated throughout her body. She sat, breathed and focussed on it. When she opened her eyes, she was still in the square, but it had a slightly unreal quality that caused her to question the time of day... and even the year.

Karla knew where she must go. She knew the village and passed effortlessly through the narrow streets and lanes as if on a mission, which in some respects was unknown to her. At the edge of the village, she started to ascend a small hill where she knew he would be waiting. Dark of hair and skin, handsome and charming, he would remind her more than a little of her stepfather. This she knew to be appropriate, for there was something he had started that this man would complete. More than that, she knew her stepfather had trusted in this possibility and had to deal with some very awkward feelings and physical responses in himself during the times they had spent together. A sense of admiration for his courage and commitment overcame her and, one day, she would communicate this to him.

There he was, as she had seen in her mind's eye. Silently he took her hand and led her down the hill by another path to a small farmhouse building overlooking the bay and the village beyond. Karla felt at ease with this man as all fear and doubt swept away, whilst she continued to experience the 'otherness' of time and place that embraced them. As they went into the house, she became aware that it was prepared for a visitor and realised it to be her, Karla.

There were no preliminaries. He led me straight into a large bedroom that was rich in a sort of mediaeval sense; deep carpets, an older style wooden bed with rugs and classic pictures on the wall. The solitary window overlooked the bay beyond a garden that was somewhat wild; a little like this man I thought. We lay on the bed and looked at each other for what seemed an age. His dark eyes had a stillness and depth that I could almost fall into. The sense of time and space continued to change and become more ethereal as a tear would occasionally well up and drop from my eye. I looked at him unblinking and could see his tears likewise.

Then slowly he undressed me. He took his time and didn't focus on my breasts or pussy. When he had finished, he stood and removed his also, placing his clothes casually, yet neatly over the back of a rocking chair that faced an unlit fire. The day was full and warm as I could see his cock to be also, although not yet fully erect. I started to tremble slightly in anticipation, but my pussy also responded with first warmth and then secretions of welcoming lubricant. First, he moved between my thighs and gave my pussy a repeated suck and accompanying kisses before moving up to kiss my neck, face and then lips. All the time he watched me and I him, it was only as his lips met mine and his tongue made its gentle entry into my mouth that I closed them involuntarily.

The kissing lasted and lasted, as it neared its end, I opened my eyes to see his closed; he was as transported as I, we were equals in this quest. Slowly he mounted me; gently he entered me as his now fully erect cock slid easily home assisted by my now abundant lubrication. I whimpered, all noise that issued from me was a reflex; there was no need to artificially heighten or make theatre of what was happening, and he likewise. He gazed at me as he started the slow incline of pumping within me, as my hips rotated forward and met his every thrust. Our eyes remain locked during this whole time and quietly, assuredly and mutually we both fell over the mound at the top of the incline as I felt his juice flood the mouth of my womb.

We dozed a little. I awoke first and disengaged from his cradling arm. He did not stir. I made my way gently down the bed to savour the mixed juices that had dried on his cock. His manhood stirred to life and became fully erect again in my mouth. He stirred also and followed my ministrations with gentle thrusts from his lying position as moans escaped his mouth. I responded by sucking him more deeply until I felt his cock at the back of my mouth. I began the breathing pattern that I knew would help the process of taking him in my throat and then completely withdrew. This I repeated on several occasions, the last of which I held him in my throat for longer than I had any man. On the last withdrawal I gently wanked him with my free hand and could feel his energy rise. I took the head in my mouth again, withdrew my hand and slowly slid down the length of his cock as it started to convulse and cause me to swallow repeatedly. It tasted of nectar, so rich, warm and wanted.

Over the remainder of the day there was some limited talk between us. The similarities in our experiences were great and what seemed to have drawn us together. This man was a farmer, yet lived a solitary life. He tended his small farm and animals diligently, but from his great aunt he had learnt something of nature magic. It was this that he taught me and which our sexual contact heightened for me. Over the weeks that followed I was able to harness my sexual energies in ways that before had simply been a release or dissipation, often leaving me drained and dissatisfied. Together we were able to concentrate and focus them into the ritual and ceremonial processes we undertook. I realised my vocation in that time; in the past I might have been called a witch.

The contact unwound as it had started. The cocoon of time and space that had held us gradually dissolved and we both knew it was time for me to leave. Our meeting was sweet and tender. What I came to realise was that the modern age and its discomfort with a spirituality that was naturally and sexually based had led to a disruption in both of our developments in our art and destiny. Somehow, we had found each other, or the forces seeking acceptance and progression through us had brought us together. It mattered not, it mattered only that it had happened and that we had both reconnected with our lineage and heritage.

As I flew home, I came to know various things. I would never marry, yet I would have children. I further knew that one of these children would carry the seed and it would flourish in one of his children, a son, and that I would have to be involved in his development, but in this case his father would understand. My art was to be my love and passion, sometimes it would embrace others, but only if they were in some way connected with or open to the art that I espoused. I knew I would be misunderstood and judged. I also knew that I must prepare myself, leave my present work and engage in study to help ground the art in the present and foster its continued passage into the future. There would be pain in this, of course, as the comforts of the average man seemed taken away from me, although I realised this was how it had to be.

Snake's Eyes

Gloria reached up to the top shelf of her cupboard and, with only a minor amount of rummaging, pulled down the latex dress she had been wearing when she last fucked Guy; if you could actually call it a dress, she thought. It had been one of those glorious days where they roamed around their relationship and finished with the light dress-up clothing they often employed when they knew their lovemaking was to be intense. Guy had worn that little leather thong 'number' with the zip at the front; both for easy access to his cock, or letting it out of its restraint if the tension was too much. Gloria kept it simple: the red latex dress, easily discardable knickers and high-heeled shoes, although she didn't remember them lasting long!

There had been a fair bit of tension in their relationship of late. Guy was preoccupied with his academic career and the frustrating lack of opportunities. Also, his research into the nature of the venom of a particularly enigmatic South American snake had become frustrating. Originally it seemed to hold promise in immunological research, even toward the holy grail of cancer treatment, but the effects it had on the student volunteers was inconsistent. Some reported heightened arousal and even sexual excitement, whilst others documented visionary experience that had an almost hallucinogenic quality. Guy did not know where to go with this mixed bag and it hadn't been helped by one of the female volunteers propositioning and pursuing him after her experience. This had caused more than a little ruckus on campus and not helped Guy's career aspirations.

University politics; how he tired of it.

Gloria had taken that in her stride. Jealousy wasn't a feature of her personality. She was sexually confident even though the twins had stretched her resources in more ways than one! She also knew that they fell back onto the core erotic dimensions of their relationship when the going got rough. It had taken them a while to recall this 'formula' when the recent difficulties they had been experiencing surfaced and she wondered why. It was almost as if they had forgotten, which seemed silly as she reflected on this point. She wasn't going to analyse it away into a 'denial' format, or rationalise that it may infer a deeper problem in their relationship, as she wasn't that sort of person. Her easy nature accepted it pragmatically and after a little diffidence Guy saw fit to join Gloria in her request for 'time out', put his work concerns on one side, and arrange for his mother to look after the kids for a day's stretch.

The day had been easy. Kids dropped off, downtown for coffee and planning of the day. Some shopping aimed at buying for each other and then to the adult sex shop where Gloria picked up the new latex dress. The last one had virtually rotted away, probably from lack of adequate care to the product. Funny, it seemed to slip her mind after steamy sex! Then a lunch, a glass or two of champagne and a walk before going back home: all precautions were taken. Phones on message bank, cars locked in the garage and cat outside as a statement of 'nobody home'. They undressed, bathed together with another champagne and some soft music, then dried and dressed each other with no sexual foreplay. Downstairs they finished their drinks while nestling in each other's arms and felt a return to the familiarity of being.

As Gloria now sniffed the dress the mixed scents recaptured the afternoon and evening. Although near the end of her period Guy had not minded and he added the small amount of the bleeding to the mix of juices that were released in waves from her cunt. First were the responsive secretions to enable his foreplay and digital exploration, and then was the gush that felt almost like pissing, which came when she sucked his cock deeper into her mouth. And last were the waves of flooding, which came from she knew not where that accompanied her high arousal and ultimate orgasm. These gushed, flooded and swamped her legs to form sticky pools on the inside of her new dress. Guy withdrew and masturbated to his climax above her, the sperm gushing in streams over varied parts of her new dress. In her tranquil state, Gloria rubbed it into the new material reserving some for her mouth as she sucked her fingers clean.

They slept.

Now, two days later, life seemed a little more even, yet she remembered she had casually discarded her knew dress and forgotten to clean it according to the 'manufacturer's specifications'. Fuck! This is what had caused the demise of the last one, so whilst the twins were ensconced in front of the television, she retrieved it with the intent of cleaning it. As she fondled it Gloria smelt the scents of their fucking more deeply and sniffed odours with successive in-breaths. She closed her eyes and continued the slow rhythmic breathing; it was almost as if she heard drums in the background providing a beat that matched her breaths. Instead of taking the garment down to the laundry she found herself, almost involuntarily, removing all her clothes and putting it on. Then she lay back on the bed and started to idly masturbate.

Gloria started with a slow circular motion around her clitoris using the index and middle fingers of her right hand. The dress was chafing her wrist a little so she lifted her bum off the bed and allowed it to rise up to her hips with a light bouncing motion. She resumed the clitoral stimulation until she felt some of her juices quicken. She was going too fast; she could tell with her breathing. Slow down girl! You've got a while, the kids love that show; but the arousal was high, so she quickly returned to her prior rhythm. As her left hand started to gently explore the outer cunt lips with an occasional dip inside, her right hand moved from the clitoral station and took one of the pillows to place under her bum. When the hand returned it ignored its prior place and moved to her arse. After a little play around the anal ring, she quickly lifted her hand to her lips, applied a generous dose of saliva to the middle finger and immediately returned it to insert in her anus. A little tweak of discomfort and it was in. Gloria had the rhythm now, her mind flirted to the use of her vibrators, but her hands felt enough. She briefly thought about the kids and remembered that Guy was going to be home before their show ended so she could get to the bank before it closed. That may have to wait as she started to whip up a lather.

There was a fragrance coming from the coiled dress below her hands. She recalled that her juices had pooled there when they fucked and had dried with the occasional smear of her menstrual blood. The mixture had been rich at the time and accompanied by the sweet yet sour smell of Guy's cum scattered over the outside of the dress. Yet it was her mixed and rich juices that she smelt most and it brought back images of their recent fucking. The smell seemed to come in waves as she now had her eyes closed with her fingers still working frantically at her pussy and now two in her arse. As the smell became stronger and her breathing faster it seemed to her like it was a mist in her mind's eye emerging from her obscured pelvis. It was a grey-white colour, if you could call it a colour. Then it seemed to coalesce into a long shape. Was this a human form? Was she recalling Guy as he withdrew to project his seed over her belly and breasts? It seemed at first that it was he, but as the shape became firmer a shock went through her being: it was a snake, and not any old snake, it was one of those that was causing Guy so much angst!

It didn't stop her fingers working her pelvis though; in fact, it seemed to compel her to work harder and faster. She obliged. The snake rose above her pubes with the misty haze still surrounding it and looked directly at her. She felt her eyes flicker frantically against the closed lids and her heart pound ever stronger. Still the snake rose and she saw its dark eyes engage hers without moving or blinking and the tongue to periodically flick out of its mouth. It was forked and it scared her, yet also excited her deeply and she felt the fluids that had dried below her pelvis to coalesce into a ball of heat in her arse and start to gently throb sending waves up her torso.

Now Gloria was totally engaged and the snake looked at her and became still. The heat in her arse started to feel liquid and slowly started to creep across her lower body and upward toward her breasts. As it did so the snake dropped down onto her belly to meet the inner energy and started to slowly crawl toward her chest in unison with the heat, which was now becoming more concentrated and like a rod in the front of her backbone. It seemed to Gloria that it was white hot with a redness that took over with each pulse. She could not see the snake but felt its undulating movement, as it seemed to her that it went to each sperm deposit of Guy's and sucked it in. The fragrance of his seed was now mixed with hers as she breathed it in deeply, yet still the snake moved on the tracks of energy deep within her body. Moving between her breasts it slid off the latex onto her upper chest, throat and then crawled to her chin. What happened when it got to her mouth? This was now agape and she wondered briefly if it would go inside and the fear arose again.

She need not have concern. The heat passed her mouth and settled in the middle of her head and, as it did so, she felt the snake again on her brow. As the shock of this hit her Gloria was immediately propelled into a landscape she did not know. She looked around; it was like a jungle. The foliage was rich, moist and deep. As the snake seemed to stop at her brow, she heard drums beating in the distance and the sky become darker. Shapes moved across the heavens like large shooting stars and the drums increased their tempo, almost now matching the beating of her heart and sending shards of colour into the atmosphere. She felt so aroused, so excited; this seemed better than any sex she had ever had, in spite of the background of fear. Then, emerging from the jungle thicket in front of her was a huge head, the head of a snake. The snake, the snake that was resting on her brow, but it was huge! And then it turned its head, flicked out its tongue and she looked into its profile at a huge red eye. The energy in her skull reached an intensity beyond which she could cope. She could not even scream. She passed out in a liquid orgy of sheer bliss.

Guy looked in on the kids; they were enraptured by the show. He looked at his watch; a further fifteen minutes before it ended. He almost stole upstairs and opened the bedroom door. Without looking to the bed, he shut and locked it, discarded his clothes and turned toward the bed. His erection was stronger than he could ever remember; yet he felt calm. He stood at the end of the bed and looked down at his wife; how he loved her! It was so cute how she was lying there, in a light slumber with her new dress around her hips and a satisfied smile on her face. He put his hands behind her knees, lifted and separated them and then dropped between. His mouth briefly savoured the richness of her cunt before he raised himself again and with one sure motion guided his cock within. There was no resistance and with one even stroke he moved the full length along her passage until he sensed the opening of her womb. Without moving a muscle, he focussed on his cock and the involuntary spasms released the full content of his storage sacs into the deepest recess of her cunt. Gloria gave a light peaceful groan and smiled whilst opening her eyes to look at him.

He realised in the vision that then came to him what exactly he must do with is work.

Initiation

I look up.

The sun is almost immediately overhead and scorching. I know I'm lost now, as the bush is getting even thinner. I don't know how I got here. Then, on the horizon I see figures. I'm saved. They carry me to a camp and humpies are around. I'm given water and some sort of bitter drink, which they exhort me to take. I do not understand them, but they know my needs. I'm feeling better, I say. I want to go home, but I don't know where home is.

Never had much contact with Aborigines. I sit in the shade and they chatter around me. Then one comes up and stands right in front of me, it's a girl. Well, not exactly, she's a young woman. She takes my hand and I stand up then she leads me away from my spot in the shade. Where are we going? Where is she taking me? Why is she taking me? The others: men, women and children, seem oblivious to what is happening. She takes me into a humpy and I can hardly make out her features in the shade. She gets me to sit and then sits opposite looking at me. We do that for a long, long time.

It's getting a little dreamy. She moves forward and grasps my manhood. Like her I am now wearing nothing, although she hadn't much on before we started. How did I lose my clothes? Well, I did and here she is with a firm grasp on my dick that starts to respond as she starts the up and down strokes that I know so well. I keep looking at her and she at me; the dreaminess starts again. I'm on my back and she is riding me.

Her cunt clasps my dick like it would never let it go. Her movements are rhythmic and she's softly humming. She has small scars above her breasts and one on her forehead. The ones on chest are symmetrical. I look down; I don't think she's born any children yet. Unusual, she's old enough, so why not? Drumming starts outside.

She leans to one side without disengaging. She picks up a large container and indicates to me to drink. She stays still on my dick while I raise myself on my elbows and taste the sour fluid she puts in my mouth in sips. She follows this with a kiss that traces the fluid in my mouth and takes a draught herself before resting the container down. She then resumes her position and starts rocking again. My prick remains consistently hard whatever she does. Am I attracted to her? Yes, but it doesn't seem sexual, so why is my dick saying otherwise?

The drumming increases, as does her rhythm. I respond with light thrusts of my pelvis. I think I'll reach the top of her cunt and touch her womb as she's only a slight thing, but I don't. There's a depth there that it doesn't seem my dick will fill. I'm well endowed, I can do this with just about any woman, so this little thing should be a pushover, but she's not. She keeps the rhythm going and I accept the status quo as the dreaminess intensifies.

She's singing a song like a cross between a chant and a lullaby. By now I'm enchanted anyway with this little surprise on my loins. Where is this ride leading, I wonder? What's making me so passive? I indicate I want to rise. I move into a sitting posture supported by the humpy beam and some clothing for padding. She remains astride me and now our bodies are closer. I briefly fondle her breasts; she doesn't stop me, but it doesn't feel right, so I stop and just meet her rhythms. Then I relax and it seems that I just 'know' her song so I join her and we sing in unison.

I look into her eyes. They are expressionless. I look deeper and then I feel like I'm falling into them. I see the vastness of the landscape and move across it effortlessly as one would in a dream. I come to an outcrop and now walk up to it. I begin to circle it and then come to a point where a large rock divides and a stream from a recent rain is gently dribbling down the crevice. I lean forward and place my mouth under a point where the dribbling makes a stream and leaves the rocky surface to fall into a pool at the base. I drink and drink deeply. It is rich and immensely satisfying. I move away and watch the stream for what seems a long time as it dries up under successive rainless days. The moon rises at one point and I watch the fullness traverse the heavens and warm the earth. Animals move silently in the background and I begin to weep.

I am still looking in her eyes and she gives the slightest of smiles. We have stopped singing. My body feels fluid and I can't feel my dick, although I know it's still inside her. She puts her hands on each side of my face and holds me very still. There is no resistance in me, I am totally accepting. She silently disengages from me and puts on the light cloth she was wearing earlier and sits to one side as the flap opens and two older men enter. There is chatter between the men and the girl, which stops abruptly and they all look at me. Silence. Then the men come to me and I rise and they walk me out into the evening air. There is a slight chill now and the fire softens this whilst warming the lightly clad drummers behind. The women are dancing in a slow circle around the fire in a sun-wise direction. I am slowly led toward the fire.

A younger man, heavily scarified, turns from his task at the fire's edge and looks at me. He turns back and picks up a sharp flint and sweeps it across my chest leaving two cuts, one above each breast. The blood begins to trickle down and he applies some ash and I know these are the tears of the sun. Then my attendants turn me around and bend me forward whilst each then supports me in this awkward posture. There is a similar sweep vertically below my arse at the base of my penis. It is painless. I turn back and watch the blood from this wound drip steadily on the sand below. I know this is the bleeding of the earth, the mother who sustains us all.

I awake feeling very rested and settled and then I remember the dream. I recall it and then get up and write it down, more or less as I have done above, but not without first checking the base of my cock: no wound, that is one virginity I still have intact! Strange dream, I have so little in common with Aboriginality, even though I have lived most of my life in this great land. I go to work, but somehow it doesn't seem the same and I have less enthusiasm than usual for the tasks in front of me. Pushing numbers around a computer screen, meeting deadlines, dealing with fictitious gods... Good job it's Friday, it'll give me time to get my bearings as the dream is beginning to unsettle me.

That night at dinner I find Jane to be just prattling on and she finds me 'somewhere else'. We've been down that path before, but I am not in the mood tonight to counter the sort of arguments that will inevitably come my way if we continue the evening together. I take up the option of an early separation and go home, put on some jazz and pour myself a malt whiskey. Her eyes begin to dance in front of me. I feel the vacuousness of her sex and the landscape of her vision, I experience the challenge of the initiation and then a deep welcoming of the land. I know I am changed and that all about me will change.

I have found the dreaming or, more correctly I realise, it has found me.

Delphi

My training was arduous. I had been selected for initiation as a priestess because of my natural beauty, silent disposition and psychic aura. I had been considered by my family a natural "muse" and taken for presentation to the Oracle as my body began to attain womanhood. She accepted me, this regal and powerful woman, adorned with robes of varying colour and long dark hair that reached to her waist. Her eyes were almost as dark and her countenance unimpassioned; that is, whilst not performing her duties. I felt a deep stirring in my body at the sight of her and would have let her do anything to me; so strong was the passion I felt.

The next year or so was not spent much in her company. It was shared with several others of a similar ilk to myself, who aspired to be priestesses and even the High Priestess herself with her oracular skills; considered the gift of the Goddess. We learnt the rituals of our caste, ways of dress and deportment. The Oracle herself taught us the art of sexuality. Initially this was the gentle exploration of our own bodies, and then those of our companions. We used tongues, hands and fingers to explore all of our being, accompanied by herbal drinks, oils and heightened by incense and sometimes music.

Sometimes this became frivolous and we would experience the ire of the Oracle. At other times it excited in us a passion that was soft, feminine, yet very powerful. She taught us to handle this power and raise its intensity to a peak where the subsequent release would transport us; initially we knew not where. Later the Oracle gave us visual pathways to follow in this heightened state of ecstasy and caused us to use our latent power to move objects, see into the body of others and to see into their future. All this and more was taught us, yet we remained intact; no object mechanical or the member of man had passed into our bodies. Indeed, it was rare for us to see the male-kind, confined as we were in the precinct of the Goddess.

The ritual moved to ceremony, particularly those of the seasons and the fire festivals that marked the social and religious transitions of our people. Occasionally we waited on the Oracle as men and women of import in the community consulted her: sometimes to deal with clan and tribal conflict, or to direct ill peoples to her trained acolytes for healing. I wondered if this would be my path, but the Goddess was to direct otherwise.

One night I had a dream where I was kneeling with my head bowed in front of the Oracle in her sacred chambers. I looked up toward her and, although it was within her chambers, it was also not. Her features changed to appearances of innocence, wisdom and terror. This took me through a range of emotions in the dream from love, to awe and then to fear. Then she made a terrific roar and pointed her hand and a long-manicured index finger toward me, as she looked deep into my eyes with eyes that were red, fiery and passionate. I awoke in a cold sweat. As was in our instruction I sought audience with the Oracle and told her my dream. It seemed to me that she looked upon me kindly with a familiarity I had not seen before. She said little, but my tasks were to change and become more closely involved with her: it was then that I started to perceive that the dream had foreshadowed my destiny as a priestess of the Goddess.

She took me to her bedchamber and instructed me more deeply in the sexual arts. From behind the bed, she produced a silver phallus that shocked me, but I knew what was to happen. She lay me down, parted my virginal thighs and used finger and tongue to help me overcome my trepidation and cause my juices to flow. And flow they did, more than I had ever experienced. My shock had briefly turned to fear, yet then to excitement as I knew this silver tool was to take my virginity and explore my femininity in a way that indicated all before had been a preliminary and not a finality. The Oracle worked the tip into my cavern and with a short firm thrust it was within. I could feel a trickle of blood mingle with the other juices and my excitement rose further and further to a crescendo I had never experienced. I briefly looked at the Oracle who was now working the tool vigorously within my channel as her eyes between my thighs looked deep and still into mine. Then I fell over the edge and the dream came to me again.

When I came to, I was covered and the Oracle was seated next to me with a warm drink in a large chalice, which she presented to me, instructing me to drink. She told me that the silver phallus marked the initiation into the outer circle of the God who was the consort of the Goddess; he who took the women into a state of divine frenzy and ecstasy. She further informed me that one day I would meet the golden phallus that would mark my initiation into the inner circle of the mysteries. As she completed telling me this, I started to feel the effect of the drink: I had a vision of a man, a great warrior, who was to come to seek counsel with the Oracle; yet it would become a battle of wits and he would depart in anger leaving the Oracle concerned. I told this to her, she nodded and instructed me to sleep. I did; a deep, peaceful sleep I had never known.

Our interactions grew in intensity and I was to perform on her the duty of initiation that she had given me. She seemed insatiable, but never dissatisfied. The days continued with my prior ritual and ceremonial duties, but my status with my peers distinctly changed and they knew it, offering me a quiet reverence that initially confused me, but then I grew to understand. At other times our sexual interactions and associated rituals became more intense, as my abilities to enter the otherworld in a trance state increased. There were occasions that men from the priesthood joined us, sometimes singularly and sometimes collectively. The rituals took on more and varied form and my repertoire, both sexually and as a seeress steadily increased. I was even awarded my own chambers and allowed some autonomy in these activities, although the Oracle asked that I continue to share all with her. So, she monitored and tutored my progress over the next few years.

There was a sense that our relationship was not personal; indeed, I seemed to lack a personality altogether as the Goddess became my life, as mediated through the Oracle my mentor. My life became encased by ceremony and enacted in ritual that included all expression of my body and mind. I became skilled in the art of trance and vision, what took longer to master was the ability to interpret what I saw into a language that could be communicated, although its reception and understanding would depend on the maturity and wisdom of the recipient. If too bound to the ways of the earth they would seek counsel for their own ends and be often left confused; I even wondered if this stood behind the anger of the warrior of my first vision with the Oracle. For those less earthbound and who saw their existence to connect with and be informed by a greater reality, then the stuff of vision and its expression in language would be understood on its own terms and respected as such. It was our experience that told us the maturity of the seeker and whether to engage in counsel.

Then one day the warrior chief arrived with little prior warning.

He was young and sharp, yet very much confined by his own

needs and knowledge, about which he had a great deal of confidence. He sought counsel with the Oracle. As was her custom and that of our tradition, she initially had me interview him from behind an opaque veil, as she sat in the wings. He asked of his conquests: he had already achieved much, yet desired more. His requests were received for our deliberation and he was asked to await the Oracle's instruction.

It seemed to us even then that his intent was the conquest of the known world and even beyond. As we later conferred, it also seemed to us that this was a representation of his being that he did not see: he wanted to gain power and control not only over his entire being, but also over the mysteries that would remain forever beyond him. Yet his literal way of seeing did not entertain this when I made subtle inquiry and it would have been our custom to reject such a man from counsel with the Oracle. Yet he had been insistent, and we knew that with his power he might destroy our community should we refuse. Under such terms my mentor had then reluctantly agreed to counsel him.

She prepared herself with baths, scents and delicate foods. I assisted her and continued my learning, yet I had never seen her this unsettled. We retired to her chamber and began the preparation with some gentle ritual lovemaking and then went to the counselling chamber, she retired onto a great couch. I took the golden phallus from the place of ritual concealment and stimulated her to the heights of sexual intensity. We then paused and she kept her eyes closed and breathed deep and fast as she entered a trance state.

On gentle command the warrior arrived with his entourage. I greeted him to bring him to my Mistress and informed him he must go alone. There was a stutter in his gait; this was not a man to take an order readily, but he followed. I sat him on a couch some feet away from the veil that separated the Oracle from him and retired into the recesses of the chamber.

I could see from my vantage point that my Mistress was deep in trance and now was the Goddess herself. He did not know this, concerned as he was about his own being and deeds. He asked the obvious question: Would I conquer the known world? Yes, was her response, for that is your destiny. What about the worlds beyond, will I not only discover them, but conquer them too? You must acknowledge the line drawn between yourself and the Gods, was the Oracle's reply, it is not always for us mortals to know such things. But I know you to be in the realm of the immortals now, woman! Thus, he yelled, so tell me the answer! My Mistress did not respond to the taunt, but I knew that this was a crucial time and had been the one that had provoked my vision.

You will gaze upon the unknown worlds, yet must then ask of the Gods whether you should venture further. I know you to carry a portable oracle, which I will infuse with my power for just this purpose. If they deny you, you must retire with what you have achieved. Should you contravene the wisdom of the Gods you will die an early death with your spoils passing to others. Yet my achievements would make me a God! Why should I then defer and kneel one more time! Beware my wrath, Oracle, should the Gods not favour me! With that, he rose and strode from the chamber.

I went to the Oracle. She came out of the trance and looked at me with a tear in her eye. She knew he would contravene the will of the Gods. She also knew his retribution would be swift and deep, and that she would forfeit her life. As we talked, it became clear she had visioned more than she had spoken and this she wished to share with me. She was aware the community of the Oracle would be devastated and the time of the Goddess diminished by the actions of this man who would champion the tyrannical One God to Her detriment. It was necessary that the Goddess be worshipped and honoured from this time and it was to be my task to take the core of the community on my travels for this purpose. My Mistress would remain and accept her fate, as it would further the survival of She whom she served for some future time, which she may have seen but told me not. This was mine to discover.

I took her back to her chamber and we made love one last time. As a parting gift she gave me a package that I knew contained the golden phallus. Then I summoned my charges around me and we started our preparations for the pilgrimage.

The Seance

I had always been attracted to Sheila. We had almost grown up together, although she was mainly my sister's friend. I watched her blossom into womanhood, but whilst I found her extremely alluring and sexually attractive, she seemed unofficially off limits, because of this association. I certainly watched her pass through the gamut of encounters that marked her development and maturity, although I wasn't sure as to how much she watched mine. Then she seemed go what I term 'mystical', with time in India, a Guru for several years culminating with some sort of career as a psychic. It was then that I noticed that whilst men seemed increasingly attracted to her that few, if any, became close. Whether this indicated she was celibate or took casual lovers, I wasn't sure. If I'd had any real passion to pursue the matter at this time, I might have looked to her Guru's utterances to determine which, but I was too career-oriented and ambitious. At another level I also didn't want to find out, which alerted me to some deeper feelings.

After my medical and psychiatric training, I became more interested in the forensic side of my profession. I had discovered that patients actually bored me beyond a point, but that understanding the mind and mental processes was of great interest. Maybe I would have been better off as a detective, but it wasn't the criminal activities of the mind that interested me and I didn't have a penchant for violence. Mysteries, however, were a different matter. At one stage when I was seconded to the police, I came across a man whom the force used as a psychic in unsolved murders. His success rate was very high and this I found intriguing.

I had always been somewhat dismissive of psychic abilities as I was of a scientific and rational bent, plus the fact that, in my experience, I had found much in the area to be fake and it to be filled with con men. I initially put Sheila in this category, although I did notice there was an emotional undercurrent to this judgement that wasn't usually present. It was intriguing that our interests had converged somewhat, although I initially paid this little attention. In hindsight it was because I was finding her increasingly attractive and I needed to defend myself from my feelings.

This was a time when my profession began to busily police itself or, more correctly, police those who it felt were invading its domain. Initially, as a man of science and logical outlook, I accepted this position and was even employed to track down those who purported skills that my profession believed that only it should possess. The main area of contention was the therapeutic encounter. As psychiatry had early in its history eschewed any relationship to the paranormal and hence parapsychological studies, anyone with so-called psychic abilities was able to practice under that title, provided they didn't use it in a therapeutic or prophetic manner: that is, didn't call what they were doing psychotherapy or claim to be able to see a client's future.

This appeared all quite reasonable, it seemed to me, until I came across evidence that the separation of these two worlds was only recent and marked by the acceptance of a psychoanalytic model of the psyche that included the paranormal, but reduced its operations to mental processes. As I matured into my field, I became increasingly uncomfortable with such a division, but it was far from overwhelming and I was inclined to the view that ultimately an expanded psychoanalytic and psychiatric model would explain phenomena in the paranormal and supernatural fields that were yet to be explained. After all, science had been so incredibly successful in the twentieth century that it seemed only a matter of time.

Sheila may have been oblivious to all of this, although I suspected not, as she was very intelligent and insightful. Yet, in spite of my suggestions, she had no desire to pursue a psychological training that would give her both acceptance and protection. I wondered whether this was denial on her part and indicated that her psychic abilities were toward the fake end of the spectrum. She certainly had an element of the showman about her, although by now I had come to see such personality features as commensurate with the territory.

I was rapidly getting a reputation as a "ghost buster", even a "cult buster", and followed this with articles and then a couple of best-sellers for the popular market. This success took me on to a circuit of functions, seminars and other deliveries, even radio and television. Yet this success seemed to raise doubts and conflicts. My colleagues began to question my integrity and sincerity, even to the point of considering me in the psychic camp when I validated and supported someone that I considered authentic. That was the conflict, but the doubt was inner and deeper: How did I truly feel about psychic phenomena? With all the research and investigation, I had undertaken, how was it that I didn't have the ongoing confidence that my profession would one day find a model inclusive of the psychic?

When I brought such issues up with Sheila she simply smiled.

"After all this study and investigation, you still haven't seen how I operate. I have frequently wondered why this is…"

"Why don't you look into your crystal ball?" Ouch! That was unnecessary… and hurtful.

Sheila was not fazed, which piqued my curiosity: "Why don't

you come to an open evening that I conduct?"

That was why I was there on this moonlit evening in her lounge room. There were six others seated around a circular table on straight-backed chairs, Sheila's chair was a little more comfortable I noticed as she entered and took her seat. She looked gorgeous. Her dark hair was gathered at the back of her head, but still flowed over her shoulders and the gypsy-like long dress she was wearing, plus a liberal adornment of jewellery which made her look like a stunning witch. After my attraction subsided a little, I became concerned about this theatre; was the appearance designed to obscure what was going on? It was also in her darkened living room; were there other props concealed? This, and more, passed my mind as Sheila took her seat.

"Can we join hands and close eyes please.

"May the blessing of the uncreated one, the created word and spirit that is the inspirer be with us tonight. I declare this ceremony open."

The others muttered something similar to, but different from, amen: I was unable to ascertain what it was exactly. Then Sheila, eyes still closed – mine were the only ones open I noted, even in the darkened room – said, or half-chanted, a prayer or song in a tongue I did not recognise. By this time my suspicious hackles were rising.

We let go of our clasped hands and sat back, most eyes were on Sheila now, although hers remained closed. At least there was no Ouija board and handholding that could restrict, divert and disguise what was going on, which lessened my concerns temporarily. What followed seemed routine fare. An older man asked a question about his deceased wife. Sheila responded to him by relaying messages to him from his wife in the spirit world. Ho hum, I thought. There was plenty of this and I was getting bored, but then these sorts of questions and interactions ceased. Maybe it was because those with pressing questions were now exhausted of queries and satisfied by the answers they were given? Or maybe it was because Sheila seemed to deepen her meditative state and start to show trance-like features as her eyes and mouth twitched and her body lightly shook.

"There is someone from the other side who wants to make his presence known... He has a message for someone called Janice?"

"That's me!" This exclamation came from a thin and nervous-looking girl seated opposite me. The impression was that Sheila did not know her; I could verify this later, if need be.

"It's Uncle Alex!"

Janice's gaze was fixed over my left shoulder, between Sheila and myself, who was seated next to me on my left. I turned to look at where Janice was looking and a shock like a bolt of electricity passed through my body. Next to the large curtain that obscured the rear of the room was the vague silvery shape of an older bald-headed man. The shape seemed to fluctuate as a collective gasp rose from the table. I noticed if I looked at the shape intently then it became more obscure, but if I let my gaze become less focussed it became clearer.

"What message have you for Janice, Alex?" This was Sheila's command.

"The diamonds I left for your mother are in a box, in a fake panel, behind the Soldier's portrait." The voice was husky and vague, but became clearer as it repeated the sentence a further three times. I looked to Janice; she was ashen and her mouth agape. The shape dissipated and silence reined.

Time to collect my thoughts. This was something else I could easily verify, if I could get to Janice before she departed. But that didn't obscure the fact that she may have already put the diamonds in their hiding place and that this figure of "Uncle Alex" was a prop. My doubts took over and reached a crescendo; I knew I had a short time to act and the curtain at the rear of the room was looking increasingly suspicious. I quickly and quietly rose to my feet. Everyone seemed still and not to notice me, Sheila was still in a trance. I tiptoed to the left of the curtain, where the figure of Alex had materialised, drew the curtain back and entered the space beyond.

I was flabbergasted. Seated on a lounge chair that seemed to be the only piece of furniture in the room was Sheila. I quickly turned to my right and pulled the curtain back a little. I could see the rear of what seemed like Sheila still in her place at the circle. Although my seat was vacant the others were still looking to Sheila as she was announcing the presence of another psychic visitor. It certainly sounded like Sheila. I let the curtain fall and returned my gaze to the Sheila I had discovered behind the curtain.

"You believe I am faking, don't you?" Her voice was soft.

"Yes." I also kept the tone of my voice low.

"You always have. How do you explain this? Can you? I'm sure if you consider long enough, you'll come up with an explanation, but maybe before you do, I can help you alleviate your doubts." She leaned forward and took my hand, pulling me toward her.

It is difficult to describe what happened next, but I will do my best. Sheila sat on the edge of her seat and looked intently at my crotch. She then raised a hand and started to massage my growing erection over my flannel trousers. My cock responded quickly and completely to her gentle stoking as her eyes remained on my crotch. Then with the other hand she undid my fly and pulled my dick free, a relatively easy manoeuvre, as I was wearing no underwear. Sheila continued her stroking, now with both hands and, it seemed to me, that her face took on the trance-like appearance I had seen earlier, except that her eyes remained open on this occasion.

It was peculiar: I could still hear the 'other' Sheila talking in the main room and conversing with a man. I turned and looked down to see 'this' Sheila's head move toward my cock, her lips gently part and my erection to disappear into her mouth. She stopped as it reached the limit of her mouth before her throat and gauged this distance with one hand around the base of my cock. She maintained a rhythm up and down to this point for several minutes; slow, methodical and entrancing in its own right. Then she removed my cock and licked its length, then just the head and finally paid attention to my balls, individually and collectively. She sucked first one then the other, and then both before returning to the shaft before finally guiding my length back into her mouth.

I watched her, silently and enraptured. I could feel the heat and intensity in my loins, but strangely there was no incipient feeling of ejaculating. I found this odd, as I had never had a blowjob of such dedication and intensity. Then Sheila looked up to my eyes for the first time and I met her gaze. Her hand came away from the base of my shaft and she positioned my cock-head at the junction of her throat. Then she seemed to swallow the remainder and I felt the head slip into her throat whist she kept up her constant gaze. My cock felt like it was falling into a void; I was following.

I was floating in an ethereal void. I didn't feel that I had a body, or any senses that I could immediately detect. It was dark and still, very still. I felt in the grips of an infinity that seemed beyond or behind the reality I had left and stretched into eternity. I felt the aeons pass and basked in the stillness and peace. Then there was a ripple in the stillness and I could see an impending light encroach on the darkness. It was total, the light penetrating the darkness and merging with it until it reached an intensity that felt like a monumental scream and explosion as the two realities merged. Then I began to detect forms in the darkness, swirling balls of light as the emanation moved into creation. I was in awe.

Then I was suddenly back in my body as the last convulsions of my orgasm sent rivulets of semen deep into Sheila's throat. Throughout her gaze never altered and she swallowed my offering. As the convulsions in my being ceased, she withdrew her gaze and her mouth, quietly to suck my length in her mouth alone and render it pure. I stroked her head and tears came to my eyes as she looked up to me again. I knew that she knew that I had experienced creation through the eyes of the divine. I would never be the same again, nor would our relationship. She returned my cock to my trousers and did up the fly, then settled back into her seat with a smile on her face. I waited until the tears subsided, then with a sigh I moved out from behind the curtain and returned to my seat. As I did the Sheila' seated in the circle came out of her trance to briefly look at me and smile the same smile. I could not explain what had or was happening and I didn't want to. I knew that henceforth my life would change, as would my future relationship with Sheila.

Madness

Another strange bed: how often will I do this before I wake up to myself? I look across at last night's conquest; at least he's asleep. He has tats down his arms and across chest, and smells like a brewery... and I don't even remember whether the sex was any good! Fuck, could have got a disease from this boy if the state of his room is anything to go by and with my cunt so sore; so is my arse... fuck! Whoa gal, what's that on the floor, a condom with his stinking spunk leaking out onto the carpet? At least that should mean I could avoid the doctor's this week, the umpteenth STD check-up; I wonder if I've broken the national record for this yet? I feel more than a bit nauseous; time to leave. On the way out I see my mobile number on a notepad near the phone. I rip the page out; continue out and down the stairs, as the fucking lift is out of order – of course.

My psych will love this. Penhaus is such a patronising arsehole.

"If you don't take your lithium, what do you expect?"

Fuck you, arsehole.

"I'm not manic depressive, I keep telling you!"

"Sure, Linda." My name is Jemma, but he keeps referring to the first name on my file: Linda Jemma Golding, "So when did you qualify as a psychiatrist?"

Like I said: Patronising arsehole.

"Well, if you're not going to take lithium because it "makes you sick", then at least try a mood stabiliser; it might keep you out of strangers' beds."

I take – snatch – the prescription and leave. The pun on the word 'snatch' is not lost on me.

Why do these bastards want to pigeonhole me? First up, when my fucking stepfather hauls me to the psych ward, I'm a schizophrenic: needles in the arse, then the pills. University becomes a struggle, but when sex starts to provide a – meaningful – distraction I then graduate to being manic-depressive. Rather like a company changing its name and logo. I'm now the more socially acceptable fucking "bipolar disorder". Sure, I get moody, but I'm an artist; aren't we all? And yes, I'm driven by my emotions and this includes what I consider to be a very healthy sex-drive. Certainly, most of my boyfriends don't complain!

But this is different. It's not promiscuous behaviour, as I can be that and remember it. This is high-risk sex, self-destructive and anonymous. One smart psych started talking about borderline personality and tacked in onto my diagnostic profile. Thanks, now no self-respecting therapist will touch me and my funds don't stretch to private therapy. I don't remember what happens in these states. At first, I thought it was too much drink, but that was easy to check out as a possibility and my drinks couldn't really be spiked every time; even I'm not that paranoid!

I give Gary a ring and arrange to meet. He's gay and won't try to fuck me, but he's also a good amateur analyst.

"Hey Jemma, how are you?" Theatrical kiss on the cheek, dry and accompanied by an audible "Mwaaaa!" "Coffee, sweet?"

Yes, I reply, as I watch him mince to the counter. Don't get me wrong, I love the guy, he's so "out there"! Maybe that's my problem, I can't own where I go when I trip out?

"No, I don't think so, sweetie" is Gary's reply to that idea in question form, "I don't think you'd have trouble owning your behaviour! There has to be more to it than that, but I can't put my finger on it."

"You wouldn't know where it is to put a finger on it!" I quip.

"Bitch! Now be serious Jem, I have an idea. I met this guy last week; he's gay though not my type, but he practices some sort of hypnosis that might help you to explore all this. His name is Dyon and this is his number." Dyon's number materialises on the back of a coaster. We continue to chat for a while, then I pocket the coaster and leave.

It takes one more encounter to convince me: This one leaves me with a black eye, plus bloody pieces of skin under my fingernails. I ring Dyon and arrange to meet him. I'm strangely nervous when I drive to his house. He lives alone and I wouldn't have picked him for being gay.

"I'm not," is his reply to my query in that regard.

"Gary thinks you are."

"Well, he may have presumed that because I was with a gay guy when we met. I have swung a little, and nothing would stop me if I was so attracted but, in general, women are my thing."

This put an interesting complexion on the man; he seemed comfortable moving around different components of his personality, something that was to emerge importantly in our relationship.

We have an initial preparatory chat about the nature and intent of hypnosis, then he appears to undermine himself:

"But I don't really call what I do hypnosis."

"What is it then?"

"It's really getting people into trance-like states so they can explore other dimensions of their personality, or other personalities."

"Other personalities? You're kidding me!"

"Not at all, Jemma, from what you've told me there's at least one other personality in you having her say without you knowing it."

You could've knocked me over with a feather. After all the psychs and their fucking drugs here was someone, not a formal professional, who seemed to have an angle that was at least worth exploring and made a lot of sense. The "at least one" comment was a bit unnerving, however.

It wasn't long before Grace emerged. She didn't want to talk at first, but Dyon had ways and means; a bit of emotional blackmail goes a long way.

"I'm not happy about this," Grace said to Dyon, "You've brought me out against my will."

"Hardly against your will, Grace, and I do have Jemma's welfare to consider."

"That little tart, she thinks she can upstage me sexually, but she's not even in the race."

"Maybe I can discourage her?"

"Well, it might help, if she lets me have full reign in the sex stakes."

"Can you explain a little?"

"Well, when she was the serious student all was going well. I came into my own, but she decided to take on my skills and use them as her own."

"You mean sexually?"

"Yes."

"What's not OK about that?"

Grace pondered a little before replying. "It's OK that she has her own sex-life, but after a few drinks she often starts to believe she's the whore of Babylon and that is strictly my territory. What she has to do is let me take over, then I can indulge myself, but when she resists and sees it all as 'her' then I get mad and pissed off and turn the screw."

"You mean act self-destructively?"

"Yes, it's aimed at her, but it can backfire on me too and that I don't like."

Dyon was sure he had a handle on Grace and her personality, but his therapeutic responsibility was now to get Jemma to see it, or more correctly Grace. He knew that if Jemma could do this then the self-destructive behaviour would diminish and Jemma may even be more aware of what was happening when Grace took over and maybe get to enjoy it! Dyon was not surprised to find that it was Jemma who was more reluctant to accept Grace's presence, than Grace was Jemma's. This was his experience: The dominant personality was always more reluctant, as she or he did not enjoy relinquishing control and power, but if this didn't happen there was the danger of self-destruction, which he knew was quite real and a distinct possibility in Jemma's – and Grace's – situation. It took several hours before he broke through and was able to get the three of them on the same page, conversing freely.

Well now I know she exists it's a little easier, though it took me a while to acknowledge Grace as part of me. Enough of that "part of me" gal! I'm as real and substantial as you are, Jemma my girl!

For a while the process worked quite smoothly. Jemma lost her aggressive edge and re-engaged in her studies at university. Her thinking was that this quiet, innocent side was more her inherent personality. It was one her stepfather saw as being odd and the psychs as pathological, when she spent long periods of time withdrawn from the family. There was more than a little irony in this, as her stepfather's attention had a sexual edge that may have accounted for her withdrawal, but also for Grace's emergence.

Grace was inclined to agree. She pointed out to Jemma that it was more than a "sexual edge"; it had been full-on sexual activity that started when she was about fifteen, though was latently present long before this, and continued until university.

Both came to the conclusion that his subsequent actions were a punishment of sorts and that Grace had not yet emerged enough to voice the injustice. Instead, her sexual awakening sought expression elsewhere and she encouraged Jemma in this. The subsequent promiscuity and mood changes as the personalities alternated led Dr Penhaus, the most recent psych, to label her manic depressive; sorry, bipolar disorder.

So, study and play went on for many months, with Dyon's ongoing tutelage. Both found Dyon's place in the whole scheme of things interesting. He appeared always to be there for them alone; surely he had other patients or clients, reasoned Jemma? To date there was no evidence of this. Maybe he's a voyeur! This was Grace's contribution, but this also didn't seem to explain his involvement. He remained enigmatic and, for the time being, both were accepting of his support and guidance.

Jemma had the good sense not to discuss these possibilities with Dr Penhaus and this was assisted by Grace's suggestion that she should be present at the next visit; Jemma could have a break from her patronising psych!

"How are you today, Linda?"

"Great," replied Grace, "had a fabulous night out. Got these two guys to spit-roast me, next time they've promised me a double penetration."

Grace looked at Dr Penhaus; his face was blank and mouth agape.

"Not to worry, doctor, I made sure they used condoms!"

Jemma laughed herself silly when Grace recounted the consultation. Penhaus had found it difficult to maintain his professional stance, because there really was little from the psychiatric position he could comment on. Instead, he lapsed into the father, read moral, role. Grace took this with a smile, acknowledged his point of view, took his script and quietly left with a wink back to Penhaus over her left shoulder; she couldn't resist it!

It was Grace who experienced her first. Jan was a motherly type who wanted to protect this rather wayward girl and her flagrant behaviour. It wasn't that Jan judged her in the same way that Dr Penhaus implicitly did, it was more a "for her own good" attitude with attendant advice. At first Grace had heard Jan as a voice in her left ear and been a little concerned about her own sanity, even to a vague sense of guilt about her sexual proclivities. But, with Dyon's assistance, it gradually became obvious that Jan was another personality requiring a voice and integration.

With Jan came Briney, a troublesome tomboy of a girl, who did not want to grow up. When she dominated proceedings Briney stopped eating and created outrage from her hungry co-selves. She could even get to the point of stopping menstruation and with it any sexual feelings. The tension ran high between Briney and Grace for a while; Jan tried to moderate, but things remained tense.

Here Dyon stepped in. He had been taking a rather passive role toward his charges, but now recognised things had to change. This was heightened by the fact that the girls had overplayed their hand with Penhaus and he was now becoming interventive with threats of committal because of a 'schizophrenic relapse'. Maybe the only thing that prevented him using his authoritarian powers was his deep-seated unacknowledged attraction to what was happening. He was a voyeur; what more did he want?

Dyon acted quickly and took his charges away to a neighbouring town where a friend of his had a rural property; he hoped Penhaus was thrown off the track. He was wrong. There followed a period of withdrawal where Dyon instructed his charges to prepare for a ceremony that would finally release them from the yolk of authority. The collective purpose over-rode their differences and they agreed. There followed a period of quiet, meditation and care with diet. They assisted in the house and gardens. As this progressed into the second week something strange started to happen.

It was Jemma who first noticed it. Over time she had become close to Grace and they had become like sisters, which, in a manner of speaking, they were. Jemma was putting some washing on the line and talking to Grace when she noticed that the responses were coming from a vague figure on her right, who was also going through the motions of hanging clothes out. Jemma stopped, the figure continued and became more substantial as Jemma realised this figure who was talking back to her was Grace, but in her own – another - body.

Grace also stopped her activities and looked back. She was now quite substantial and Jemma noticed her beauty and how in many ways she was so different from herself. Her hair was longer, facial features were similar though slightly rearranged to give the impression of someone maybe genetically close, yet different. Her breasts and hips were fuller and her mouth rich. Grace was accentuating all the features of sexuality that were present in Jemma, but latent. Jemma turned to her left as she heard Briny enter the yard, similar, but appearing younger and more boy-like. Then, of course and now not a surprise, came Jan, the mother.

"Dyon," started Jemma, "I think you may have some explaining to do."

Even he was starting to look a little different, his appearance was gaining a wildness and his eyes had a piercing quality they had not seen before.

"Nothing you probably can't intuitively know and work out yourself – yourselves."

That enigmatic response simply heightened the confusion

and mystery of what was happening, although they knew he was right: this was a situation that demanded not an explanation, but experience. Gradually they noticed his other charges as they began the preparatory rituals. Dyon became the conductor of an orchestra that included all manner of people.

When Jemma – Linda – didn't attend her next appointment with Dr Penhaus his suspicions became further aroused. He could easily just enact committal proceedings and get the police to start the ball rolling. Yet he hesitated. He tried to convince himself that this was for care of his patient, or even professional interest, when really it was vicarious. These thoughts he tried to dismiss, particularly when they aroused deep feelings in his body and occasionally produced an erection. He put this down to fatigue, stress and professional anxiety.

It was a little difficult tracking down their movement away from the city, but the police owed him more than one favour. He decided to go there by still of night and dress casually, even with a little disguise. The drive simply raised his anxiety because he had no idea what he would face when he got there. He tried to give it all a simple psychological explanation: His patient had fallen under the 'spell' of this Dyon, a figure who the police gave a guru-like picture of, although he had committed no crime.

When Penhaus arrived near the farmhouse he parked his car a discreet distance away and made his way on foot toward the building. As he got near, he began to circle it as lights were on, but there was no obvious activity. He passed some fifty yards to the left beyond the garden and then noticed light emerging from a hollow some two hundred yards further on. Stealthily and under the guise of darkness he moved toward the light. As he came closer, he could make out voices chanting and the sound of drums. To the left of the hollow was an outcrop of trees and large boulders. He clambered onto one, but had to traverse several before he could gain a relatively relaxed lying position that gave him a view of the entirety of the hollow.

Below him and beginning some ten yards away was a throng of people. They were only lightly dressed in gowns and some outlandish costumes. There was a mixture of the sexes, but a general accent on youth. The men generally marked the periphery and were drumming or using sticks to create a regular rhythm. Toward the middle was dancing, although in a semi-ritualised manner. They are all on drugs, assumed Penhaus, with their eyes closed and that stupid paint on their faces and bodies. However, the only drug he could see present was alcohol, as he presumed the great goblets in hands and standing free contained wine from the vats on the periphery.

Then he looked to the right. There was a raised area and a male figure, whom he assumed to be Dyon, was seated in a great chair. His arms draped casually on the armrests and one held the greatest of all goblets from which he periodically supped. His eyes were open, still and wild. His matted hair was raised to the sides giving the impression of horns and creating in Penhaus the sense that he was mimicking the devil. His legs were parted. Two female forms walking toward him, both looked like Linda! One was more voluptuous than he recalled, although a little like how she had looked at their last consultation, so maybe she was her sister? He thought quickly, he didn't recall that she had one. Then the women dropped to their knees and in unison crawled toward Dyon, up onto the raised dais and toward his parted legs. Whilst he watched into the distance and throng in front of him, he casually lifted the cloth that covered his genitals with his free hand.

What an erection! Penhaus was startled; it looked huge, like a sabre. The women were now close to it and he parted his knees even wider and moved his lower legs further out to give them comfortable access. Penhaus did not know it, but it was Grace who first toyed with his erection and then engaged it with her mouth, before holding it and offering it to her 'sister' to do likewise. Penhaus' mouth was again agape, but he was transfixed as the women alternated their endeavours then joined to a simultaneity that made his head spin, as one sucked the other attended his testicles, or ran a tongue up and down his thighs. Dyon remained impassive.

The drumming increased in intensity and the dancing women casually discarded what remained of their clothing. Some continued to dance singularly while others engaged with each other in dance, which rapidly progressed to kissing and fondling. Bodies slipped to the ground, pairs and sometimes multiple numbers explored each other with mouths and fingers and the groaning started. Penhaus started to sweat, but he also had an erection. His eyes could not leave the scene.

Men came from the periphery and joined the women. Genitals became organs, penises cocks, and vaginas cunts as Penhaus started the slippery slide into depravity. But the throng was exalted. The men sucked and were sucked; they fucked the women who were simultaneously fucking each other or other men who joined the throng. The elders continued the drumming at the periphery, which formed a circle that enclosed this writhing mass in front of him. Eventually all the bodies seemed as one and Penhaus came into his pants without any stimulation.

Dyon looked to the rock. He knew Penhaus was there and he could now see the head droop and eyes close. He looked down to his two charges who continued uninterrupted as he stood. He looked in front of him, felt the pace and rhythm to be reaching its climax, so he passed his goblet to a waiting attendant and raised his arms in the air. The drums reached a crescendo and stopped; he clapped three times and allowed his sperm to issue forth onto the tongues and into the mouths of the two acolytes below him. As they turned to share the emission of this god-man with each other all around the throng were the sounds of heightened groaned and then the daunting sound of individual orgasms becoming as one in a vortex of sound and light.

Dyon was satisfied.

With his left hand Dyon pointed to the rock. The drumming slowly recommenced and Penhaus lifted his head somewhat; he was dazed and confused. He did not have any time to gain focus. The women, led by Jemma and Grace, screamed a low guttural noise and dashed toward and up the outcrop. Penhaus made a vague attempt to retreat but was easily surrounded. They carried him down to Dyon; he was bereft of any struggle and looked like a corpse lying across the shoulders of the women. They stopped in front of Dyon, holding aloft this man as they would a coffin. Dyon looked deep into Penhaus' eyes, which looked back in fear, but also acceptance. Dyon nodded to the crowd. They turned on Penhaus then, threw him to the ground and tore him limb from limb. He barely screamed, his body became a mass of parts and the crowd had their fill.

The ceremony was complete.

The Dream

Penny awoke with her heart pounding. She had dreamed of Michel – again. This time he was bringing her to orgasm with his tongue. It was darting around her pussy lips and then giving her clitoris a gentle nibble, using his teeth in a light and tempting manner, then engorging it with his mouth and gently lifting it from its moorings as if to swallow it. Then back down and back to the darting. She came and came, screaming his name loud and long, as his tongue did not miss a beat.

When her heart settled a little and the sweating subsided Penny let her hand investigate. She was wet with the juices of love. She brought her hand up to her face and smelt the juices as the texture confirmed her suspicion that it was not just in the dream that she had come. She then let the index and middle fingers enter her mouth, as she savoured the product. Her mind ran back through the dream. They had been dining, chatting across a candlelit table. How very chic, thought Penny! Yet it served to show her the depth of attachment that she had to Michel. They had then materialised into a bedroom – as you can in dreams – and their lovemaking had gone through a range of activity before the culmination that awoke her.

This was not the first time. The dreams had begun some time after Penny had met Michel, who had been referred to her by his local doctor for psychotherapy. On their first meeting he sat opposite her with eyes downcast, still of movement and offering only short responses to her questions. There was no doubt that he was depressed and this from a therapist reluctant to make such a diagnosis when it seemed so fashionable. But with Michel it was different; he had the sort of depression she had seen in psychiatric wards. Penny recalled the type; rarely moving from their chair, disinterested in all activity around them, avoiding eye contact and rarely displaying any emotion, particularly smiling. This was in spite of the fact that the doctor had commenced antidepressant medication and was probably the reason he had referred Michel, because he was not responding to the treatment.

Michel had the psychological history from hell. His father had committed suicide when he was a baby and he was an only child. It seemed that the responsibility of being a father was just too much for a man Michel had been told was quiet and loving: Not a very loving act to his son, thought Penny! Nor to his young wife, who then went through a succession of relationships masking her probable post-natal depression and producing two daughters to different fathers. The first man was never in the picture, the second moved in to live with Michel's mother, but resented and beat Michel, once to the point that he ended up in hospital.

That his mother stayed with this man in spite of this outcome made Michel feel betrayed. He retired to his inner world, performed well at school, but his social life was truncated. This extended to relationships that he formed after adolescence, which were rarely sustained and often similar women to his mother or diametrically the opposite. This was not surprising, mused Penny, he was a very attractive man physically, with a reserve of emotion that felt untapped and unexplored, and so women would naturally be drawn to him. That included his present relationship with Christina, which had produced a son. There were all the hallmarks of impending and repeated disaster here, so Penny realised she would have to tread very carefully.

Their first few meetings had been quite pedestrian. The most Penny had been able to achieve was more eye contact. The first time it happened she was quite startled, as she hadn't expected it. Michel quickly looked directly into her eyes without moving his head from its downcast position when telling her about a dream he had the previous night. She felt a shock go through her body that settled in her pelvis. If she had not been with Michel she would have automatically scratched at her crotch, so strong was the feeling that settled there. Penny felt some heat in her cheeks; she hoped she wasn't blushing. Probably not, as he continued to recount the dream and she felt that he was looking through and not at her.

"I'm walking across a marshy landscape and it's raining. I'm looking for someone, but I don't know whom. Then from behind a dead tree a man appears and walks toward me. I can see it's my father, I recognise him from photos. He walks up to me and silently embraces me. I wake up crying."

Well, no need to be a Sigmund Freud here, thinks Penny! Her initial thoughts go to the father: she would like to think this is some sort of change for the better, that Michel may be coming to terms with the loss of his father and this could liberate him from the pattern that was besetting him in his life and relationships. But she had some nagging doubts, as it was not Michel who was embracing his father, it was the other way around and this thought sent a chill through her.

"Maybe the rain is like the tears you sometimes wake up with?"

Penny had decided to look at the emotional level of the dream. If she could facilitate his emotional recognition and development then the deeper symbolism of his relationship with his father may clarify and lighten from its present ambivalent and concerning depth.

"Maybe." This was all she was to get.

After the session Penny made some notes, but felt troubled. She wondered if continuing with dreamwork was a good idea; it certainly would be a safer option if she did not. At a professional level she knew that unless these deeper issues were engaged that Michel would remain depressed and at risk. She felt she had no choice but to proceed and at that level her professional clarity was definite; it was her response to Michel's look that troubled her. It was then that Penny started dreaming of Michel, initially in a dark and enigmatic way, but rapidly becoming sexual.

Of course, she interpreted this in terms of a counter-transference; that is, when the therapist starts to have feelings about a patient or client that may indicate something of an unresolved nature in their own psychology. What surprised Penny was that there didn't appear to be any overt transference from Michel: that deep initial look was powerful and enigmatic, but it certainly wasn't a display of any overt emotion toward her and specifically not as a woman. Even the demise of Penny's recent long-term relationship didn't feel an explanation for her response.

And what was her response? At one level it was obviously sexual and could be explained by her current status. Penny pondered this and wondered whether she should go and talk to a supervising therapist about the relationship with Michel, but she decided not. Harry would inevitably see it in the sexual transference and counter-transference context; that was his way, after all. He may even recommend that Penny stop seeing Michel and refer him elsewhere. She understood that as an option, but felt it would betray Michel. Penny also knew that such an act might be in the interest of the therapist, even the supervising therapist, rather than that of the patient; she had seen that often enough. At least, that was her thinking, and it supported her choice not to see Harry about this issue. Her reasoning on this was that they were engaged in something deeper, as she recognised in the dream and his looks. She had to see this through.

Of course, when her dreams started Penny had to rationalise her position even further. She had gone too far to turn back now, but she was certainly troubled by her ongoing motives. Whilst she had sexual dreams, these were different. There was usually a romantic component, but the sexuality was often quite mixed and sometimes alien to her experience. In many ways her sexual development had been quite conventional, even restricted, and was reflected in her long-term relationships. She was also still childless, although by choice, so she believed. The dream that awoke her on this occasion frightened her with the intensity of her orgasm; it was more than she had ever experienced. In the dream before she awoke, she even recalled Michel looking up at her from between her legs, with the gaze that had startled her in their session together.

Other dreams she had of him were more edgy than her experience to date. Michel would spank her, throttle her and take her anally. None of this she had experienced in her waking life, but she enjoyed it in her dreams. Penny now felt she was in over her head and there was no going back. Harry was no longer even an option; she would press forward with a vague and increasing fantasy that therapy may finish with them establishing a personal relationship. My god! This is so obviously counter-transference, thought Penny, what the fuck am I doing? Something deeper troubled her, however. There was something beyond the obvious: something deep and mysterious about the masculine realm. It seemed to embrace them both – and Michel's father. It had features of anger and violence, but was broodier and darker. There seemed to be a net into which the three of them were entwined and Penny could only see some of what this was.

The last time she saw him Penny felt there was a shift for the better, which was why subsequent events so shattered her. Michel had volunteered a dream that had lighter and direction in it; the brooding presence of his father was not there. Penny felt relieved and this was reinforced by their eye contact. For the first time that she could recall, he smiled at her. Penny recalled going home to her unit that night lighter of mood; she also felt a relaxing of the sexual tension between them. Maybe she would stop having those dreams!

She did not. That night she dreamed that they were again making love. Making love: whom was she kidding? He was fucking her like an animal. Her hands were gripping the railings at the head of the bed and she was on her knees. He was ramming into her cunt or arse; she knew not which. He was yelling like an animal and gripping her throat, stifling any sound. She turned to look at him and his face was engorged and eyes protruding as he looked at her. She awoke shocked; she had not had an orgasm, it simply felt deathlike.

Which indeed it was: Michel hanged himself that night. He had left the partnership bed in the middle of the night, barely troubling Christina; it was common for him to get up like this she was subsequently to admit. He had gone to his study in the garage and put a noose over the central beam, kicking away the chair. He did not seem to have made any attempt to disengage himself in his death throes; so deep was his commitment. The note on the desk was an apology to all, Penny included.

Maybe it was the note that stopped any inquiry beyond the necessary. Christina seemed relieved. Penny wondered whether she might perpetuate the pattern of Michel's mother. Penny could not be sure either way, so she gave Christina her card and phone numbers, although for whose benefit she was unsure. Penny was left with her feelings. Now she chose to see Harry, although she did not tell him her dreams, there was a sense of something enduring with Michel, or the world he represented, that she didn't want violated. Somewhat surprisingly, given her training and conservative background, she did not feel any guilt about this.

In the weeks that passed after Michel's suicide the immediate outside ramifications settled fairly quickly, which was a pleasant surprise to Penny, as she had plenty to contend with in her 'inner' world. Unusual for such a traumatic event was the lack of recrimination and anger that emerged. Everyone seemed strangely at peace and even Christina, whom Penny was concerned might take the path of her mother-in-law, seemed quite content to move to a small country town with her son and start a small cottage industry business with the insurance money from Michel's estate. Christina saw Penny before she left, although she was prepared to do this on a professional basis, Penny was adamant that the meeting be informal and outside of any clinical setting.

"How are you, Christina?" Penny started the conversation at the coffee shop on safe ground, setting the agenda in a somewhat accustomed manner.

"Much as you'd expect. What about you, you look troubled. "Was the surprising reply; the roles were quickly reversed.

Penny found herself to be opening up to this woman, and as she did, she opened up more deeply to herself. She told Christina that she often dreamed about Michel.

"Me too," was Christina's response, "usually with a fair bit of raunch! Bit of a surprise really, as he wasn't very energetic in the sack. A man with great depths, that's what drew me in when I first met him, but I don't think we ever tapped much of it. I wondered whether I was just imagining what I was feeling and I still do... a bit. But when I let myself, I think he was like a window into another world, like a doorway or channel."

The conversation drifted on a little, but not for long. They both realised in each other that they had touched something deeper and more mysterious than either had experienced in their lives to that point. Maybe that was Michel's parting gift. Each left the meeting knowing they had more to explore.

That evening, with a glass of wine, Mahler in the background and the privacy of her own thoughts Penny looked back on the day... and beyond. She felt settled about Christina, whom she thought "got" Michel in a way that Michel's mother had not appreciated his father. Maybe that is why she came off the rails with her sexuality and relationships, so perpetuating a pattern. My god, was she looking into "karma"? Christina would be all right, that she knew without doubt or hesitation so should focus on herself with her professional coat on the hanger.

Penny's first thoughts were a recapitulation of her professional involvement with Michel. At an obvious level this had been covered with Harry, but she wasn't going to delude herself about this, as she was well aware there were levels of her own feelings and experience that she had not shared with him. Although she had given this considerable examination, they warranted a final review. As she did this she felt little in the way of awkwardness or guilt, even the dream recall brought a smile to her face and an itch to her crotch. She was briefly tempted to lift her skirt, part her panties and masturbate, but resisted the temptation and instead poured herself another wine. She just loved Mahler and the depth of feeling he evoked.

There had been no more dreams of Michel since his death, which surprised her a little. The last one had been disturbing, as it seemed to almost predict his death; something she found unsettling. Although many in her profession were given to such paranormal inquiry and even take it into the consulting arena, she had been disinclined and to this time dismissed such dimensions as 'mystical' in a somewhat derogatory manner.

Penny now had to rethink her position in this regard as a result of her recent experiences: Maybe that was one level of the gift that Michel may have left her.

The other level? The strange and mysterious world he had opened up in her dream life. Penny came to realise that from one perspective the eroticism of her dreams was an initiation into this world, as well as the paranormal in general and her sexuality in particular. She knew, irrespective of where this experience would lead her from a professional perspective, her personal life would change. She would expect, even demand more from her sexual encounters than she had experienced to date and that Michel had been significant as a guide and initiator.

Time for bed: Out came the vibrators that she had purchased only a few weeks ago. The larger made its way around her clitoris and into her cunt – how she had grown to love that word – raising a minor storm of sensations. The smaller she slowly edged into her arse and started a dual thrusting rhythm that culminated in an orgasm she now expected as routine, whereas before it had been a constant struggle. She placed her little friends back into the silk scarf and into the bedside cabinet before falling asleep without her usual night-time preparations.

She was walking across a misty landscape wearing a light flowing gown. It felt warm and even though she could not see in front of her there was a destination in her mind. The warm wind billowed through her dress and scattered her hair in differing directions. The landscape seemed to hum, almost talk. In front of her emerged a great tree and out from behind he stepped. Penny had not seen Michel for an age, it seemed. He walked toward her never losing contact with her eyes and a smile on his face. She was welcomed into his arms.

They made love and they didn't, the whole atmosphere was lovemaking, it didn't require sex. They walked around the landscape as the mists cleared revealing a rich and lush countryside where they seemed to be the only occupants. Michel was constantly talking to her, but in a kind of mindless or telepathic manner. She took it all in and it was then she realised that she was asleep. No, it wasn't a sleep; it was something else, something she may only realise in her own future. Still, she took it or, more correctly, drank it in. There was wisdom in his 'words'; wisdom that she knew would guide her in all aspects of her life into an unknown yet welcoming future.

Onanism

Clare remembered the words of the song as she undressed:

"Last night I lay in bed a-masturbating. It does me good, I knew it would..."

She might need to follow that advice tonight.

It had been a long time since she had felt a man – a cock – buried deep in her pussy, mouth, arse, anywhere. She had that twitch in her crotch – her cunt – that just ached for something to be stuck inside. She started with her fingers, but that didn't seem enough even when she had four in there. Full, yes, but it wasn't providing that edge of satisfaction that she craved. Ben's cock had done it; it was yummy. But the self-serving dick-head (she found the pun amusing though) had serviced more than her pussy, as yet she hadn't found any available woman in the district who hadn't been accommodated by his more than capable manhood. So, she lay here aching.

Clare turned to the bedside cabinet and pulled out a dildo. "Monster Kong" had been one of Ben's parting gifts, a memento maybe? It mattered not, she took out the black tool and without preparation plunged it into her cunt. That was better, she felt full but still it didn't create the relief she was craving. Kong went to the floor as she played idly with her pussy wondering where she should proceed. A finger in her arse, that often got the show on the road. No, not even two, fuck! Where to from here?

In the cabinet was her storehouse of personal secrets; some shared with lovers, others to her own needs only. Ben had used Kong; it hadn't threatened his ego, maybe reinforced it and that was the purpose of the gift. Mind you, she thought, he had enough going for him for that not to be a threat: Bastard. A rumble in the drawer: what was this? A jar? A jar of – for – what? Quick look at the label: "Rhiannon Gifts." That helped, then she recalled that funny little wizened grey-haired lady in the markets who still oozed sex in spite of her age: "You might have need of this sometime, Love." Yeah, right, with Ben on my arm? Maybe now I reckon she saw more than I did.

Casually Clare read the label: "A soft herbal preparation for the enhancement of sexual pleasure." Didn't sound much, so to the directions: "Gently massage a small quantity around the clitoris whilst in the reclining posture." Simple for starters, thought Clare, so she dipped her right index finger into the gooey mixture and rubbed a little around the entrance to her cunt. She was feeling a little tentative; her thoughts of Ben had disappeared. That in itself surprised her; his image had been a constant companion and not been lessened by the various transients who had occupied her bed, although for never more than one night. Fucking Ben!

Her fingers took gentle tours around her clit; she was more kind to herself than others who played with her treasure. Faster the fingers moved and then darted inside her cunt-pit to invite fluids to join the greasy mixture: she was whipping up a storm. The mixture gave her a deep welcoming warmth and caused her to become gentle; to her cunt but also to herself: Were the two that different, after all? Clare's mood softened, the greasy mixture soothed her in both body and mind and she settled to a slow gentle rhythm, almost musical.

Clare found herself flying. The sense of her index finger gently stroking the length of her pussy channel was comforting, but also strong. She felt her finger enlarge and stay within her loins as Ben's dick had done, but without being inside her, just pushing persistently and gently as if there were some sort of obstruction in front, as if she were a virgin. Her finger felt harder, stronger, bigger, and deeper, as it thrust itself up and down her channel, as she flew. Below she saw the houses; plumes of smoke dotted the night sky as she passed over and beyond. She looked down and realised the broom that held her was an extension of her finger even whilst she gripped the stave. She was high: not only above the rooftops, but also in her core, her being. She laughed.

And there he was on the hilltop. He was more than a man, and more than Ben could ever be. She now realised the relativity of her feelings, and as her fingers stroked her clit, massaging the greasy mix into her core, she knew that Ben was of her past and before her was a power as none she had known: She was in awe. Clare was alive, her body vibrated and enriched her; Ben was gone. This man who stood before her with his horned head, darkened features, and a cock that surpassed anything she had seen, appeared to her as her equal. She continued the stroking of her clit as he came toward her. The massive member tore into her, but was welcome. The pain at the base of her pelvis ignited a fire that lifted her awareness up through her head and beyond.

She came, and came, and came. The horned god withdrew his member and with a scream left her on the hillside; she was replete. Her aching cunt was quiet. She slept. When she awoke, he was gone and her finger vibrant yet sore. Clare looked at the jar: Thank god there was a phone number on it; she would need more.

"It does me good, I knew it would.

"Tonight, I will repeat the operation..."

The Ancient

She had never seen him like this before and it frightened her. They had been in a relationship for several years now with its predictable ups and downs, although the sexual attraction had been consistently strong. In the early years she had asked more of him, something she had experienced in the only prior significant relationship of her life: the intense eye-gazing and feeling of merging. He had dismissed that as romantic rubbish and championed a "post-romantic relationship".

What do you mean? She asked.

He explained: The merging is a psychological projection, he said, all well and good, but to be realised as such. She did not like this, as it had been so intense and passionate before. But, then again, that relationship did founder and she was still unsure as to the mechanisms of this. He explained more, about a different level of discovery beyond the gender identification 'thing'. She wasn't sure she understood and wondered whether he was resisting: maybe too hurt from a prior relationship that had ended with a death. Still, she hoped, as she felt he had that potential, otherwise she would not be with him.

Their relationship settled into a patter, bore children and each progressed professionally. Their lovemaking remained intense and exploratory, yet still she felt that lack; something remained missing for her. He appeared recalcitrant, so she had a decision: should she stay or go? He was a good man though, maddeningly frustrating at times, so she decided to stay and she accepted the lack of romance. In fact, it seemed to diminish in importance, although she could not countenance that he may have been right in his deduction; she assumed it to be her accepting and tolerating nature.

The night had started as countless others before. Kids asleep, the night young, some mellow wine and reading in bed. It was a still night and they got to contact, rubbing legs and then it simply started. She enjoyed it when he ate her pussy as he wasn't given to it much, he didn't seem a very oral man, although he enjoyed his wine. This reinforced her psychological assessment of him, so she accepted this too. But when he did get into it, he really did, and this was a further level of reinforcement for her views. Tonight, he was energetic in his enjoyment and she was lapping up the attention. Maybe because it was a consequence of the sucking she had earlier given his dick, as she had taken it beyond the limit of her mouth in a way that caused that unusual gushing between her legs that she had once thought was urine, but now could not identify. It did not matter, so she lay back and enjoyed, simply savoured his tongue roaming around her pussy entrance and then engulfing it as he made his way deeper into her recesses with his tongue.

He also knew she had showered and cleaned her ass; it was her custom. So, a reaming of her anal ring with an occasional darting into the rear pit like a snake's tongue only served to increase her pleasure. Then back to the long slow tongue-lashing of her cunt. This was good. She held each side of his head whilst a small surge of energy crept up from the well of her pelvis into her back. As this happened, he finally disengaged and slowly she saw his head move up to meet hers. Their eyes engaged without blinking and with a practised ease he placed his cock at her pussy entrance and gently thrust the whole length in.

Briefly she recalled this to be a time that eye gazing and merging could occur. But his expressionless face did not invite it. As she often did, she gave a try and opened up her gaze, feeling she was exposing the depth of her being. Normally if she did that, he put his head next to hers and broke the spell she was trying to weave. She would then give up and simply enjoy where the experience would go, as orgasm was usually the consequence. Yet on this night he did not avert his gaze, neither did he open up and merge; he simply continued his rhythmic pumping of her cunt in a slow tempo. What was he doing? It was her turn to avert her gaze; she was beginning to feel uncomfortable. But he did not allow that and with his hand slowly turned her averted head back to meet his. He remained expressionless. She was anxious... she could feel it in her pelvis and he knew it.

He had a sense that his pumping was like drumming. The drumming took him in a spiral and took him down, in and past, past to somewhere deep and ancient. He was standing in the middle of a circle of near-naked dancers with elaborate headdresses who were stomping on the ground and moving in a sun-wise direction, although it was dusk and nearly dark. The drummers were outside the circle and only dimly recognisable. There was little vegetation and the moon was set above them and his gaze. Before him she lay on a bier that was not to take her to her grave, even though she looked like a corpse. Her eyes were closed and breathing almost undetectable. He knew that draught she had taken created this impression.

He moved toward the platform and lifted her from it to lay her on the purple rug festooned with animal skins that covered the ground. The chanting of the dancers rose above the drumming and started to gain a melodic quality. He took some herbs from a bag that was slung from his shoulder, ground them to a dust in his palms and scattered them over her, whilst offering a prayer in an ancient tongue that beckoned a vision of a cracked and lonely path that they both walked, crying with a joy that transcended all they had left behind.

The vision enveloped them as he gently parted her legs and raised the brief garment that adorned her loins. The hand that graced her mound and the fingers that explored the quarry beneath aroused her. She looked at him expressionless. He tore his loincloth from his waist, knelt, raised her pelvis and entered her in a movement continuous and symphonic in its intensity. He let her pelvis rest on the skins and she welcomed him deeper as he dropped between her thighs and completed his entry to the core of her being. All was well; the land would survive and be fertile as his sperm flooded the entrance to her womb.

As the bed creaked a little beneath her, she came back. He was above her and spent; she could feel his juice forming a bridge between her womb and his cock. That was some orgasm, as it wasn't usual for her to have visions. She looked up at him and his gaze remained incessant. She wondered if it had remained like that when he came and knew that he had. She looked into his eyes and he became ancient. At first, she didn't recognise him and became anxious, but she took a deep breath and realised she did know him, from where she knew not.

Then he came back and rolled to one side. As she nestled into the crook of his arm, she knew now what he had meant all those years ago. She appreciated her role and understood it as the maintenance of the world and the life that existed in it. She had realised her place in the truest sense of the word. She felt content and she slept.

Stonehenge

Diana shifted uneasily in her bed. Sleep eluded her again and the heat in and around her vagina was unsettling her. To her it still was a vagina; many of her friends referred to it as a cunt, but they were well past the virginal state, whereas Diana's love channel was still in its pristine state. Those same friends had long since stopped teasing her, as she did not respond to their sexual baiting and always seemed to have her head in the clouds. This was not an arrogant position, however, otherwise the teasing may have led to the loss of friendships, and rather it was something almost beatific, although even Diana struggled with terms like this.

That was all very well, thought Diana, but these feelings had their downsides. The exalted states that she often experienced were quite blissful, sometimes accompanied by visions and impressions of events that seemed so distant in space and time, but then she would often crash into a depressed state. She struggled to make sense of these mood fluctuations and the events she experienced. When they first started her parents took her to the local doctor who immediately referred her to a paediatric neurologist.

This rather severe man came to the conclusion that Diana had a form of attention deficit disorder and recommended medication. These certainly reduced the number and intensity of her experiences, but left her lethargic and depressed. Her parents came to the conclusion that the treatment was worse than the problem, if indeed there was one, and after discussion with Diana decided to cease the treatment. Diana, for her part, learnt it was best not to talk about her experiences, which suited her parents, as they could believe she had 'grown out of' whatever the problem had been. The only legacy was the serene smile and distant look that often engaged her.

Now she was in the middle of her teenage years and a virgin still. It wasn't that she was not sexually appealing; she was. In fact, not only good-looking, but she also exuded a sexual vitality that grew to accompany her exalted feeling states. Diana did not recognise this connection in those early years, although she most certainly felt the sexual states in her bed at night. This was the side of her that others did not see: she felt tormented as the feelings increased and her restless pelvis gave her images of sexual unions with many people and of varied forms. These both tormented and sometimes disgusted her, so she sought solace elsewhere.

Her involvement with Christian youth had been intense, but did not resolve the torment. It did give her some access to the visions and an understanding of them, but she gradually came to see that the content was not fundamentally Christian in orientation. What this interlude did confirm was that what she was experiencing had a spiritual flavour; it was just that the content remained outside what she was being taught. As this involvement did reduce the sexual tension and lessen the disturbing night-time fantasies, she decided fairly early on to continue some of the practices she had learnt, but also to continue her spiritual exploration elsewhere.

Then one night something strange happened. Her pelvis began its familiar heating and the intense sensations in her vagina started. She began to think of Liam, that handsome young man from the Christian youth. She imagined him kissing her, awakening her passion and then putting a hand on her breast... then she snapped out of the reverie and began a chant and steady breathing. This worked for a while, but Liam reappeared and this time had her breasts exposed and was kissing them. She started to respond... No, no! I can't do this! Back to the chanting and breathing for you, my girl.

There was a crash near her wardrobe. Her guitar had fallen down; how had it done that? As she picked it up and leant it back against the robe the light suddenly went off. Damn! The globe must have blown; I'll get Dad to fix it in the morning, she thought, but just as she did it came back on and the window started to bang. Diana started to become distressed, went back to bed and pulled the covers over her. She sobbed deeply, being both frightened and confused, but she also noticed that the heat in her pelvis was subsiding and the strange events in her bedroom had ceased. There was obviously a connection.

Diana did not tell her parents, then or on the subsequent occasions that these events happened; the memory of the neurologist and his 'treatment' remained strong in her mind. Instead, she found a level of comfort in her visions, somehow they seemed to harmonise with the feelings in her genitals and she was able to have both simultaneously: Indeed, the visions became stronger and clearer when she did have those feelings and they no longer took on the strong fantasy elements they had previously.

The strangest thing though was the movement of objects when she was in these heightened states. Although initially disruptive and sometimes frightening, she found that they somehow were connected with the physical and visionary intensity. Then something even stranger began to happen; if she somehow 'held' the energetic state, then she could often control the movement of objects in the room. This was initially haphazard, but with practice she gained a proficiency that surprised and pleased her, although she still had little in the way of an explanation for what was happening. She determined to simply 'go with it'. Things then started to calm down, at least Diana felt more settled. The genital heat was directly connected to the movement of objects, which she discovered had a name: poltergeist phenomena. When she explored this, though, she realised that it had changed, developed or evolved to something called psychokinesis. It then began to dawn on her that she had unusual powers and her sense of concealment and secrecy increased.

One night shortly after that the visions became unusually clear, to the point that Diana was no longer an observer, but was actually involved. I'm wearing a long flowing gown; it is white, with a light blue over-gown. I have flowers woven into a band around my head and my reddish locks are longer than usual, reaching to my waist. Intricate jewellery adorns my neck, wrists and even my ankles. This seems like gold with circular or patterned symbols carved into the metal. My hands are free and really delicate, obviously I'm not doing much in the way of housework, wherever I may be.

I raise my gaze and realise I am standing in the middle of a clearing in a wood or forest. The day is overcast and cool. There are several figures, both male and female, standing around the perimeter of the circle and they are hooded and chanting. One, a man, has a staff and his gown is purple. He is not chanting but looking at me intently. I feel I know him well not as a lover, but a mentor, as he is appreciably older than me and I also know I am still a virgin, although my hold on that state seems tenuous. I know I have been prepared for this time and that my skills are somehow to be used for this group standing around me and yet others.

The man raises his staff and the chanting stops. He turns and heads out of the clearing that marks the West and I immediately follow with the others filing after in a sort of order that is unknown to me. We walk along a forest trail for about half a mile or so as the density begins to thin and we reach the forest's edge. We are on a hilltop and there is a wide clearing on the top where a lot of industry is in progress. Men are taking the last of some huge wooden poles out of the ground, whilst most of the others lie around or are being slowly towed down one hillside toward a small settlement in the valley.

This must be an ancient time, I suddenly realise.

The settlement comprises many simple huts, mainly in a circle and enough to house fifty to one hundred people, I would guess. There is smoke emerging from apertures in the centre of the woven roofs of some of the larger buildings and people are milling around in a mixture of socialisation and light industry. I stand to the right of my mentor as the last of the great poles is brought down and removed. This area has obviously been used on many occasions and over a long period of time. It has a stillness, almost a sanctity, that is very peaceful yet pregnant with expectation.

To the right I notice many huge boulders on logs that have been their method of coming to this place from the river below. Their bluish tinge marks them as foreign to this region and they had been brought to this place with intense industry and manpower. Most are long and have a squarish or rectangular shape and they are strangely familiar to me from another time; maybe the present I have left to be here. I notice people from the settlement starting to come up the hill and gather at a seemingly respectful distance and many others join them, presumably from other surrounding settlements.

My mentor moves to the centre of the large space and holds his staff aloft. The surrounding crowd becomes silent and watchful. I move forward to join him, he is the Pendragon, the head Druid of this land: I know this without a doubt. His eyes are of fire and his staff has the dragon carved and coiled around it. His reddened eyes look toward me and from under his robe he procures a wooden instrument that he begins to make sound from by blowing down its length. I turn, look to the stones and begin to chant in unison with his playing.

The heat starts in my groin, it is welcome and intense. I let it arise and concentrate and then assist its movement up to my throat to join and direct my chanting. Still, I gaze at the stones and the heat moves to the centre of my brow. I am ready and the chanting falls away, although the Pendragon keeps his pattern of wind-sound. I focus on one stone and ever so slowly it begins to lift off the ground and hover in the air some foot or so above the grass with a slight rocking motion. I hold it there and then slowly move it into the space occupied by Pendragon and I. I know where it must go. When it finds its place, I turn its massive form to the vertical as a few of our male entourage move forward and guide its base into a prepared hole in the ground. I repeat the process with a second similar stone and it is placed a few paces to the side of the first, upright and parallel.

I stop and pause. The next step is the huge horizontal cross stone that bridges and unites the two pillars; this will require all my focus. I feel still and confident, moving the stone across and in front of its two supports. Then with even more precise focus I move it up and gently allow it to come down on the two uprights. The first structure is in place. I relax temporarily, before the task of moving the remaining stones as the day begins to dim and the moonrise. We continue into the end of the day, yet the people do not move and remain silent. After many hours and sustained effort, we are done and the henge of stone is complete.

The Pendragon leads me to the centre of the circle and to a garland setting that looks like a grand bed. I look at him and smile, and then I pass to the centre and lie on my back. The man, who in another time and place will be Liam, comes to the edge and looks at me. Around the stones people are dancing, drumming and singing. Fires mark the outer perimeter and the atmosphere becomes rich and intense. Liam removes his clothes all but his loincloth. He leans forward and slowly undoes my gowns and removes them. I am passive and offer no resistance; indeed, I anticipate what is to come. I am now naked; Liam's eyes do not leave mine. He removes his cloth and kneels before and above me. Slowly he lowers himself and parts my willing legs. He knows I am already moist and he enters me simply and completely, negotiating the impediment of my innocence in a smooth stroke of his manhood. I am full and complete. I look to him; he is a god and I a goddess, we are joined in a holy union that will mark the completion of my duties, as now my gifts will leave me as I move into this new phase of my spiritual existence. Liam comes deep within the heat of my loins and soothes the fire to a gentle flowing water into which I slowly dissolve and he with me.

Diana comes out of her vision. It is time. She knows that tomorrow she will seek Liam out at College. She knows he will know and that he will take her from girl to woman. Beyond that she could see nothing in her vision, but is aware that this act will mark the beginning of a new path she must take in her journey.

She sleeps a peaceful and dreamless sleep.

The Healing Goddess

Troy wasn't sure what life held in store for him now since the accident. It was now nearly a year and the driver at fault was shortly due for release. He was drunk and came across the road so far that the front left-hand side of Troy's car took the full impact, leaving him a paraplegic and his girlfriend dead. Mitigating circumstances and two years only? Jen dead and him with a wheelchair-bound life, no job to speak of and a dwindling circle of friends: Justice? What fucking justice!

The grief for Jen was emotionally quieter now; their relationship was a little on the wane anyway and the fight in the car on the way home wasn't a great parting gift. He felt guilty more about this than anything, but that didn't bring her back and he had to move on. When he felt this shift the suicidal thoughts began in earnest. He was a bricklaying surfie and both were now out of his reach. Compensation? That would last a while but not forever; with such a bleak outlook death seemed a viable option. Whilst he recuperated with the rounds of hospitals and physiotherapy, plus the odd catheterisation and urinary infection, he had plenty of time to think... and read.

Troy had not done much of this; he had sacrificed his innate intelligence for a lifestyle that supported his love of nature and the wide-open spaces. It was an irony that these options were now severely restricted for him, so to counter the depression he took to reading and self-education as a way to find a path out of this morass. Luckily, he wasn't on a respirator and his limited hand movement allowed him this independent luxury, so when his family and friends asked what they could do for him he often replied with a book list. His flat was just about adequate for independence, so with the help of a supportive even if somewhat emotionally distant family, he settled to what he could see as a foreseeable future... at least until the money started to dwindle.

As his circle of interests, largely due to his altered circumstances, and his friends started to shrink Troy felt increasingly confined to his flat, but found the depression lifting and any thoughts of suicide started to dissipate rather more easily than when they first arrived. What marked that change? The books had something to do with it, but there was more to it than that; he felt it was the awakening of his imagination. No, that wasn't quite right it was 'the' imagination, rather than 'his'. He played with the word a little: imagination – image – mage – magic. The last appealed and even though not versed in the history, structure or art of magic and magicians, it appealed to him.

Troy took to active meditations utilising imaginative approaches, art, poetry and philosophy. He was hungry, he read the classics and their concerns about human direction, morality and the place or otherwise of the divine principle. He drank heavily from the goblet of knowledge and it inspired wisdom. He made use of libraries and the Internet, and undertook tertiary courses that spiked his interest and creativity, rather than those that had a goal or career as the outcome. His life started to become rich in a way he had not imagined, but he remained paralysed.

In spite of all the knowledge and evidence to the contrary he could not come to terms with the apparent permanency of his situation. Early on a psychologist had accused him of denial with his attitude and belief. Troy didn't see her again. Yet there was an interesting side to his belief; he was not emotionally racked by it and didn't spend hours on the Internet scouring research and information. He remained quite still in his belief, supporting it with diet, limited exercise and contemplative practice.

The magical dimension seemed to offer much at the beginning, but then seemed to dry up. He saw this as due to the repressive elements in Western society and the resulting censorship of unorthodox spiritual practice and behaviour, particularly when this involved sexuality. The sexual dimension intrigued him in this context, as he was impotent. Well, not exactly. He could get an erection, but it was entirely out of his control as he found in the hospital shortly after the accident, with the pretty nurses and the bed baths. Some of them found his responses fascinating and he had more than his share of contact here, but he had to inform them there was nothing in it for him; he could not feel anything, it was simply a reflex and out of his control, bugger it!

Then he began to supplement his Western spiritual researches with some Eastern input and he came across the ancient Indian practice of Tantra. This appealed to him, strangely, as he obviously knew he could not conduct the sexual practices described, but there was something about the energetics and imagery that was enormously appealing. That night he dreamed of the goddess: well, maybe not the goddess, but certainly an appealing dark-skinned woman with a painted red dot over her third eye and a twinkle in the others. For the first time in nearly two years, he had sexual urges. Not that he felt them in his body, of course; they were entirely in his mind.

He awoke: Mind-sex, is that all I get? He laughed to himself, but he also immediately focussed on his condition and had the first inkling of a relationship between the two. The woman in his dream stayed with him, she was called Lila. He meditated and conjured her in his mind; it proved remarkably easy to establish an image of her. She smiled and he blushed. Lila told him that he presently lacked only one sense, all the remainder were there for him to appreciate her with and he found this to be the case. He could see her and was listening to her, and she heard him.

Lila asked him to lie down. He did and closed his eyes in response to her further instruction. The smell of exotic oils and perfumes entered the room. He then smelt the aroma of a woman's sex and it reminded him that it had been so long since he had his face anywhere near to a woman, let alone her pussy. He drank deeply of her smell.

"You're forgetting taste, lick me, but keep your eyes closed."

Troy tentatively put out his tongue and met the softness of pussy lips above him. They moved in response to his gentle strokes and he lifted his head to suck deeply. But he could not resist and he opened his eyes... all was gone.

It took several days for him to meet Lila again. At times he despaired, but at the periphery of his awareness she told him to be patient.

"Be patient and follow my instruction." These were her exact words.

Again, he lay on his bed:

"Look at me."

Lila slowly materialised at the foot of the bed and slowly came around to the side, bending to kiss him. He responded tentatively, scared she would disappear amidst the perfumed aura that enveloped them. Lila stepped back and he could hear music of an unknown stringed instrument as she began to dance before slowly melting from his vision.

The play continued in this manner for some weeks. Then one day she climbed onto his bed and lifted his gown. He could not see his penis, so it wasn't erect. With a sweep of her gown, she was astride his pelvis facing him. Troy was shocked; he had no idea what his cock was doing.

"In India we believe that the soul of a man lies dormant at the base of his spine."

He knew this already, what was surprising was that, for the first time since the accident, he felt a small burning between his arse and the base of his cock.

"It is my task to awaken your soul, Troy, of which I am the image."

She raised herself, her lower gowns slipped away as she guided his now erect penis into her dark pussy. He felt nothing, of course, but she resumed her seated posture and smiled.

"Close your eyes Troy. Take the Kundalini fire you have begun to feel behind your manhood and allow her to permeate your loins and focus on the head."

Warmth moved from the quiet fire and seemed to move into his groin to fluctuate to and fro.

"Open your eyes, Troy."

Lila was rocking side to side in perfect unison with the energy movement he felt in his groin – loins.

At the same time the remainder of Lila's gowns came away and he drank in her deep and dark beauty. Magnificent breasts with even darker nipples slowly rocked side to side with the swaying of her pelvis on his erection. Then the upper and lower bodies alternated in their movements and the breasts synchronised with her pelvis.

Troy was transfixed.

"Do not lose the focus on Kundalini. Move her to your manhood."

Lila was right, her beauty had taken him away from himself and he made the reconnection. For the first time in two years, he started to feel his cock. The energy moved from his loins to the base, but the head remained lacking in feeling. His focus became stronger as Lila continued to sway above him and at last, he could feel the tip. More than the tip, he was nestled against her womb. Troy felt Lila's warmth flow down and through him, a reversal of his energy movement yet mixing with his in a divine dance into which he melted. Lila instructed him to sleep and dissolved.

The instruction continued in this way for many weeks. Troy augmented this with study and meditative practice. Gradually the sensations became more continuous and not confined to Lila's presence. She did not answer questions in this regard and instructed him to remain silent and receptive. He remembered what had happened when he had opened his eyes prematurely; he obeyed the command with ease. He felt gratified with this, though quietly disappointed that the sensations were not translating to any movement.

Lila must have read his mind:

"I, the goddess, must ascend the golden path and unite with you, the god, which is the ultimate task. It is the ultimate healing, anything else is secondary."

Indeed, he could feel this. The sensory changes moved up his body weaving and periodically igniting at central points, which he recognised as the chakras. The progress was slow, yet progressive and he was heartened, no more so than when his heart opened and he felt an outpouring of emotion toward this form above him.

She responded.

Troy woke up one day with an itch in his left big toe. He cried. He sobbed an unknown happiness, even when it disappeared. Shortly afterward the itch was in his heel. He looked down and focussed on his toe. Slowly he tried to move it and it responded. He sobbed again and again.

Lila's instruction continued. His creative expression increased and she asked him to recite his poetry whilst she continued to excite him. Then she asked him to open his inner sight and respond to what she was thinking. He found he could read her mind: not only her mind, but also those of the visitors that came to tend to him.

"This is power, magic; do not abuse it. Use it to guide others and heal."

Then one day Lila sat above him and casually announced this would be her last visit, but that she would always be with him. At first this paradox jarred him, and then with his inner vision he knew what she meant. By now Troy was skilled and could even move his pelvis and thighs a little in response to Lila's movements. This did not seem to surprise her and she engaged more deeply. The energy moved up his spine and this time stopped at the point in his neck where he knew the cord was broken. The heat was intense, but gently dispersed and moved to his third eye, where he concentrated it again. With a supreme effort he moved it beyond his eye and above. Then as it moved beyond his head, he experienced the most shattering orgasm he had ever experienced.

Troy did not see Lila again. But he knew she was with him: no, she was part of him and united with him. They were as one.

The neurological specialists disguised it well, but they were dumbfounded. Eventually they came to the conclusion that the cord break had been incomplete and the nerve tissue only bruised. The apparent break on the scanning was considered an "artefact" and the machine underwent an extensive overhaul. They felt reassured that such an error would not happen again. Troy was not perturbed. If they had concerns about any legal consequences, they would not voice them, even though he could easily reassure them if that were the case.

Troy simply got up from his chair, shook each by the hand with a polite and sincere "thank you" and walked from the room.

Eastern Wisdom

"You know there's something about erotic material we, or maybe I, just don't get." Kieran was in one of his musing moods, thought Joan, so she decided to lighten her response to see how serious he was.

"That's just because we're getting on a bit and you like to look at those young bunnies getting up to all the mischief, we like but with fresher, more lithe bodies." Her reply was quite measured.

"I knew you'd think that," responded Kieran, maintaining a serious air, "but it's more than that."

"OK lover boy, please explain."

Joan knew he was in a serious mode now and she felt she ought to go along with it, as she had always been intrigued by his fascination with the erotic - films in particular.

They were actually in a good place in their relationship over the last few years and the sex had improved progressively, so Joan was interested about Kieran bringing up the subject at this time. They had just watched a pornographic movie together, but rather than making love – or fucking more likely – Kieran had just leaned back on the lounge, taken a sip of his wine and come out with the above question. The movie had been good, although they rarely watched anything that didn't have high production values these days and he knew what to get with his experience in erotic material over the years. Joan had been the passive consumer to his tastes and initiatives, partly because she wasn't as interested as he, but also because the sort of material they enjoyed usually expressed a common interest.

This particular movie had a fairly simple plot (most do), being a group of people at a team-building weekend, which ends up as sexual team building. Joan had a smile; as such plots were quite common and an excuse to string together a series of sex scenes, but usually with no depth of narrative. The production was good, the actors not too young – which helped the acting – and good looking, with most seemingly enjoying their work. There were the usual combinations; a couple of girl and boy scenes, threesomes, a gangbang and a small orgy at the end; again, all fairly standard fare. The lesbian contact was integrated in the threesomes and orgy, the ejaculate plentiful and usually facial, plus there was a regular ration of anal sex, a couple of double penetrations and a smattering of dildos.

It was probably one of the best they had seen, yet it had left them both in a reflective state, rather than engaging in raunchy sex, so that Kieran's opening comment was not really a surprise to Joan, as she was similarly pensive. Before he started his explanation, she had been wondering whether the relative lack of arousal was because the film wasn't pure "raunch", as well as the fact that they had been exploring Eastern spirituality of late, Tantra in particular.

"But before you do, can I throw a couple of things into the ring?"

"Sure." Kieran turned to look at her, as she was already looking at him.

"Do you think we'd be having this discussion if it was raw porn?"

"Yeah, I wondered that too," was Kieran's response, "I reckon we wouldn't be talking now, we'd be into it."

"Why's that do you think?"

"Because the movie has all the right elements from my – our – perspective and is trying to achieve some high though not clearly identifiable values, but isn't quite getting there. I think this is objective; that is, I have a sense that the director was trying to make a bridge to mainstream movies with an integrated sexual component, but it's still stuck in the "porn movie" style and format with insufficient narrative and acting. I also think it is subjective in that we've been looking at sexuality somewhat differently since we've been exploring Tantra." Joan realised they were on the same wavelength, so the conversation was in full flow.

What followed was a comparison between pornographic sex scenes and Tantra. What they discussed was that there was really nothing in Tantra that wasn't also in porn. Although some Tantra was restricted to couples and uncomplicated sexual acts, the more exploratory end of the spectrum was inclusive of all the kind of material that was present in the sort of movie they had just watched. Kieran and Joan hadn't been in an orgy together, although they had experimented early in their relationship with threesomes. These usually became emotionally awkward and left them with a choice to join a club or some other outlet that would cater for these proclivities, or to confine their sexual experimentation to their relationship, augmented by erotic material. This was not just pornography, but also clothing and toys as well as a common interest in erotic art and the history of eroticism; which is how they stumbled upon Tantric sexual practice and made the decision to explore it.

"It's not what's in the movie, it's how it's put together." Kieran had broken the silence.

"Explain?"

"Well, it could be the context. In Tantra we know about the use of dress, food, alcohol, spices and perfumes – I'm sure I've missed some – and these are in the movie to a greater or lesser extent. For example, dress in porn is a common feature and food and wine is sometimes evident. There was the scene in the movie where the maid – wearing no panties I might add – crawled down that long table between the guests and then learnt forward and down at the end to suck the host's dick. Then there was the time the blond rubbed oils into the brunette and stuck a dildo up her cunt before the guy came in."

"You're saying the elements are there, but in the wrong order, or not integrated?" Joan chimed in.

"Yeah, something like that. I think the director is making a step toward mainstream and that is his goal, but he's using the hackneyed porn movie formula. If he, or his colleagues, were aiming for mainstream I suspect they should do it the other way round; start with a good narrative and make that the backbone of the movie and then extend the scenes into sex, rather than having it like a musical where the plot is a kind of excuse for the songs.

"Look, we could go down this line a lot, but I'm not sure whether that's what we're both responding to, I think it has more to do with the ritual context, or lack of it. There's some there in a basic form, such as when that girl was kneeling, surrounded by four men standing with their stiff cocks poking out of their trousers and then sucking them in turn. But it's a bit basic and there's more in other genres."

"Yes," replied Joan, "that's why, even though I'm not into bondage, discipline and sadomasochism – to a point lover – there's more intrigue there because of the ritual and the avoidance of any pretence to a plot or narrative. And, although I'm not much into gay stuff, the TV sex soapies on gays have that fascination for me, as you know, and I suspect that's for similar reasons."

"It's almost a two-pronged thing then: On the one hand porn hasn't established itself properly in the wider movie genre, possibly because it is holding onto old formulae, but also it may lack a depth in ritual process?"

"It would seem that way. Mind you, we shouldn't forget the vested interests of the porn industry and the associated psychology!" Joan chuckled as she said this.

"I think I get what you mean, but explain please?"

"Well, at one level it's fairly obvious. The industry is about profit, so it's going to help if it has a semi-addictive kind of quality. Mind you, it probably doesn't need to think this through too much, as the consumers probably consist of a high percentage of addictive personalities anyway. But I suspect that's why they keep to the formula of putting in all the apparently right elements, which we know are valid in Tantra, so that gets the guilt element out of the picture, but does it in a haphazard sort of way and in scenarios that the average viewer would find difficult to achieve. I know we've had a few threesomes, but it's tricky in mainstream society, as we found out."

"You're hinting at another level?" Kieran interjected.

"Yes I am." Joan responded immediately, then paused to consider before going on. "I don't reckon the industry would give this much reflection, they'd be driven by markets, formulae and profits. There's something more subtle and maybe we should look at the Tantric model and then back into porn?"

"Good idea."

"In a nutshell we know Tantra is about spirituality and using sexuality to achieve this. At an obvious level porn doesn't make that connection and keeps the sex at a basic level where it becomes addictive rather than transformative.

"Yet porn has all the elements. Anal sex stimulates the first chakra and *arouses* the Kundalini energy, which is the start of the spiritual journey and is also to do with *power*. Vaginal sex – in a woman – is more about the second chakra and *sexuality itself*. You could say oral sex has to do with the fifth chakra and *expression*: so, what about the others? Maybe this is where fetishism comes in, not just as a ritual support, but also in spanking, choking, pain and pleasure and the like. I suspect all the elements are in porn, but they don't necessarily *match* the scene or aren't in the *right order...*"

Kieran noticed, almost in passing, that Joan was in her *School Ma'am* mode.

"I think that's true," Kieran could understand what Joan was trying to explain, as she was expressing more clearly some vague intuitions that he was having. "I have a sense of this too. You know, some of the best scenes in porn are where they don't follow the standard sex scene formula. For example, in a standard and straight boy and girl scene, the girl and boy emerge from the flimsy plot, maybe kiss, then she sucks him for a while, after this he fucks her in two or three positions, maybe gives her arse a poke and then comes on her face; how often do you see that and how boring is it?"

"Too often!"

"And I think this leads to a couple of things, too. One: I often find a scene more enticing and intriguing when it is only sort of partial, so maybe that is because it focuses on only one chakra? I'm thinking out loud, but bear with me. There's a scene in one movie where it opens with a secretary coming out of an office and walking up to two waiting men. She squats and removes their cocks as they stand each side of her. She masturbates them – no sucking – and they come on her blouse. She stands, puts on her jacket whilst they put their dicks back and then she ushers them into the office. There's another where the woman is kneeling on the ground with her head also on the ground and her arse in the air. Her skirt is up over her back and she's masturbating. You see the lower half of a man, naked and with an erect cock, come into view. He squats – not kneeling – over the woman's buttocks and lowers himself down penetrating her in one slow steady motion. She continues to masturbate and there's a crescendo of excitement as she comes. The man withdraws, stands and leaves."

"Careful lover, you're turning me on!"

"But maybe that's the point?"

"OK," responds Joan, recognising a seriousness and intensity in his voice, "and point two is?"

"Point two is: Maybe an expanded scene with a guy and girl should take a different sexual order, if it is more complex than the simple and direct scene I just recounted. And maybe in more complex scenes, involving other people, it could be more ritualised. I mean if several guys are attending to a girl, they don't all need to get a suck, fuck or arse fuck. Remember the scene in that movie where there was an audience who didn't ultimately join the sex actors on stage, or necessarily turn around and fuck each other? You know, there's more of this in some of the older classic porn movies than the modern ones."

"You're right, so maybe they don't do that as much now because it's too close to *giving the game away!*"

"You joke, but there's more than a grain of truth in what you're saying."

The discussion petered out at this point, although various points that were raised were returned to over the course of the next few days. Instead, they went to bed and made love; they didn't just fuck.

Kieran suggested they have a sex ritual that would employ some of the issues they had discussed within their own initiative. Whilst the Tantric model was valid, they both understood that they were Westerners and so wanted to explore what they had come to understand in their own cultural context. They also didn't want the experience to be too formulaic, it needed to include spontaneity and respond to the demands of the occasion. Kieran, in particular, was interested in how they could employ sexual techniques and acts they had learnt from pornographic movies, but to put them in a context that followed the energetics; that is, to be fundamentally creative and see what happened at a spiritual level.

They chose their evening carefully: The night of a full moon, as Joan had started to explore the Goddess tradition in Western culture, and a meal at one of their favourite restaurants. They both dressed for the occasion, Joan in a slinky black dress, her favoured necklace, bracelet and gartered stockings, but no knickers (although Kieran was not to know that at the time). He was smart in a casual suit and open-necked shirt, although he did have underwear on! The food was simple, with the meat lightly done and red wine sipped beneath the candles on the table. The conversation was gentle, based on their relationship and where it was headed. They talked of their intentions for the evening, although both were a little unsure about where it would take them. A taxi took them home, phones were on message-bank (with no volume) the music went on and they went to their bedroom, which had been delicately prepared by Joan with soft lighting and the fragrance of burning oils.

Joan quietly allowed Kieran to disrobe her, although he stopped when she had only bra and stockings remaining. He stepped back, admired her and removed the bra only. He then stripped himself down to his jocks as he began to touch and kiss Joan, to which she readily responded. This interaction was relatively brief; more like an acknowledgement or re-familiarisation process. Kieran led Joan to the bed and knelt her forward so that she was kneeling on the edge with her arse raised. He placed a pillow below her head and she allowed herself to drop onto it. He moved behind, kneeling on the ground he allowed his hands to roam over her buttocks and toward her pussy. He parted her lips with his fingers and slowly inserted first one then two fingers into the recess of her cunt. The juices began to flow as did quiet moans that issued forth from the pillow. At this point Kieran moved forward and licked her cunt from below up with long strokes of his tongue.

After some minutes of this he started to include her arse in the ritual. He knew she would have cleaned herself well here as his tongue darted through the rim and tasted the contrasting sharp aromas that met him. Then he placed an index finger in her arse and the remaining three fingers in her cunt, slowly moved them back and forth whilst offering words of admiration in response to the gentle moaning that continued to come from Joan. After an equivalent time, he stood, put some saliva on the tip of his cock and placed it at the entrance to her arse. With a slow rocking motion, he gently expanded the restriction of her anal rim and the head of his cock slid into her. He moistened the shaft of his dick with more saliva and slowly moved its length within her passage. The moans became deep groans, but Joan's arse was accepting once the delicate balance between pleasure and pain that marked the intruder was overcome.

Kieran felt his cock to harden further and felt like it was growing to fill the cavity. As this happened, they were both still and silent. They knew this to be the point of awakening; that the mystery of her – their – core was being stimulated and awoken by the expanse that filled her. As this happened, she exhaled deeply and audibly and he removed himself with the careful deliberation with which he had entered. Joan sighed and maintained a deep and slow breathing pattern as he moved to one side to a bowl and flannel with which to clean his manhood before the next stage of the journey.

First Kieran turned her over and placed the pillow under her buttocks in the middle of the bed. He crawled on, between and within her in a fluid motion like a prowling great cat. Joan held her arms up and welcomed his head, cradling it to the side of her neck as the deep thrusts began and he filled her alternative passage in a similar manner reaching up to her womb. Joan felt the fire that had begun in her arse now radiate through her cunt and become molten. She closed her eyes and focussed on her breathing as she noticed Kieran was doing until they breathed together in a rhythm that matched the strokes of his cock in her pussy.

The arousal was deepening. Kieran was also experiencing the molten fire of her sex and it seemed to swamp his cock so that it's defined hardness also became fluid to the point that he wondered whether he was still erect, as they seemed to merge. Waves of fluid began to leak from the entrance of her pussy and dampen his balls, as they met the space between arse and cunt, which now became damp and sticky. He felt his own juices begin to rise from the base of his cock and the revived head of his dick became highly sensitive. If he lost his awareness at this point, he knew he would come, so he constricted the muscles at his cock base and around his arse until this sensation quietened, aided by Joan's index finger inserting itself beyond his anal rim.

Kieran was now in a zone. His cock regained its previous hard sensation and the orgasm was now distant. He was able to focus on Joan as he felt her whole pelvis become more mobile and the mutual sense of the molten energy began to fill both their pelvises and then to concentrate somewhere deep in Joan's back. Kieran felt like he was in a hypnotised state now and time seemed to stretch and dissipate. He didn't know how long he continued like that, or when they rolled over so that she rode him and he was able to play with her breasts. He watched her; her eyes were closed. He squeezed her breasts as she gripped his arms.

Both felt the energy begin to move up Joan's body, seeming to pause at points where she increased her rhythm and the ascent continued with a progressively faster pace. Kieran closed his eyes and focussed on this movement too, he was now responding to Joan, who was dictating the pace, or maybe it was the movement itself that was governing the whole process. They both fell into its sweet clutches and saw the movement writhe and ascend becoming first white and then golden. As it reached Joan's throat it seemed to him that her groans were like utterances of a foreign tongue, which he could not understand, yet seemed so familiar. Then there was a sharp rise; the writhing image dispersed and there was a brightness beyond comprehension. Joan screamed… and screamed. It seemed to both that they were formless, floating in some unknown ether that held them both, or maybe they were as one. Slowly, ever so slowly, this state softened and a sense of angelic voices filled the void. Then, from the nothingness emerged a brilliant soft blue light that condensed into a ball and pierced them between and above their eyes in a space deep within.

Neither of them knew how long this state lasted. Both opened their eyes as they came back. Joan was still sitting astride Kieran and he was still cupping her breasts. She leant forward, kissed him and dismounted to cradle her head into his armpit.

"Did you come?"

"No." He responded.

It didn't matter it seemed. Sometimes, when he had focussed on her orgasm, he didn't come. Often, she would then, in the aftermath, move down and suck his cock and their mingled juices to add his sperm to the richness within her mouth, to then swallow deeply and lovingly as a kind of "thank you". But on this occasion, it didn't feel necessary and neither wanted to move into that space and dissipate the experience. Somehow her orgasm had been for both of them. They both felt energised, he put on some music and poured them both a nightcap before they settled down to sleep.

It wasn't until a day or two later when the heightened state that they experienced started to wane that they talked about what had occurred. Neither felt the need in that immediate time to try and repeat or recapture the experience; they felt surfeit. When they did discuss it, they both realised that they had captured something important, commensurate with their prior discussions, and that would be a basis for future exploration. Not that they wouldn't have a raunchy fuck, should the mood take them, or continue to look for the elusive "perfect" porn movie. It was just that they had discovered something more that transcended all of these patterns.

Eden

"What do you mean, 'kidded all this time'?" Eve was a little shocked and sat down on the grass below the apple tree. The snake remained silent until she composed herself, which he recognised when she finally looked at him again.

"It's all in the terminology really. If it had been a legal contract then you could have referred back to it and maybe not got in this mess. The actual word the creator used was 'hidden', not 'forbidden'."

Eve looked around her and then saw something strange, although it didn't shock her. Some small distance behind the tree she saw Adam's naked back. He was lying on a rug and his big frame obscured the person he was holding, but she knew it to be herself and confirmed by the arm around his waist. This had happened to her before: when their lovemaking had been particularly intense, she sometimes experienced herself 'out' of her body, although on this occasion it was particularly clear and less dreamy than her prior experiences.

It was Eve's birthday and Adam had not gone into work so they could spend the day without the children. They took lunch and a bottle of wine down to that secluded patch with the lone apple tree in the centre, which was a favourite spot for daylight intimacy. The sex had been simple, tender and respectful, leading to a mutual crescendo that seemed to come from nowhere and surprised them both with the intensity and the mutuality of their orgasms. Naked, they had played with each other's body with fingers, tongues and genitals. Adam had paid special attention to Eve's pussy with his mouth as a sort of follow-up birthday present. After, they both slipped into a light doze until Eve found herself standing under the apple tree a few yards from her body.

On this occasion the experience was particularly intense and clear, so she took advantage of it, walking around and watching her senses of smell, hearing and touch. It was then she heard the voice in the tree and looked up to see a large snake lazily coiled on a horizontal branch with its head drooping down and toward her.

"Well, I'd better fill you in a bit. The creator has no input into the creation: none at all. Now these are buggers of terms, 'cos the creator is kind of both and neither: He, or she, is actually present in the creation. Where? Hidden. So how do you get back there, back to the source, that's the question."

"I think I know."

"You're quick, gal. The question was actually rhetorical and I was going to impress you with my arcane knowledge! OK, I'll give you a chance. Pray tell?"

"Sex. Well, not just sex, but you know what I mean. Sex is the pathway to the occult wisdom, or is contained within it, or the divine is hidden in sex... I'm getting confused, but I bet you know what I mean."

"You're good! Remind me to look you up for a job sometime once you've finished this life journey!"

"I could well do!" Eve laughed audibly and saw Adam stir and turn over. He then opened his eyes and simply looked in her direction, but she was unsure whether he could actually see her and, as if in response to this thought, the arm that embraced him gave a light squeeze and he closed his eyes again.

She continued: "I'm not sure whether I get the 'hidden and forbidden' bit though?"

"I'm told the devil is in the detail. Heh, that's a good pun, even for me!"

Eve reflected on his jocular character and was enjoying the impishness of the exchange. There were times it could have been an elf or a leprechaun who was gracing the bough. She even imagined a long clay pipe.

"Well, things were going well with your ancestors. Creation achieved, time and space fashioned to give you a place to exist, then this pleasant little planet to ground you and enjoy the fruits of the creation, so that the creator could experience 'his' creation.

"It was all going well. You were told about the fruit of knowledge and ate it. Being the woman half of the equation, you then inducted old Adam there (a flick of the tongue went in Adam's direction) in the art of sex, love and transcendence, and creation overflowed into humankind."

"So, what went wrong?"

"Difficult to say with any certainty, maybe a technical flaw in the creation process, maybe something or someone else unanticipated: more an energetic thing really. We noticed it when the whole play of sexuality started to become encoded. Then we could see the split starting. There were those who kept tabs on the sexual play and its pathway back to the divine, but also those that chose to use the power option to their own advantage: actually, it was to the advantage of what we call the 'flaw'. Bit of an irony really: those who should have been custodians of the divine actually servicing the flaw and duping the creation. That's when 'hidden' became 'forbidden'.

"We kinda know and are trying to rectify it otherwise we might have to do the whole damn thing again. That's where you come in. Rather than wipe the whole experiment I thought we could close the loop and start again from the 'Garden of Eden' scene."

Eve took a step back. The snake remained quite still. She let what he had told her digest and beneath the vernacular presentation of his – or her – sermon, she felt she 'got' it; whatever it was.

She was back in her body. The transition had been instantaneous, but the experience both continuous and complete. Her arm was still around Adam's waist and he turned back toward her.

"I just had the most amazing dream!"

"I know." Eve replied.

"How the hell do you know?"

"I was in it, wasn't I?"

"Yes... "

"Adam," she said in soft tones, "there's something I need to show you. I think the apples are ready!"

Eve rose and held a hand out and back down to him. He had been resting on his elbow and, after a brief pause; he took her hand and rose to join her. She reached up and gave him a light and very tender kiss and their naked forms embraced. She took hold of his hand again, then turned and led him toward the apple tree.

The Sign

He needed to come up with a name for the new movement: He knew that. It was a quiet time, a lull in the fractious political storms that were sweeping the barren countryside, but on the shores of this still lake he pondered what he must do. It was a small space of quietude in the hectic pace that had swept him up since he had returned. Those many years in the community had enriched him and Maria, and given them a depth and appreciation of life that he felt would sustain him on his return.

He was wrong. His heritage was too much to overcome and they had asked – demanded – that he lead them in their plight against their oppressors. Whilst he was away, he realised that such temporal issues were perennial and he did not want to lose the taste of eternity in matters temporal. Yet they demanded: He was of the royal house, even though in exile, and his duty was to lead them. He remained internally divided. Maria comforted him, but could offer no avenue of resolution with his dilemma. So here he was sitting on the shore of this ancient lake that he had fished those many years ago with his brothers and friends, but was now se-quested in monasterial surroundings that alternatively lifted and depressed him. This had not been the case in the community.

It seemed they would be comforted with a sign; a name for the movement that was forming around him, yet was already taking on a different guise to that he had envisaged. At this point he felt that if he gave them what they wanted they would leave him to his destiny. He knew they would contrive myths of his sanctity, even divinity, and construct them in a manner that reflected their oppression. He hoped they might also contain the transcendent element, although about this he was not optimistic.

Maria joined him at the lakeside. It was the time of the moon, which, from whence they came, was a time of honouring of all things feminine. In this present community these were progressive and seemingly subversive trends. All did not augur well for the future, yet his destiny was to be involved and offer something.

What could this be? He looked at Maria who simply smiled, took his hand and led him back to her tent. She massaged his feet with oils and worked her way up to his cock, which rapidly attained its full manhood. The massage was gentle and two-handed, with an occasional darting tongue to the tip. This woman enraptured him; he looked to the future time when she would bear him the child who would be the culmination of their fates and their genuine contribution to the future.

He moved his manhood from her lips and laid her on the carpeted earth, lifted her gowns to expose the treasure he had realised in the community. He looked at its shape, enshrined by hair that provided an invited mystery. He dropped to his elbows and his face furrowed into the channel before him. He gazed, then closed his eyes and savoured deeply. The scent was enticing, engaging and demanding. He recalled his time on the boats on the lake outside and the sense of the fish that they had caught and had sustained them. Then the rich smell conjured an image of the fish and he knew this to be the sign he would leave the movement as they moved to their new life: but he would be gone.

The Fourth Temptation

Satan was racking his brains.

This one had him stumped: he'd shown the full hand of his temptations, all of which this man had managed to resist. He'd been through the Kabbalah and tested him out with the ol' "power and glory" routine, plus a bit of political and temporal stuff. Now it was looking ominously like his brother, the bloody Almighty, might win the day. Ever since these guys had got out of Egypt it had been trouble with this One God mantra. That left Satan out in the cold, even though he was the "bringer of light" in the creation scenario. He was offended and now seriously pissed off. Now this Joshua had been sent to test him, although to young Josh it was the other way around.

He decided to take a break and ponder where to go from here, while Joshua meditated on his empty stomach. He could always give up and go to some other lands and cultures and just leave this one to the Almighty. It was a serious consideration; all that piousness didn't make fertile ground for his ways. But that was all too easy, victory for the Almighty and by default! There must be another way...

Well... What were the cultural roots of this people before the One God had usurped the pantheon? Had he forgotten his pagan roots so quickly? Was this — forgetting — one of the Almighty's new techniques? All these questions tumbled around in his mind as he tried to remember those halcyon days when spirited beings played under the sun, worshipping it and then copulating under the moon in reverence to the plenty and magnificence of existence. Then the alliance had fragmented and his bloody Almighty had triumphed, throwing him – his only brother – out of the hyperborean paradise along with any of his mates who objected to this authoritarian rule. Those that agreed with the Almighty were put below him in rank, although they still enjoyed the fruits of paradise.

So here I am, the once mighty Satan, light-bringer to the human race, supporting them in their quest for immortality and a place among us, when he consigns them to Earth for the duration and a possible – and I do mean 'possible' – place in paradise; providing they submit to his sadistic punishments of guilt and the fear of eternal damnation. Why the hell doesn't the creator of all of us step in and clean up the mess being made, before it's too late? I know, I know, the 'real' creator steps back from his creation, but why does he, she or it (or a combination of all, after all he, she or it is omnipotent and omnipresent) let this counterfeit get away with it?

The bloody Almighty has already got a foothold. He's well and truly buggered up Egypt's progress in that way. Moses proved his General on earth in no mean way and that tablet thing was a great trick; even I would be proud of that one! But now, as things start to wane a bit, he sends down some dreams to young Joshua here who then thinks he has to be the Saviour or Messiah of his enslaved people. Whatever happened to the old ways? I'm getting nostalgic...

That's it, that's it! Sex. God-forbidding fucking sex! I'm losing my marbles, why the hell didn't I think of this before? That was what made the wheel go round for the pagans, brought smiles to their faces and joys to their hearts. More than that, it was a doorway to the divine; that is, before this interloper stole the show. Now he's trying to cement his position with Joshua and establish a temporal dynasty to match the fascist regime he has in paradise. Well, fuck him, not if I have a say!

This is going to take a bit of work: Joshua is no pushover;

he's now so imbued with goodness and the three-card trick I've already dealt him hasn't cracked any ice. Mind you, he did spend a little time in Egypt before his triumphant return, so maybe he had a taste of what I'm talking about. I'd better pull out my trump card...

Joshua's meditation had been still and undisturbed. The small ripples on the edges of his mind's eye were easily put away. He thought then of Martha, the blessing of his life... That is, behind his maker who was guiding his life and destiny. He knew that the enemies of the Almighty would be seeking to unsettle and even destabilise him. That was why he was spending time on the mountain, so that they could throw their all at him and he could proudly defeat the enemies of his God!

Martha's image would not leave his mind. This is a distraction; it will pass. But it doesn't, it just hovers there... I take her hand and we cross the field. Even though both she and I are virgins of our second birth, I have a sudden sense of what she is like under her gowns and dresses, so I wonder whether it is time. We move into the orchard and I lay her down in the luxury below the apple tree. I kiss her and she responds: a kiss so sweet that it flavours my very core and touches my soul. I pass a hand onto her breasts. They're substantial and soft, so I slip my hand under her gowns and feel their tenderness as the nipple hardens under my fingertips.

Before Martha there had been many. In Egypt the festivals demanded response of our entire nature: animal, human and divine. The priests had glorified and sanctified such action and in the temple precincts we indulged in divine orgies, the like of which I have tried to eradicate from my being in an attempt to fill this role now demanded of me. But now I begin to question whether that is my path... In the temple the goddesses in human form disrobed to sweet music as we supped even sweeter wine.

Then their lips supped of our manhood's and liberated the nectar of immortality.

Martha stands in front of me. It is no longer an image in my mind's eye. How did she get here? If I think too long about it the moment may pass. I take her hand and we find an olive tree under which to repose. I can see that her thoughts are as mine and we are connecting with our time and experience in the Motherland. Yet we had never shared each other in that place, only numerous others. Ourselves we kept for our initiation into the pharaonic priesthood, until that fateful day when the word came from our birth-land demanding we return to fulfil the destiny of our heritage. I had welcomed it; with some regret, but the demands of my people were too great. Martha's reluctance was greater, yet she accedes to be with me, as we still perceive our union as part of our fate.

Yet the demands have become greater and the union postponed. We both learned to channel these longings into our meditations and the will of our people. But not until this day did, I sense this void at the core of my being. Martha looks at me as I join her on the ground. Her eyes look welcoming and relieved. I undo her robes and bask in her nakedness. I smell her essence and then her womanhood, it lifts my spirit and raises passions in me that have been dormant too long. Her deft hand takes my manhood and guides it directly into her being, then approximates her womb: legs behind my back, arms around my neck, groans in my ear, heaven. I let go a torrent of pent-up fertility and know instantly she and I have brought into being a spiritual child. I know then that my destiny is not that ordained by our people, but with this heavenly creature. We may have to leave this land to further our destiny and leave it to another to fill the Saviour void.

Satan rests. All is good; it worked.

Inquisition

It was Mike's turn at Irene's dungeon, his responsibility to construct the sexual theatre for their evening. They'd been treating themselves to this particular brand of entertainment for a couple of years now and, after a few failures with venue and production, they had found Irene to be an ideal Mistress and her dungeon to be atmospheric, varied and suitable to their tastes. Irene was in her late thirties they guessed, very soft mannered and with a well-maintained figure, yet once she took her role, she developed an edge of severity that was both subtle and attractive to them both and she quickly earned their mutual respect. She was also capable of producing something unknown into their individualised dramas that accentuated the excitement and challenged the producer, be it Mike or his partner June.

As they were packing to go June asked Mike what she should take.

"Nothing special tonight, love." He seemed to pause and frowned slightly. "Maybe if you can keep to the basics in terms of the style we like, but add a puritanical edge."

"I thought you'd 'dealt' with that religious upbringing of yours!"

"It's not that, so stop trying to second guess the drama. This is still an evolving thing. The sort of edge I'd like is someone in a religious order, maybe a nun. I don't expect you to pull a 'habit' out of the wardrobe and I wouldn't like it to cloud the erotic background. I'll leave it to you."

Mike seemed equally preoccupied with his choice of night

attire, but June was now in a state of mild confusion, even apprehension; she opened her wardrobe, took a step back and started scanning the material in front of her.

When the doorbell rang announcing the cab's arrival, they were casually seated in the lounge listening to some blues Mike had selected and enjoying a cocktail. Their life had settled into a comfortable rhythm over the last few years. Irene's establishment represented something they had introduced into their relationship to explore their sexuality beyond the routines that could kill a committed long-term relationship. Apart from any mutually constructed 'play' they considered themselves and were otherwise monogamous. There had been the occasional 'straying' at the beginning, as they were finding their feet, so to speak. Neither was sure at the onset where the relationship was headed, nor was either particularly looking for any long-term partnership or commitment. It was if they drifted into it as any sexual encounters elsewhere dropped away and they were pleasantly surprised to find themselves together in this comfortable apartment.

Children were still a possibility, but each had a brief failed childless marriage behind them and had become aware of the dangers of the sexual routine and boredom of a long-term monogamous union. So, when it became obvious that they were 'mates', and that the sexual boundaries of their relationship had settled quite naturally into fidelity, they decided to explore the boundaries in a manner that was both safe and creative. Of course, there had been some failures in this and they stayed clear of anyone where an emotional involvement was a possibility. This had proved almost impossible to predict, in spite of their respective professional skills, so they explored the 'paid' options and eventually found Irene.

Irene ran an unusual enterprise. It was a small bistro in their local 'village' or collection of shops in the inner-city suburb where they lived. There were several staff, a mixture of men and women, who served from the bar or waited at the tables. It had a discrete atmosphere and was not particularly busy, yet it suited them ideally. One evening when they happened to be discussing future possibilities in the wake of a recent failed evening out Irene asked them, when they had finished the meal, if they would care to be given a tour of her establishment. This surprised them both, as it seemed to be simply a self-contained small bistro with a delightful range of attractive staff, but their interest was piqued and they agreed.

Irene led them down a passage past the toilets and under a sign that read 'Staff Only'. Everything started innocently enough with a look into the kitchen, a private drawing room for functions behind and an adjoining small home theatre area with several comfortable sofas: the drawing room made sense to June, the theatre did not. Irene led them on through a door at the back of the theatre and to a spiral staircase in a shaft that took them directly underneath the bistro. A locked door was opened with a code and they stepped into a large space that appeared like a dressing room, but of a particular kind. The walls and shelves were adorned with an array of devices and some clothing that reminded June of the 'back room' at their local sex shop. There were whips and cuffs, masks and restrainers, and some clothing that could be used as an addition to whatever a person may already be wearing. There were a couple of seats and one curtained changing area. June gave Mike an expressionless gaze, but neither hesitated in following Irene through the door on the far wall and down a couple of steps into what was obviously a dungeon.

Neither June nor Mike had been in such a room before. Of course, they used many of the accoutrements that lined the dressing room in their own private play and had occasionally made use of these in some of their earlier experimental 'outings', but this was beyond anything they had experienced, although not to their knowledge as both were familiar with erotic literature and art; indeed, they boasted quite a collection. Irene discretely stood to one side and with a slight hand movement invited them to explore. Both knew they were moving into new territory and June's heartbeat gave her internal confirmation of the excitement that she was experiencing.

Their exploration of the dungeon on that evening was relatively cursory. The selection of equipment was impressive and emotionally challenging. This did not stop them both looking at the X-shaped cross against one wall, fingering the cuffs at each periphery and then turning to separate and begin an individual exploration. When they came back together in front of Irene, she silently ushered them out and they retraced their steps to the drawing room. When seated Irene enquired of their preference of drinks and in a matter of a minute a handsome youth delivered their requests and each took a long sip. Irene seemed to have only a glass of mineral water.

"Well," began Mike, always one to take the initiative when there was any potential for confusion: "I think an explanation might help!"

He could not resist a smile, which gave the game away for Irene and she took a deep breath through her nose, crossed her legs and looked deeply at each of them in turn.

"There's always a bit of a risk factor," she began, "unavoidable, but I'm fairly experienced now and don't often get it wrong. Even when I have it has been a case of 'thanks, but no thanks'. Sometimes I lose the associated bistro custom, but not usually and our relationships deepen anyway. I find it better than advertising and all I ask, at this stage, is that if this is in anyway disagreeable to you, we simply close the evening and I ask for your respect and confidentiality in what I have shown you. It is a source of satisfaction to many and I would not like to put that at risk."

Mike looked at June and they exchanged an understanding, so June picked up the initiative: "We're in, please explain." Irene visibly relaxed; she had made the right decision.

She explained how her background as a call-girl specialising as a dominatrix had eventually got her into a bit of trouble, although she was reluctant to go into any detail even with Mike's subtle prompting. This didn't particularly perturb either of them; Irene was relieved and warmed by their lack of persistence and when she found out their professional backgrounds, as they got to know each other, she reflectively understood there was no particular need. Mike and June both worked in the psychological fields and this is where they met. Mike was an academic and research psychologist who was experimenting with high arousal states in animals and the application of this to human health, whilst June was more therapeutically inclined with an interest in dysfunctional, rather than pathological sexual behaviour. Their interests and careers intersected as, shortly thereafter, did their bodies.

And that furthering of their 'interests' is what had brought them into Irene's company. June deduced that Irene had been a high-flyer in her trade and very successful. She also gained the impression that she may have flown too high and got into a spot of bother with the more nefarious personnel who had a significant and sometimes controlling interest in trades such as hers. She speculated: Irene had accepted a graceful retirement package, which included her being able to continue to ply her trade – which she had a passion for – but under restricted circumstances. The mutual agreement was that any additional 'trade' that she could develop from her own restricted activities in the restaurant business was mutually acceptable.

This all seemed to explain the nature in which they had become involved to this point and engendered a confidence in both June and Mike about their involvement in extended activities in Irene's establishment. This was reinforced when, after they agreed to make use of the extended services at the bistro, Irene was insistent that they do not confide in anyone else without her express permission.

All these facts, impressions and 'working guesses' rapidly fell into the background when they had their inaugural 'night out'. This was by nature of an induction and mainly involved the staff and Irene performing a show, with June and Mike only involved in the latter stages. There were times when other couples – and it usually was on a couple only basis – were involved: this was an area Irene kept a tight control over and was part of the agreement of involvement. The last year or so had seen a wide range of experimentation, which was to their mutual satisfaction.

They arrived at the bistro and went to the bar for a drink. When the small bag they brought was placed on the bar it discretely and rapidly disappeared. As they finished their drink a convenient window allowed them to slip around the bar to the drawing room and from there down to the dungeon dressing room. Irene had not been upstairs, nor had the saucy Clare, as requested by Mike without June's knowledge. They could just make out the techno music emanating from behind the dungeon door; the soundproofing was efficacious; he knew it would be significantly louder inside. The light above the door was red and they both knew the door was locked and could, in this circumstance, only be opened from the inside. Irene certainly ran a tight ship!

June took her clothes from the bag that had been deposited there in advance. She had been a little bemused about the 'nun' direction and had to do a little improvisation. She had a white nurses outfit and found a black top from her 'normal' wardrobe to create a 'sexy habit'. Her psychological background made her appreciate several levels of innuendo and humour to that phrase! It also served to soften her mounting anxiety, as she used a black handkerchief on her head held in place with a fine white headband. She was already wearing black stockings with a red garter-belt and matching G-string and she ducked behind the curtain when she took off the skirt, she had arrived in to put on the habit, so as to provide a level of surprise at a suitably later time. Finally, she gathered her dark locks and allowed the large kerchief to partially conceal them. The final touch was the large wooden crucifix that was in her box of therapeutic props that she had found a suitable necklace for. Ironically, she felt more of a sacrilege about using a therapeutic prop than she did about the fact that it was a crucifix; she was additionally amused that her catholic upbringing now had so little emotional hold. Her old training therapist would be proud! The heeled black shoes rounded off her endeavours.

Her preoccupation did not afford her much opportunity to see what Mike was up to, so by the time she sought him out he was wearing a large black cape and black boots that went up beyond the hemline of the cape. By contrast the top of her stockings barely met the lower reach of the skimpy nurses outfit and any movement revealed some whiteness of thigh and redness of suspender. Mike was ready before she and he felt relieved, as he had previously felt quite anxious that June would see what he was wearing and express some surprise, even shock. She was also a little quizzical about the white studded collar he was wearing. Mike pressed the button next to the dungeon and the red light went out a short while later: it was time to enter.

Mike led June across the room to the cross. He turned and put her against it so that she faced the room and then slowly put each arm and leg into its appropriate position to be restrained by the manacle. The back was lightly padded and her feet firmly on the ground, so June was physically comfortable, although emotionally far from it. Mike finished, put his hand under her habit and stroked her pussy from outside her panties whilst giving her a deep kiss. In spite of her nervous state and desire to remain a little restrained and watchful, her pussy start to ooze. Mike felt this, finished the kiss, withdrew his hand, savoured the aroma and turned to walk back into the room with a parting enigmatic smile as the light that highlighted the cross became dimmer.

To her left a light was raised and June saw a comfortable armchair on a slight dais, where Irene was seated comfortably with her thighs parted and thigh-length booted feet firmly on the ground, raised by the long heels. Irene was wearing a tight leather bodice, studded and belted. It constrained her moderate breasts and continued up the front only to end in a substantial collar that sported further studs and a circular hook at the front. Her blond hair was tightly groomed into a ponytail and she wore a skullcap mask that finished at her cheeks leaving her nose exposed. All was black and in her right hand she had a long whip with which she was casually flicking onto the buttocks of the crouching figure between her legs. It was Clare who was simultaneously working Irene's pussy with her tongue, as her position meant that her hands were occupied in keeping her torso and head raised to the level of Irene's genitals. She was wearing a maid's pinafore and white cap with stockings and high-heeled shoes.

Mike had taken his cape off and emerged into the light, now June was shocked. He was wearing gartered stockings under his calf-length boots and satin knickers of the loose French style that barely contained his significant erection. Above this he was wearing a simple and slightly small sleeveless shirt that continued up to the white collar at the front. Apart from the white collar, all was black. The effect was stunning; to June he looked like a priest in drag. She quickly gained an inkling about her outfit, but was more involved in the theatre in front of her. Mike went over to Clare from behind, lifted the pinafore, and parted her vaginal lips whilst with his other hand pulling his erection out of the knickers. With a little added saliva, he then placed his cock at Clare's pussy lips and with one thrust entered her fully. At the same time Irene increased the flicking and Clare the sucking. This was all done with a silence that would have been partially deafened by the background music, should there have been a vocal accompaniment.

His fucking Clare didn't affect June. She had seen it all before and knew this to be theatre, although she was a little unnerved when he looked directly at her in an expressionless manner and she now noted that he was wearing lipstick that gave his mouth the smile of a clown, although he wasn't laughing. It was all becoming a little surreal. What was portrayed before her was like a silent black and white movie with a modern soundtrack and only the occasional splash of red to break the contrast. June moved her pelvis against the cross; she was uncomfortable, even itchy. Mike noticed this, disengaged from Clare and moved around to her side. Irene stopped the flicking as he whispered in Clare's ear whilst she continued sucking Irene. Slowly she stopped and got up, walking toward June with a demure gait, not unlike a waitress, she thought. When Clare arrived in front of June the light on June went up again as she leant against her and thrust her tongue deep in June's mouth. Initially she felt compelled to respond and could taste Irene's pussy on June's tongue. As the compulsion changed to attraction Clare disengaged, dropped to her knees, then squatted between June's legs and started to eat her now molten cunt around and over the soggy panties. June felt herself slip, as if into the mouth below.

Mike had taken over Clare's duties as well as receiving the

flicking whip on his satin-clad buttocks. It felt good, but he briefly wondered about what was to come... June watched with interest, not only had Mike never dressed like this before, he had also never asked to be even play-smacked. Her confusion was mixed with the pleasure of response to Clare's experienced tongue that acted like a balm. Then Irene abruptly disengaged Mike's head from her pussy by grabbing his hair and lifting. She then rose and led Mike by the collar with a leash; June hadn't seen her put that on, maybe she had her eyes closed for longer than she thought in response to Clare's tongue-lashing. Irene led him to a newly illuminated bench-like piece of furniture that reminded June of a gymnasium horse. Irene bent Mike over lengthways and clamped his wrists to a pair of manacles near the bottom of the front legs. Then she disappeared into the shadows.

The music continued, Clare's tongue did likewise and June wondered what was going to happen next. Mike was quite still and, although in profile, he chose to look away from June toward the far wall. Then Irene returned wearing a black strap-on dildo to which she was applying a liberal amount of lubricant. June knew what was going to happen next and she was all eyes. After a few preparatory licks of his anal rim Irene positioned the head of the dildo at the entrance to Mike's arse, then, in unison, both turned to look at June as she gently penetrated his anal ring and then continued up and deep into his arse. June's emotional response was too confusing to describe as her mouth stayed open and her breathing increased.

Clare stopped her oral attention, undid the ankle manacles and then rose to do likewise with the wrists. Then she led June to a similar but slightly shorter apparatus that left June's head free when she was strapped in a similar way and position to Mike. As Clare was doing this, she noticed that Irene had extricated herself from arse fucking Mike and released him. Clare then lifted June's head to show her a swing that was a foot or so in front of her face and set at the same height. Clare sat in the seat facing June and gently started to swing so that on the up-swing her pussy was right against June's mouth if she looked at her. In that position Clare would wrap her legs around the front apparatus legs for varying periods of time, aggressively hold June's neck and push her head into her cunt. Although June needed little encouragement, the scene carried all the appearance of a violation.

Then June felt a dick – it had to be Mike's – against her anal rim. It hardly required lubrication by now and with a few short thrusts Mike was buried deep in her arse. He held that position for a while, allowing his cock to stretch her inside so that he could obtain the maximum penetration that would ease any unnecessary friction when he began pumping. And pump he did, whilst June periodically had Clare's cunt to savour. The pleasure was there, but there was an edge of pain that was different to what she usually experienced when being arse fucked and also usually subsided once the long strokes started. This surprised her, but it was not – yet – overwhelming. Then something changed; she suspected, but did not know till later, that when Mike stopped his deep pumping on an in-stroke that Irene was coming back into the picture. There was a noise above the music. Irene was spanking him with something a little more substantial. With each smack his cock surged deeper in her arse than she had ever experienced before. It was growing; becoming gargantuan.

June's rhythmic attention to Clare's cunt now became continuous as Clare had somehow engineered herself to be both stationary in front of June's mouth yet also in a reclining and free-floating position. Clare became quite passive and receptive and the mouth and tongue that were providing such lascivious attention seemed to go into an automatic mode in rhythm with the music. June could feel herself becoming entranced, then the smacking stopped and Mike's cock resumed its normal shape and position. Was this the end of it? She thought not as Clare for one remained glued to her and Mike was not moving. Then she felt his cock grow again, but the stimulus to this seemed different. There was a push, a pause, then a deeper push and she suddenly and assuredly she knew that Irene was arse fucking him again.

From there it took the three of them a little while to get the rhythm, but get it they did with Irene's expertise and they then settled down into what would seem like a marathon to all concerned. The pain factor was back for June and now, mixed with the intensity and excitement the trance state seemed to deepen. She let herself go. She was the still object of this gyrating mass around and inside her and she felt she could allow herself that luxury, but more than that, the state she was moving into felt compelling.

It was like when you wonder whether you will get back to sleep, then do and only realise it afterwards. June looked around her and then at her clothing. She was wearing a full nun's habit and she was lying on straw in what seemed like a prison cell. She ached all over and her buttocks felt raw like they had been bleeding. She put her hand under her habit... they had. What was going on? Why are they doing this to me? Then, like a dream, it came back to her. For many years she had tried to conceal her visions, but it had not helped when the stigmata appeared on her hands and it was only a short while after that when the Pope's police paid their initial visit. At first things seemed to go well, but her visions also increased and she found it difficult to disengage from her Master's suffering and his command that she should suffer too.

So, the punishment started. Gently at first, a few beatings

followed by interrogation. Who was her Master? I serve only Our Lord was her consistent reply. It must be the Devil, as only Our Lord suffered the passion so this is a cruel mockery, they countered. The stigmata did not release her and she knew she had no answer, so when her Master visited her and commanded her to join him in his passion and ultimate victory, she acceded. Do with me what you will; I can say no more. Reluctant shaking of male heads and she knew she was consigned to her fate when the head priest signed the document in front of her. A little turning on the rack, just to loosen her up, a couple more beatings and she was back in her cell.

She had not been a virgin when she joined the order. It was her passion and lovemaking with Alfred that had awakened her sensibilities, where she first had visions of her Master and his instruction to do his bidding. It was with heavy heart that she told Alfred; he was silent and shortly after went to sea. Her time in the convent had always been difficult and many times her superiors questioned her sanity. The stigmata were the straw that broke the camel's back and provided the excuse the Mother Superior needed. It was a short time afterwards that the instruments of the Inquisition arrived.

What happened next violated her in a manner that the rack and beatings could never do. The monks and soldiers who accompanied the papal caravan despoiled her in every way possible. As her anus ached from the repeated sodomisation and her vagina bled from sheer abuse, she would lay whimpering in the corner of her cell only to be comforted by her Master that all was well and how it should be. It was at times like this that her faith was stretched to its utmost, but as she realised it also as her fate, she became resigned and submitted to the abuse. Sometimes her Inquisitor watched. It was painful, but it no longer hurt. She could look into the eyes of the perpetrators with a peace and clarity that was usually met with a slap across her face. Sometimes this would make them angrier and they couldn't sustain their erections, so they resorted to beating.

Then it stopped. It was the calm before the storm. She knew her fate was to be the stake. The nuns came and dressed her in a worn and dirty habit and once again placed her crucifix around her neck, although this time upside down. She quietly wept. She was led from the cell across the courtyard and out of the gate. In front of her was the funeral pyre with the thick stake in the middle. The soldiers took her from the nuns and led her up to her cross. Her hands were tied securely behind the stave and they retreated to a safe distance. Then the inquisitor stepped forward and lit the fire. Not once did her gaze move from the people in front of her, yet only fleetingly did their eyes meet hers. The flames rose making vision difficult and she started to feel the heat, yet she felt no pain. In front of her, separate from the crowd was her Master. He was smiling. The flames took to her habit and the heat moved upward from her feet to her soiled pelvis where it felt to her that bliss started. It was to rise with the flames and engulf her in a circle of bliss so powerful that only the Master's form could be discerned. Then all dissolved, as the ecstasy was complete.

She felt the intensity in her head reach an overwhelming state just as Mike released his sperm deep into her arse. Then she was calm, incredibly calm and still. Mike slowly withdrew as Clare undid the clamps on her wrists and pulled an extension out from underneath the apparatus so that her head was now supported. She allowed all this to be done to her with no thought or question. She was in bliss.

When she came to, she was lying on her back on one of the large pieces of furniture that seemed like a day bed. The lighting was mute and the music now a soft instrumental. Clare was stroking her head with the kerchief discarded and she opened her eyes to see Mike in front of her with a glass of water. He took her head from Clare and lifted the glass to her mouth; it was very refreshing. Then she gathered strength and returned her head to the pillow under her own momentum. Mike was now sitting on the bed next to her and holding her hand. He looked like a kindly priest. In fact, if she looked deeply at him, he looked almost like the epicene Master of a vision she had experienced somewhere. She chuckled: if he was her Master then she was his Mistress!

Confession

It had been a long day in the confessional. The Mediterranean heat was permeating the building in spite of the thick stone walls and Father Alfonse was starting to feel weary. The succession of petty issues that came through the grill hadn't ignited his sense of devotion to his flock, or his sense of humour. There was nothing that he had heard that would even excite the gossipmongers in this village that supported his order, let alone any sins – venal or carnal – that warranted more than a few hail Marys. A bit like dealing with kids in a family, he thought, as he reflected back on his childhood. As the oldest he had always been earmarked for the Church and, when nothing else beckoned to excite his passion at the chosen time, he willingly joined the order, although his decision had a hidden complexity.

Then Sister Maria took her place in the confessional. He briefly wondered what this sloe-eyed innocent could possibly have to confess? He could make a few suggestions, but repressed the thoughts and images that they conjured; otherwise, he would have to take his place on the other side of the grill.

"Forgive me Father, for I have sinned."

He sat and made the standard response before settling into an idle fantasy of how Sister Maria's body really looked underneath the obscuring habit; there was something familiar about her that took his memory back so many years, even a generation. Had it been that long since he had known Angela?

As Pietro his sexual experience had been meagre. He didn't have anyone more seasoned to guide him through his adolescence and his hen-pecked father was no help. A few gropings with the dark-haired girls of his village didn't really excite him. In fact, it was the angelic voices of the pre-pubertal sopranos in the choir that stimulated him more, although he couldn't distinguish whether this was sexual or spiritual. This caused him some angst and more than one visit to the confessional, where his confessor was keen to point out that it could be a calling to the order. He even started to consider this and became an altar boy, but his faith in the advice given was severely tested one day when this same confessor accidentally spilled some altar wine over his vestments and then made an elaborate attempt to wipe him clean. Maybe it was an accident that the wine spilled in his crotch, but the cleaning was vigorous and not asked for; as well as the beads of sweat on Father's brow arousing suspicion. He left.

Back to the girls on the hillside: Gropings through clothes, mutual masturbation and even some oral succour, but no genital sex as the girls had to maintain their virginity. One enterprising lass found a way around this by guiding his dick into her arse whilst she masturbated herself. They both had an orgasm, but he was unable to repeat the exercise as the fears of his sexual orientation returned. It wasn't until his cousin, Angela, came to visit the village one summer, that these fears subsided in the wake of the visage of this most angelic creature, who was true to her name.

They became close during those months. After the initial wariness of relatives unknown there was the teasing and game playing that took them rapidly into a state of common feeling that neither had entered before. The teasing changed to compliments and the physical contact, at first seemingly accidental, became an integral part of their connection. They were cousins after all, what was more natural than they should hold hands? Tongues wagged a little, although they were relatives it was not illegal in the eyes of the state for them to become lovers, but the Church frowned upon it. His parents warned them, jointly and separately, but they were as innocents and the words fell on deaf ears and the warnings ceased.

It was as simple as crossing the village square when the step was taken. Angela plucked and gave him a flower. She looked at him intently and, it seemed to him, as she had never looked at him before. Something was changing, even as he looked back, he could feel it through his body. He accepted the flower and leant forward to kiss her cheek, but she did not incline her head and what started as a token of gratitude became a sign that they shared something more. At first it was just lips, but as Angela parted hers, she felt his tongue explore her mouth and she to respond. Their eyes closed and they sank to the grass and the sound of the birds in the trees above. They had fallen in love.

There was the last month in front of them. They found hours, even minutes to be together. They found places of secrecy and quietude where they could explore each other's bodies and beings in a state of pristine innocence. They both knew the step they were going to take. Pietro shied away from her sex; he suggested alternatives, but none they hadn't already explored and she would have no more of it. After kisses of mouths and genitals one lazy afternoon their passion took them beyond a point from which they could return, even if they had wanted to. He parted her panties as he had done so many times before, but on this occasion, it was not his fingers that moved into her pussy, instead they held his erect cock as he guided it in. They discovered each other that afternoon again, but deeper. And this was to continue the last few weeks until the time for Angela to return across the mountains. We'll write. Yes! And next summer I will come to your valley? Which valley are you talking about, you naughty boy! He laughed. It was sealed with a kiss: until summer next.

Next summer never arrived. A mere month after their parting the letters suddenly stopped and Pietro was summoned by his parents, although it was his mother who did most of the talking.

"She is pregnant." This was all his mother could say for what seemed an age.

"Oh God!" Pietro was stunned.

"And it won't help bringing the Lord into the picture, it seems to me that you have done enough defiling without that!" She was now furious; it seemed to Pietro that it was the comment about God rather than Angela's pregnancy that most raised her ire.

"She will have the child and it will be looked after by the order, which, I might add, Angela will duly join. She has much to ask forgiveness for."

It's sealed, thought Pietro, the priesthood for me. Although mooted it would now become fact, he had no choice. He briefly thought about running away and finding her, but it was beyond his means both physically and financially. What did he have to offer? If she made any contact I will go. Yes! That's what I'll do! But there was none. He was to find out later, whilst his vacillation continued that she was to die in premature childbirth. The child, a girl, survived against the odds and disappeared into the order the other side of the mountains. He joined the local Church and was ultimately ordained. His sexuality found a safer outlet, or so it seemed to him.

"I am pregnant!" Sister Maria announced, and his mind came back to the present; a present deeply suffused with his own past.

"My poor child!" This was all he could offer whilst he brought himself back to the present and task in hand.

"I'm not a 'poor child' Father, I'm so happy!"

His world sank. He could no longer distinguish the past from the present. She gave him little chance for respite, launching herself into a description of what had brought her to this point.

"He is a man of hills and nature, he tells me. I met him on one of my wanderings there and he befriended me. He is older, about your age. In fact, Father, it's funny, he looks rather like you!

"But he didn't seduce me, it was more the other way around. I have been told tales about my mother, her beauty and passion for her cousin, that I was a product of that love and survived in spite of the odds. My mother gave my life for me; I have always wanted to find a way to repay it. At first, I thought this was by joining the order, because that is what she had intended after she gave birth to me, or so I am told.

"Yet the more I thought about it, the less likely it seemed. Rather, as I heard the stories about her, I realised that her desire was to seek out her cousin, Pietro, I believe he was called, and present herself and her daughter – me – to him. I have tried to find him Father, but no Pietro lives in the village and some say he went overseas, others that he joined a distant order. I don't know whether I have been deceived and they don't want me to find him.

"I wondered at first if this man of the woods was my father. But he said it could not be, his name is Nino and always has been! That was good, because I wanted him, but I didn't want him to be my father!"

Then she went on to describe their passion. It could well have been her mother and he that she described. She was explicit, erotic and naïve. He determined there and then to help this young Sister in her plight as he realised Nino would be waiting for her. He didn't want him to experience the distress and grief that had marked his life. It took a lot of planning, but leave she did. Alfonso's involvement raised a rumour that he was the father of the child. When this happened, he did not deny it and knew his fate would be expulsion. He accepted gracefully and took her to the woods.

When they met, he could see their love and the joy in this man's face was a deep healing for Alfonso, now Pietro once more. When he announced his real name to the couple next to him around the fire, he could almost see the blood drain from Maria's face. She stood and faced him, then dropped to her knees and placed her head in his lap. Then she cried, and cried, and cried. Nino watched on, quietly drawing on his pipe.

He left them the next day. This was neither his time nor place. He found the way to her village and Angela's grave on the edge of the graveyard. It was untended. He spent days restoring it and loving it. When this was complete, he gave a stipend to the gardener to maintain it indefinitely and left. He also went to the woods, to the place where their love had been consummated. It was here that his body was found and then brought back and buried next to Angela's, following the gardener's direction in response to Pietro's request. The gardener knew his task was now to tend both, which he did after the stipend finished; not out of obligation but love.

Stigmata

Mark was just so frustrated. His life seemed to get so far and then hit a brick wall. Was this of his own making, or was it "karma"; some divine fucking joke just to tease him. He wanted to know the answer, not in some other lifetime, but now. Right now.

He'd wasted all that money on "analysis" and where had it got him? He understood – deeply – his personal contribution to the blockages. If it were just that, how come the barriers were still there? He felt suicidal, knowing that this was a call to find the solution. He also knew that ending it all wasn't the solution; he wanted it in this life.

He took out the knife; it had been a long time since he had played this game. He placed his left hand on the table, palm up and fingers spread. He used to do it, all those years ago with the palm down. He didn't know why he was changing the rules, it was a little awkward physically; but it just felt right. Then he took the knife and gripped it like a dagger and let the point rest vertically on the table between his little and ring fingers. Then he lifted it and let it come down between the middle and ring, then the index and middle and then finally between the thumb and index. Then he reversed the process, slowly and deliberately, until he arrived back where he started. He didn't stop there, but repeated the whole cycle without pausing, steadily increasing the tempo.

Mark was in the rhythm now and the speed increased, almost of its own accord. He knew he was getting in that state where he could go almost infinitely fast, yet with a precision that he felt made him immune to self-harm. It was this state in the past that somehow lifted him out of himself and the mundaneness and boredom of existence, for a while at least. He was in that state now; the knife moved and skated across the table as if moving of its own volition. His breathing was easy now and life once again started to gain a sense of perspective and purpose. Then it changed: it had never done this before. In one cycle as the knife came to rest between his middle and ring fingers time seemed to stand still. Mark watched the knife lift as if to continue its path in this transported slowness, but instead to stand above the palm. Then with a cry of confusion and anguish he plunged the blade deep into and though the middle of his palm.

Mark felt no pain. The soldier dressed in Roman garb was kneeling below his outstretched left arm and hand that was palm upwards. The soldier was hammering a nail through his hand into a wooden structure below. He knew instantly that he was being crucified and he looked to his right arm, which had already been nailed to the wood. Another soldier was roping this arm to the crosspiece; they obviously wanted him to have a prolonged experience. Still there was no pain and the soldier to his right moved to his feet, placed them together and turned them before driving a nail through his ankles and into the stave below. Still, he felt no pain, only an indescribable anguish. He could hear wailing around him and the soldier to his left telling the throng to shut up as he applied some rope. What was he doing here?

As they raised the cross to put it in the ground, he remembered. Instead of taking the option of being with Maureen, he had allowed them to seduce him into participating in their revolt. His heart was against it, but he complied; his heritage and lineage demanded it and he felt powerless to resist. With Maureen, Mark had explored some of the spiritual riches that came from the Nile delta and they had both returned to his homeland to instruct others.

He was a peaceful man, but the violence of the last day had shattered him, as had the betrayal. He was deeply confused; it wasn't as if he had found his God, the Father who was the pinnacle of his – and Maureen's – search, instead he was to die like a common criminal without having fulfilled his destiny. Mark started to thirst and they gave him a sponge-soaked drink. He wondered whether it was drugged, but it didn't seem to matter now, nothing did. He looked down at the small throng and recognised some, then he saw Maureen, his Maureen, emerge from the crowd. She had tears in her eyes as she gazed up at him, but he could feel the love in her heart and he smiled in return.

What had happened in those final days? Together they had travelled south and entered the therapeutic community on the delta. There they had explored the wisdom of this great land and its place in healing. Some of the techniques of the East had been imported and adapted to the community's needs, particularly those of a magical and sexual nature. Mark and Maureen had moved into this enthusiastically and deeply, and even conceived a son in one ecstatic ritual of love and transformation. The small family had returned to their homeland to begin an offshoot of their community, as their belief was that the conflict with their occupiers would be best dealt with in a peaceful and loving manner.

Yet in his homeland his lineage marked him out as a leader, hence his birth-name. The hostility and aggression toward the invader was still present and they called upon him to fulfil his destiny and re-establish their heritage. He was in conflict, divided, because he felt there were other, new ways, which he and Maureen had been exploring. The pressure was immense and he consulted deep and long with Maureen.

One day, after intense lovemaking with his beloved, Mark

emerged to meet his community. They exhorted him yet again. In his heart he wanted to be with this woman, who showed him vistas unseen and mysteries unbeheld. He felt this was the way to his maker, the source of creation. They continued the challenge and Maureen emerged from the rear of the building with a vase of precious and expensive oils. As they continued their challenge, she poured oil on his feet and massaged them, deeply, lovingly and forgivingly. He knew what this meant: she was giving him permission to leave their pact and to follow the demands of his lineage. He cried in the face of the self-satisfaction that surrounded him.

Mark knew it not to be he and felt deceived. When he was arrested, they wanted another, even as he showed them healing in the garden some time prior. They demanded this other when offered a choice by the regional governor, who was so reluctant to be involved in what he saw as internal and regional politics. But he was ultimately left with no choice and Mark was consigned to his fate.

Maureen sat at the foot of the cross, unlike the others she remained. He watched as he felt the life ebb from him, exasperated at his fate. He had tried to follow the dictates of both his heart and his destiny. Had he got it so wrong, had he made the wrong choice? It certainly seemed so in that moment. He railed against his fate and challenged his unseen maker about his desertion; he heard no reply and sank his head.

Mark wondered at first whether it was the effect of the drink that they had given him, or that it was a genuine experience. He awoke in a cave with Maureen at his side, ministering herbs and spices, tending his wounds and mopping his brow. He knew then that he had not missed his calling. His people would take the fable of his death and elaborate upon it, but he knew it would be distorted early and become like the usurper it sought to replace. He had left some of his writings; maybe they would discover these and they might temper the direction of the movement that would follow. He felt sad, but now knew that his destiny was for a posterity he would never see and that his son may begin a new lineage and in a new country. They packed and in the stealth of night took their few belongings, including the precious chalice, picked up their son from Mark's mother's house and began their long journey to a Northern land.

Slowly Mark pulled the blade from his upturned palm. As it left the wound immediately closed and he could see no evidence of its entry. He felt no pain, just a sense of relief. He also recognised that the blockage had gone; something had opened up. But, unlike before, he knew that he would never have to repeat this act again.

The Grail

Merlin knew his time on the surface of the Earth was nearly at a close. He had been through a long and sometimes troubled existence, and was now tired; tired of even life itself. He was leaving behind a considerable achievement, yet he remained dissatisfied and not able to put his finger on the root of this malaise. The most obvious early success was to escape the clutches of Vortigern, that tyrannical king who would have effectively sold Britannia to the Saxons, and help in Arthur's ascension to the ancient seat of kings with the establishment of the Round Table.

Yet the forces involved were not just temporal; they were also eternal. Deep in his being Merlin knew, as a champion of the 'old' ways, that change was upon him. Whilst his genetic interference, or magical influence, had brought forth Arthur from the brave yet foolish Uther in his magical tryst with the Duke of Cornwall's wife, the beautiful Ygraine, it ultimately backfired. Arthur was considered barren. Merlin presumed not, nor impotent as Arthur's sister Morgana subsequently confirmed with the abomination of a son, she gave birth to, yet doubts remained in the populace who were unawares of this fact. Gwenivere was a poor choice as Queen, against Merlin's earnest counsel, and it was infinitely more likely that she was the infertile one; caught as she was between the ancient and new Christian ways. This haughty Queen came between Arthur and his mentor and then racked her husband by her infidelity with Lancelot. That such a union was also barren confirmed Merlin's suspicion, but not the people, where the proven fertility of the King symbolised and reflected that of the land.

So, the land itself faltered and the Britons' tenuous hold on this great gift of Hyperborea became more strained, as the Saxons waited at the borders: beaten in Arthur's earlier triumphs, but ultimately not defeated. Merlin needed no crystal ball to know their time would come again. Of more importance were now matters eternal. His attempts to guide a lineage that could hold the spirituality of the land in the ancient ways were foundering, yet he must find a way. He mistrusted Christianity deeply beyond his own Druid nature. He watched in disgust as the ancient forests were felled and sites harmonious with nature disguised by Churches and their screeching bells. Gwenivere championed them, yet broke one of their fundamental commandments: How could people live such duplicity and hypocrisy? He knew not.

He poked the fire and Nimuë looked back at him. Where had this divine creature that he not yet trusted, come from? She was dark, not flaxen-haired as Gwenivere, so was of the old stock. Her petite face contained eyes that penetrated and a still mouth all framed by an abundance of dark locks. Her body was also comely, though well-hidden underneath her robes that served to disguise and hide her, as well as protecting her from the bitter cold. The women had presented her to him for instruction. He felt after Arthur, with the failures, that his responsibilities in this area were done; yet they convinced him. He bowed to their request, recognising that it may contain wisdom in the scheme of things that was beyond his present kenning.

Merlin had instructed her: "This is the Mandrake. It is in the image of a man and transports him beyond himself. It can both heighten and sustain the act of love, but death will follow if indulged beyond what is wise."

"We know it as Mandragora, the power of the dragon."

She had the knowledge; had she the sight? As yet he knew

not.

Nimuë crawled into his bed that night in their camp under the stars. It was the fullness of the moon and this was allowed. He took strange comfort in the arms of this creature that ministered to his body with her hands to relieve him of the burden and responsibility, as well as the yoke of time. It was many years since he'd had a woman, but he didn't consider this a taking. Nimuë was skilled in the art and brought him to a precipice over which he was easily and willingly pushed, before any sexual engagement was even consummated.

Merlin did not recognise where he now was. It seemed a great cave: how had he got there? He could not remember, but Nimuë was still beside him, her hands on his body, and he knew that whether or not she had the sight that she certainly had the magic. Great candles lit the walls and furs covered a large section of the floor. In one corner was a great fire, the smoke of which wended its way to a small aperture many yards above in the recesses of the cave. To one side was a table replete with food and wine; this was luxury indeed. He felt to ask no question at this time and to simply bask in this indulgence, so long overdue.

Nimuë continued her massage, which was now also tending his exposed manhood. She was using oils and a skilled hand. When more was needed a hooded woman moved from the shadows with a jug and poured the precious oil into Nimuë's cupped hands. With a nod from Nimuë she retreated backward to the darkness, awaiting any further summons. When Nimuë completed the tour of his body, leaving his organ ripe and proud, she went to the table to prepare a platter of food. A snap of her fingers and three women emerged from the darkness to continue Nimuë's work. First, they started with massage, leaving his manhood unattended and exposed. Then one parted her gown and lowered herself onto him, gyrating her hips and offering soft moans.

Although Nimuë had finished the meal preparation, she stood back and watched her servants' treatment of her mentor. He was responding softly and tenderly, as each took their turn upon him whilst in between another sucked the juices from his cock before guiding it into its new home. This dance and circular rotation continued for some time: it was a ritual with which he was familiar in the past, designed to heighten the energetic intensity of a man in preparation for the sight.

They paused: the necessary pitch was reached and needed sustaining. The women retreated and Nimuë came forward, assisted Merlin to a sitting position and placed a platter in front of him. She returned to the table, brought forth two goblets of sweet red wine and sat opposite, supping with him, but allowing Merlin to eat alone. All this was in silence. When he had his fill, he reclined and Nimuë tended to his feet; the second phase of the ritual had begun.

Merlin focussed on his breathing, the wine was strong, and he needed no more. He lay down and Nimuë stood above and astride his pelvis. He looked at her as she disrobed and revealed a perfect form, which she graciously lowered onto his erection. Her cunt was warmer, softer and richer than the others: she was well versed in the ways of love it seemed, no wonder she understood the lore of mandrake! She started softly, increasing in both speed and intensity as she ground onto his pelvis. He was aware that the herbs in the wine would sustain him and delay his ejaculation to the time of his choosing, if at all. He responded with abandon as they both entered the dance of the Goddess.

Then in perfect synchrony they both became still. Merlin took the potency of his erection and focussed on the heat. It smouldered and ignited, seeming in his vision to be the serpentine form of a great dragon that uncoiled and breathed its fire up and beyond as its great wings flapped and the ascent started. This great power came to a still point above, between and behind his eyes. He held it there and was able to connect deeply with Nimuë in this moment. Now he would source her knowing and the sight that belonged to them all, but which only those of the 'Way' could access. He would see through Nimuë's sight of what would come to pass and what they must do, if anything.

Nimuë spoke through the images that flooded Merlin, as they were common to both; she gave them shape, texture and direction.

"I will bear you a son, my lord, yet you must remain here in the underworld while I go forth and present him to our people to be fostered until his time comes. The land will suffer for many years and the people be not rested or at peace. Arthur will languish and not respond to your dreams; his unfaithful wife will desert him for a nunnery and her lover the madness of the woods. The fellowship of the Round Table you established will sustain the land and people during this time, though oft will be the Saxon insult.

"Yet it will be the internal disruption wrought by the new religion which will torment the land most. The people of the old ways will move to the country and the hollow hills. Oh, my lord! What shall we do when Arthur ignores your dreams! You will want to return, but I will not allow you. We must harness the power of the old ways at a deep level and pass them through to our son when he takes his rightful place at the Round Table under an ageing and ailing King, who is also contending with the usurper; Mordred, the bastard son of his union with his sister.

"Despair not, our time and place will come again. I will stay with you until my birthing time, when I must return to the women of my kind and deliver our son to the future."

The images that coursed through his vision matched perfectly the words of Nimuë. She had the sight and together their vision was powerful, the mandrake in the wine was working its magic well. At present it was a passive viewing of the future, though they had the potential to be actively involved in a manner beyond that which Merlin had achieved on his own; maybe that was why he felt dissatisfied with his success to date? He opened his eyes and looked at the still creature astride him. He closed them again and released his seed that would become their son, Parsifal.

Nimuë did return as promised after the birth and Merlin's dreams to Arthur fell on barren soil, as did the land. He yearned to return to his charge, yet Nimuë kept to her promise to keep him within this hollow hill. Time stood still as the world above moved on, yet they aged not. Nimuë told him of the progress of their son and they deepened their sight with acts of passion as well as their love.

In time Parsifal grew, took leave of his foster home and sought the path of knighthood. In this he was successful, honoured by the king and he took his place at the Round Table. The knights were ageing as was the king, the generation beneath them had not the strength or insight to seek the demands of knighthood, excepting Mordred's presence there, accepted by Arthur who knew one's enemies were less powerful when within sight. It weakened the alliance of the Table though, and all were aware of Mordred's association with the Saxon chiefs, who had wisely adopted the new religion. These were uneasy times.

Merlin could feel his vitality returning: Nimuë's retinue who allowed him free access to their bodies aided it. This was the way of the Goddess; sometimes Nimuë joined, sometimes she did not. At the time of the seasonal festivals, she joined him in sacred union as they continued to concentrate their abilities and intent. They visited their son with the sight and he began to feel a stirring in his heart; an intuition of what must be done. There was a sacred vessel that had been lost; its retrieval would heal the king, the land and sustain the people. It would move silently into the new religion, yet be the container of the old ways. It would pass as an undercurrent through time and history to emerge at times of crisis and danger for the land and its people. Some would see it as the vessel used by the god-man of the new religion as a way of acceptance. Those with the sight more truly understood it to contain the essence of the old ways. But where would he find this sacred vessel?

Nimuë and her three servants were priestesses of the Goddess in her union with the God. They formed a sacred family with Merlin, the lord. As god and goddess their role was to keep the cycles of existence nurtured, sustained and furthered. This was a function they grew into as they matured in skill and wisdom. The Goddess recognised the core of this to be sexual and encouraged its expression, yet always in the service of spirit.

At the sacred time of the fire festival that marked the end of autumn the veils between the worlds were most potent. Nimuë and her retinue entered into ritual with Merlin and the sight opened to them both once more. Merlin saw creation, out of the void of dark nothingness he saw and Nimuë verbalised the creation of being, vast eddies of energy that clashed between existence and non-existence. He saw the universe born and emerge within the place that prior had been nothingness. Worlds became manifest and the music of these spheres filled his sight. He felt himself on this one world that marked the centre and understood the fourfold pattern that stood behind all. He honoured and revered it.

He wept.

When he opened his eyes Nimuë and her three servants stood in front of him in the subdued candlelight, their forms heightened by the flickering fire beyond. Each held muslin, containing an unseen object of varying shape.

The servants revealed the first three:

The stone of the philosopher, which rightly sat beneath the coronation chair of the king and sustained the land.

The sword of the knight that held the land in place.

The staff of the wise man that brought counsel and knowledge to the ruler.

Nimuë came last and revealed the chalice of the heart that contained the royal blood and sustained humanity into a future supported by creation: although tools of man the Goddess stood silently behind and within them all.

These servants of the Goddess had retrieved the sacred objects when ignorance and misuse had emerged. Their source and creation was unknown and unknowable, yet together they held existence in place. They were now lost to mankind and Merlin's heart sank, although he understood this to have been the case prior to seeing them. Then hope was raised in his heart as he saw the dedication of the Goddess to once again present them to her errant children. Merlin also knew that in a dream Parsifal was having a vision of the chalice, yet was not yet ripe to ask what it beheld and so would wake in grief and tears.

The objects were laid at the four quarters that symbolised and held existence. The three women retired. Nimuë brought sacred clothing and they both dressed in silence. This sacred night they were the Goddess and God, the primal beings of existence. They faced each other and allowed their hands to join as each gazed into the eyes of the other, igniting the still point above, between and behind. They became as one, again, yet also with a sense of otherness. Tonight, this was to be transcended.

Hands moved over bodies. Tongues explored mouths, necks and crevices. Merlin laid Nimuë on the fur and took his fill of her nectar as she honoured and devoured his manhood. After a seeming endless play, they returned to each other's eyes. Merlin was above Nimuë as she held his head in her hands. He moved the last robe that veiled her and simply moved within. Their eyes remained connected and danced through creation. As the rhythm of their union built, they became as the primal forces of existence and non-existence into which they both dissolved with the release of all that was within each to become one.

The chalice was full of their passion. Each drank from it in remembrance of who they were and from whence they came. Nimuë stood, raised and showed Merlin the chalice one last time, then walked into the darkness, the womb of this hollow hill, to the still place that Parsifal would find.

Epilogue

There are several choices in the manner with which to explore a vast topic like sexuality and its association with the paranormal, and of course, much of the way the topic is tackled will be determined by personal predisposition. It is for this reason that I used the depth psychological movement of the last one hundred years or so as a starting point in the *Introduction* and have continued it a significant way in the later stories, expanding it to modern western medicine and healing more generally.

This orientation has further developed the topic by using major themes such as mythology and religion, or mysticism, to provide a broader and more encompassing perspective than you may have conceived prior to this book. The background of sexuality and the paranormal is then looked at from many different perspectives within the stories themselves, much as you would a multifaceted jewel.

From this variety of angles and possibilities there is the need to choose a more restricted viewpoint to undertake this reintegration; it would be appropriate for me to return to the discipline of depth psychology to do this. The obvious reason for this is that depth psychology is inclusive of many of the themes we have explored, particularly if the orientation of C.G. Jung and some of his followers is taken. This approach will necessarily overlap some of the points raised in the *Introduction*, but explore them further and in a more integrated context.

Yet for me there is a second over-riding reason, as well as a personal demand in this choice. I believe that depth psychology has not overcome a lot of divisions and schisms in its own ranks. Initially and at the very core of its emergence is the orientation toward the supernatural. In the nineteenth century there was much more of a co-existence between the emerging field of mental health and paranormal phenomena. There was extensive inquiry into this nexus with approaches such as hypnotism, mesmerism and the like, but with the emergence of the stricter scientific era this rapidly waned.

Psychiatry, an emerging discipline keen to establish itself within medicine, would increasingly view mental health disturbance in a scientific and rational way along the lines of the medical model and leading to its current status. Sigmund Freud, a medical neurologist, applied this model to the deeper phenomena exhibited by the mind (dreams, for example) to develop an approach that was inclusive of sexuality, but within an objective, scientific and largely pathological framework. I contend that sexuality demanded and demands such inclusion, but this was and is only one incomplete way to go about it.

This Freudian view is the one of sexuality that we have retained in the West, if we are looking from a medical, health or psychological perspective, in particular. Other disciplines had and have largely side-stepped the issue. Although Jung included religion and mystical disciplines in his life and work, he maintained a publicly professional demeanour as an empiricist and left sexuality largely to the Freudians. Reciprocally, Freud was quite dismissive of formal religion. The rise of the various scientific behaviourist approaches meant that the emerging academic and research discipline of psychology did likewise.

Wilhelm Reich began his professional career as a psychoanalyst of the Freudian school. He, like Jung before him, was to break ranks with the tradition. Unlike Jung, however, he maintained his professional interest in sexuality and took a far more directly physical and subjective approach that also extended to more therapeutic application. My impression is the Freudian approach of psychoanalysis may have served much in the way of scientific and academic inquiry, but its application as a therapy and hence efficacy in healing is remarkably limited.

By contrast Reich's approach has spawned a veritable legion of therapies, which have been embraced by the New Age and even some Eastern spiritual cults (the Rajneesh movement, for example). Reich's own refusal to accept a spiritual dimension to his life and work left him somewhat on the outer, as compared to Jung, for example. In my opinion, it has done most to damage his integration into the postmodern era of depth psychology. His movement into more paranormal fields with his investigation of Orgone Energy amplified this, with subsequent difficulties with US authorities (he died in prison) and questions over his sanity clouding the picture further, making his mainstream acceptance even more problematic and difficult.

This tour through a vast field is both simplified and personal, accented as it is towards the subject matter of this book. What you may conclude from this outline is that maybe Jung has the best overall model, because of his inclusion of the paranormal and the spiritual. Although his obvious paranormal interests and involvements seem confined to his early career, there is plenty of direct and indirect evidence that their influence remained strong and significant in the development of his ideas and psychology, somewhat hidden under his self-titled empiricist veneer. His exploration of spiritual disciplines, alchemy in particular, remains a significant overarching or supervening position to take toward sexuality and the paranormal. I would and will further contend that alchemy, in particular, will have much more to say in this regard.

The spiritualist undercurrents excluded from mental health and psychiatry are then more readily appreciated and integrated if a more Jungian framework is employed. But if he was relatively dismissive of sexuality in his psychology, then how can this be? Two indirect features bear comment. Like paranormality, sexuality was a strong feature in his personal life and interests, as well as its mystical associations, if various commentators are correct. Similarly, there is academic evidence that much of his work has been edited to exclude any such contentious material to his perceived and promoted professional and public image.

In a relative way I am left with Jung's overall approach, if not necessarily the content of his work. The discipline of alchemy will be included in my ongoing discussion and his theory of gender identity returned to (here and elsewhere), but it is his exploration of symbolism that made the most significant starting point in this present discussion. Reich may have future relevance, more from a therapeutic perspective and maybe with some discussion of his paranormal views and theories, but will be excluded from the present context. Freud has effectively put sexuality in a stream that does not integrate into our ongoing discussion, as it is too objective, scientific and medicalised.

One pioneer with a Jungian orientation, James Hillman, is inclusive of other depth psychological disciplines and the relevant trends of the nineteenth century. He is also grounded strongly in Greek thought and mythology, such that his view can be seen as more philosophical, artistic, even poetic and creative. Of interest he is the only non-medically trained of all the people discussed to date. He was to separate from Jung and his Analytical Psychology, calling his orientation Archetypal Psychology. Although not significantly inclusive of sex and the supernatural, his approach parallels many of the directions into these topics that I wish to engage from this point onward, as it takes image and symbolism as its ground: it is a soul-oriented approach, with which I resonate strongly.

It is my stated position that sexuality still has a long way to go in its reintegration within Western culture, in spite of the above direct and indirect attempts. There are some significant ramifications to this: In my own profession this failure has an impact on the way we view illness and disease, as well as the way professional relationships are conducted, such that I believe a new paradigm of medicine is required that is inclusive of sexuality in a broader and more creative context.

Medicine suffers this lack of integration generally, but the mental health professions do so more specifically. In spite of the above stated attempts in depth psychology and psychoanalysis, these tend to remain outside of mainstream psychiatry and psychology. This position is ably supported in the overall culture of the West; in many respects medicine and psychology require a broader, more holistic and interdisciplinary approach to effect any change. As a self-confessed polymath, and in other writings, I have attempted such an integrative approach with the accent toward health and healing; however, the Psychosexuality Series aims at this broader reintegration process and is directly inclusive of sexuality.

The core of this shift in thinking, or paradigm change, is to take an orientation that is more soul-centred. The concept of soul has been negated in the modern era, somewhat sidelined by religion, and ignored as a reality by science. Yet people such as Hillman have championed it's repositioning in Western culture and I readily and wholeheartedly support this; I see it is essential for the potential paradigm shifts of the post-modern era.

Our mundane day-to-day reality has been challenged by modern physics, but it is still retained; in physics, Quantum theory, Relativity, Chaos and String theories have a lot to teach us if interpreted from a psychospiritual perspective. We have a view of our existence confined between birth and death, ordered in time and space, and championed by cognition. We are constrained in the *Great Cycle of Existence* instead of being liberated by it. We exclude domains that challenge this view (sexuality) and bring it into serious question (paranormality), but if we take a more soul-oriented perspective such domains have a different relevance.

As our rather flatland worldview is literal, then the soul is symbolic; it is the world of image expressed as metaphor, paradox and in creative narrative. Soul transcends many of the definitions immediately above and helps illustrate and explain much that we need to exclude to sustain the flatland world-view. This is truly the world of the imagination, which must be seen as something different from the wish-fulfilling fantasy of flatland, and to extend into visionary and mystical experience. So, how about we approach the world of the supernatural as outlined in these stories from that perspective and see what might be revealed?

Paranormality suffers considerably at the hands of the rational flatland perspective. Science would dismiss it and certainly the inherent mercurial nature of the paranormal does not help such an outlook, especially when it is observed from such an objective, scientific, and fundamentally dismissive perspective. I have pointed out the inherent trickster nature of this reality and, in situations such as these, it is seen in full flight.

My personal experience of paranormal experience reinforces this, and as I am inclined to embrace the reality from which such phenomena emanate, then maybe I can also shed some varying light on the topic. Certainly, the trickster element is reinforced by the playfulness of many such experiences. I am also struck by the dreamlike experience of them. (I would add that I have a strong trickster element in my personality!)

For example, as a child I had a vision of (or *saw*) a UFO out of my bedroom window one night. It was circular, moved slowly in an arc, then changed direction and accelerated out of sight in a straight line. My response to this experience: I was not frightened, and it may be of interest that I did not tell anyone about it. To my memory the images of that night are clear, I am sure I was wide awake… but that may not have been the case? So, let me contrast this with one adult experience.

One day I was driving along a road past a large isolated hill that is both the southernmost point of Western Australia and forms one of three supposed connections to Gondwanaland, itself a subject of the myth versus reality debate. I could see shapes around the hill some distance away, so I stopped my car and looked again. There were several and they looked like flat oval discs hovering in the air. They were somewhat indistinct, although made clearer if I let my gaze go a little hazy. They also seemed to fluctuate in intensity, even inside or outside of my vision. At times it seemed I could influence their movement. I watched for a while, unperturbed, then simply drove off. There was no overwhelming emotional response, I simply felt peaceful and a little dreamy.

A product of my imagination? Surely. But a fantasy? I didn't and don't think so and I am – obviously – disinclined to take a deprecatory view of imagination: In fact, I give it a more elevated perspective than simple cognition, as you may have gathered by now. We're beyond flatland and in soul territory now; here imagination is a dominant feature. My experience felt fundamentally imaginative, I was not confusing it with the surrounding reality, but the state I was in was also somewhat different. When observers of UFOs describe their experience, it makes the state they were in easy to excuse and dismiss the content of their experience, I surmise.

Is this also true of the other paranormal experiences I have had? I now look through my list of such experiences and, yes, it is. Have I been in any particular psychological or emotional state at the time, or had a significant psychological trigger or trauma prior? Sometimes, but not usually. If I were to have it would be easy for the objective observer to put the experience into the fantasy, wish fulfilment, or escapist category. If severe, it could be the locked ward! Have I initiated them by my own actions? Not directly (except with sex – we'll get to this), but I have often been in a heightened state with mystical overtones. Have they changed me? In subtle ways, I believe so.

The outcome of all this? I think that paranormal experience should be viewed imaginatively and symbolically to make sense of it. I further think this is the language of the soul and we are firmly in this territory with paranormal experience. Were the experience to be in a dream we would have no such questions or difficulties (which also says a lot about dreams and our conventional attitude towards them), so how about seeing the supernatural state as moving into the dream consciousness of the soul in the waking state? I also invite you to look at the supernatural content of the stories in this light and that this symbolic language may have more to say about the situations the various protagonists find themselves in within the stories than a literal explanation could offer. It may also have a lot to say about any meaning of these experiences.

Finally, we come to the vexed question of the ultimate reality of such experience. By now it will be apparent that I consider a literal and scientifically objective view to be inappropriate, but is it wrong? Maybe it isn't, maybe it is simply very limited, so let me explain. I think a broader and more inclusive view is the imaginative perspective and for all the reasons outlined to date. I believe this allows us to position ourselves with respect to paranormal phenomena on their own terms, but who are 'they' if not just a product of our imagination as mere fantasy? What or whom are we communicating with? I feel we need a mystical perspective to even begin to cope with these sorts of questions, but here I would like to say that the imagination does engage a greater objective reality than our limited literal and rational perspective ever can. Further, that the imagination is the doorway to this reality.

Maybe these questions are better entertained by first introducing sexuality back into the discussion, so let me explore this pathway a little further. I'll start with personal experience. I have had paranormal experiences as a result of sexual activity, both with a partner and during masturbation. Of course, initially these experiences were spontaneous and seemed haphazard, although in hindsight the circumstances around the experiences were often heightened or otherwise exceptional.

These experiences are now actively pursued, although not routinely. I may disappoint you, but I am not going to take my personal experience further in this discussion. Why is this, you may ask? I don't think it is particularly relevant in the context of this present book and I do discuss it in a little more detail elsewhere (in *The Porn Users Guide to Enlightenment*), also I have only outlined two of my paranormal experiences above and neither are particularly related to the paranormal subject matter of the stories. Nor are the stories necessarily descriptive of my personal sexual experience in relation to the paranormal, although they patently reflect my creative imagination, which has some basis in the literal. I did tell you I had a trickster component to my personality, didn't I?

At times the sexual content of the stories is fairly blatant and comes from a particular perspective. I have tried to make the narrative descriptive in a way and to the point that you can readily imagine the scenes being portrayed, as if you were actually watching it. In this manner it can be compared to a pornographic movie and, indeed, a lot of the content reflects such material. However, in addition to this objective and even voyeuristic perspective is the inner and subjective one, which is described within the narrative. This is obviously not something portrayed readily in a pornographic movie and requires your imagination to now extend into a more visionary perspective, or beyond the pornographic to the erotic.

Both these inner and outer perspectives are relevant and, in some ways, parallel or reflect each other in a sympathetic fashion; the subjective-objective conundrum regarding paranormal experience we explored to some extent above. In this way sexuality can be seen to be a trigger or stimulus to the paranormal. Yet it is more than that, because it may also connect with the paranormal reality itself and be integrated with it. A brief example: my state after seeing the UFOs around the hill was similar to the post-coital state after a satisfying orgasm. This would put sexuality and the paranormal on some sort of continuum – or maybe part of an even larger one?

Rather than lapsing into Eastern views of this and employing a chakra model based on Kundalini and the gods/goddesses Shiva and Shakti, let me try and express this in a more Western idiom and one that relates to the *Great Chain of Being* – body, emotions, mind and spirit – of the perennial philosophy.

For this journey let me begin with the physical, the body. Here we have sexuality as instinct and something we have in common with the animal kingdom. One step above this on the spectrum is that of physical attraction, the 'love (read lust) at first sight' variety where a semblance of emotion is engaged and the sexual instinct is becoming humanised.

Now, of course, this is what routine pornography seeks to portray – and exploit. The general approach in pornography is to stimulate the sexual response with imagery – a statement in itself if the comments earlier about the imagination are considered – but in a way that remains confined to these levels of the spectrum. How does it do this? There are many ways, but chief amongst them would be to make the imagery relatively devoid of emotional content. Also, the use of fetish imagery would be directed toward the same end, maybe even enticing those inclined into further similar content and the road toward perversion.

Either way – and there are many other subtle mechanisms – the imagery remains base and therefore trapped, if an energetic perspective is considered. This is the genesis of addictions and perversions as well as all sorts of combinations thereof, and we will go no further down this path. I would point out that some pornography, and appreciably more erotic art, doesn't necessarily do this; it can employ imagery and acting in a fashion that can lead to the creative movement of the sexual impulse. It is not common, however, although I would point out that the attitude of the observer is important. If the observer is watching or reading such material to stimulate the imagination, then such material can be an adjunct. There is, of course, a danger in this and one the industry employs. Maybe a more enlightened view of masturbation and a mentor attitude from the elders in our modern culture would help this differentiation?

In *Sex and the Supernatural* the sexual imagery can be seen to be pornographic, or to stimulate the imagination in the above manner. Take your pick, but watch your prejudices! This is where the paranormal content comes in, as it is seen as a vehicle for this sexual energetic process to continue into the imaginative realms of the soul, of which the supernatural is an expression.

In summary: Try not to get lost in the sexual imagery. If I'd wanted this to be the outcome I would have simply depicted it more or less as would occur in a movie. How would I have kept you lost in the imagery? I would have employed extensive wording to support the basic image, but to maintain the energy there, in the manner of: "His calloused finger traced a slow arc over her delicate well-manicured yet soft pubic hair before inserting itself through the moist barrier of her cunt lips, wherein she gave a soft and seductive sigh of appreciation" ... sort of variety. If true poetry it may also get you beyond the circular instinctual level. But, if like routine pornography, it doesn't have that subtlety (and usually intends not to) then you can remain trapped. Also, if I were to have unnecessarily minimised the imagery, that could equally have been a trap, but of the restrictive and even masochistic variety by frustrating you.

However, I did not want to exclude the sexual imagery altogether, as one of the major aims of this book is the balanced reinstatement of sexuality in our Western culture. I know this is a fine line and a difficult one to judge, but if my attempts are seen in this context, maybe some of my other arguments extending from this premise can be better appreciated.

Many of the stories incite a significant emotional response. Further to the above, routine pornography seeks not to do this, because emotion takes the sexual energy into the soul realms. Indeed, aided by the paranormal content this emotional response to the sexual imagery makes the complex of sex, emotion, and the supernatural more completely parapsychological, hence also more integrated. This emotional response can be elaborated even further. As well as almost defining the sexual response as truly human, beyond the simple instinctual, as well as in the realms of the soul – which paranormality also describes according to our earlier discussion – it also connects us with the erotic.

Now here's a vexed term – eroticism – which is subject to the same flatland criticisms I have levied elsewhere, as we are commonly and currently taught to equate the erotic with base sexuality. Not so: that eroticism can include base sexuality is not in dispute; but it is much, much more than this and in partnership with the soul is the doorway to the mystical realms of sexuality. All this is reinforced in Greek mythology where the god Eros is the partner of Psyche (or Soul), lifting Psyche from the human to the divine realm. This is what eroticism can do for sexuality; lift it from the base instinctual into the soul realms and beyond, and as characterised by the emotional content.

Is this the end of the journey of the sexual instinct? A journey through the passions of sexual attraction and consummation, to the emotional realm of the soul, then the connection with the divine power of Eros and on to the realm of the gods? At the personal level it would be convenient to see it so. Here also, and as symbolised by the union of Psyche and Eros, do we have the ultimate union of the male and female, or the masculine and feminine principles?

In a relative way it is the end of the journey. As a result of this union, Psyche or soul is taken into the realm of the gods and achieves divine status beyond birth and death. This mystical realm is the completion of the ascent of the sexual instinct, where the ultimate union is portrayed as the elixir of life, élan vital, or in our Western culture as the Grail. It is reflected in the physical body with the higher hormonal glands in the brain, which are also associated with sexuality, vitality, longevity and rejuvenation.

The journey there can be arduous and not without its dangers, as the stories themselves illustrate. In most cultures and their associated mythology, this sexual power is considered to reside within the feminine – that is both in women and men – and which is portrayed in our stories, as indeed it is in mythologies worldwide. Yet not just in mythologies, it is also in spiritual systems of initiation that employ sexual techniques. That Tantra overtly displays these features, when the mystic cult of the goddess Shakti and the serpent power Kundalini are considered, indicates that we may have a similar pathway in our own culture from which we have been disconnected within the Christian era.

The Grail attempts to restore some of this balance by connecting us back to pre-Christian elements within our own traditional background, as well as connecting it to the mystical Grail. There are many who would see the latter in a directly sexual context, such as a womb. I have chosen not to, as I see it more appropriately symbolising the union of masculine and feminine at an exalted level where neither gender dominates. Indeed, it represents their ultimate union. That it is also a symbol of rejuvenation is also significant.

I would suggest that Alchemy is one such tradition. The mundane image of making gold from base metals is a literal interpretation of a symbolic reality; that is, making our inner gold, or our own spiritual transformation. Jung has had much to say and do in the reinstatement of this mystical dimension with his explorations from a psychological angle. Here I would simply add that there is a sexual pathway in Alchemy that matches that of the left-hand – magical – path of Tantra and employs sexuality in actual ritual and initiatory practice.

Alchemy can be read entirely in this manner, which is probably one reason why its secrets are so well disguised or obscured, as it would be available to the might of the conventional Church in the manner of Witchcraft. Alchemy, read in this light, sees the ultimate union of masculine and feminine in the image of the androgyne, yet another reflection of the Grail and rejuvenation.

It would be tempting to leave this work here, but I'm a trickster, remember? So, I'm going to leave you with a couple of themes that you might find a little unsettling.

The first is an extension of the paranormal argument about the ultimate reality of the material engaged. I posit that the literal approach is the first level and the second the imaginative. I suggest that the second can be seen as the territory of the soul, of a dreamlike quality and symbolic. I also suggest that the mystical level this points to may be an objective reality, the nature and mystery of which we cannot fully appreciate, and which the paranormal reality may be an initiation in – as well as transforming our attitudes in the literal world.

So, what if this applies equally well to sexuality, as the analogue approach would have it? When I engage in – say – a masturbatory fantasy that expands to an imaginative and magical experience, is the man or woman I engage with therein real or simply imagined? Does he or she have an independent existence to my imagination? And what if he or she is someone who also exists in daily reality? I'll leave this viewpoint there for the time being; there's plenty more for the Psychosexuality Series to explore and rituals, rites of passage, and initiations have only been touched on; except in the stories, of course, which are imaginative… is your head spinning yet?

The second theme demands a section of its own and is hinted at quite strongly in the tale *Madness*.

In one sense the literal world could be seen to be governed by the Greek god Apollo, the god of light, beauty and the Sun. His counterpart? Dionysus, the god of all things seemingly opposite to this, as well as the vine, madness… and much more. Of course, these two gods are not seen as opposing, but in paradoxical relationship as symbolised by the eternity symbol (the numerical figure eight on its side). In ancient Greece there was a cult to Dionysus and it was populated by women, with many of these features being reflected in the story, although the Dionysian mysteries extend well beyond this simple tale.

Why should I bring Dionysus up at this point? Partly because originally the *Madness* story did not sit well for me in the general outline of the stories and themes; but I also had a strong sense that it needed to be included, in spite of some of its more uncomfortable themes. Some of these have become obvious, such as the issue of multiple personality, but others not so readily so. Some people I have read the story to and who are unfamiliar with the myth are a little unsettled by the conclusion.

Maybe I'm a little more than the trickster of Hermes, maybe there's an element of the Dionysian in my personality? If so, what is it saying here, about the book and also about this dimension of the mystical, particularly with reference to sexuality? (I mention the last point because other stories, such as *The Pirate* contained some prefiguring themes.) It would be nice to bring together the various themes and their explorations under a comfortable structure, inclusive of the sexual and supernatural, finally to be packaged in some transpersonal or mystical superstructure. Well, a Dionysian perspective doesn't exactly destroy this superstructure, but it does place it on a slightly uncomfortable footing and probably supersedes it. Dionysus is an enigmatic figure even in mythology and he will be the subject of future work, so wide is his presence, significance and influence, and particularly his relevance in the post-modern era.

In many ways Dionysus can be related to Shiva, who was the primordial supreme god in the Hindu pantheon. Shiva was subsequently placed in the triad of Brahma, Vishnu and Shiva as the Creator, Sustainer and Destroyer respectively. Yet enigmatically he is the supreme god of Tantra, with whom Shakti unites in an exalted state of mystical consciousness. How do we explain this paradox of supremacy and destruction?

Not easily it would seem, and the parallels between Shiva and Dionysus are extensive, indicating an archetypal figure that preceded the separation of cultures and nations. Indeed, Dionysus is a god of the agricultural cycle and connected with the mysteries of birth, sex and death that demarcate it as well as define the Great Cycle of Existence. The paradox of death should be born in mind when we consider destruction, as here it intimates the precursor state to rebirth… a profound mystery. Indeed, Dionysus formed the basis of a mystery cult in Greece (and continues do so with Tantra in his Shiva-esque guise), somewhat dominated by women.

Other associated characteristics are that of wine. At one level marking nature and the agricultural cycle, but another the principle of ecstasy, altered states of consciousness and mystical experience. Another was that Dionysus oversaw mystery rituals that included death by dismemberment (often token in the form of flagellation – recalling sadomasochism), which is also a feature of the shamanic visionary state and is a precursor to rebirth and transformation, as well as orgiastic sexual activity. Maybe this puts the complex and orgiastic imagery of pornography into a different light?

I mention all of this because these images touch profoundly on fear, chaos, destruction and madness, with their paradoxical relationship with opposing and more apparently appealing Apollonian states. For example, Dionysus rules pleasure, Apollo security: although not strictly opposites from a rational and logical perspective, maybe psychologically they are. It also puts ecstasy in a complex and enigmatic light, which is also a feature of shamanism. These are all primal and existential levels to human existence, which the Dionysian archetype engages challengingly and directly. At the mystical level Dionysus takes us into an orgiastic state beyond our fear and characterised in this ecstatic realm by chaos, madness and death.

Maybe this is the ultimate journey beyond all opposites to the source of being and symbolised by the mythical dragon? Maybe it also illustrates to us how we should engage such issues in our own time, up to and including pornography?

Pornography and the erotic at some level a pathway to the highest levels of exalted mystical consciousness? Now there's a challenge!

About Drew Wynn

Drew Wynn has spent his life pre-occupied with sex, for which he makes absolutely no apology. In this book Drew presents a distillation of his ideas and feelings regarding sexuality and its relationship to varied states of consciousness in a creative and fictional manner. He anticipates this work will spawn a lineage of writing and other creative output in this exciting field.

Whilst this work approaches sexuality from a seemingly unusual perspective and with the use of fiction, it will demonstrate that sexuality is far more varied than we are given to think and this represents just one avenue that it can flow into. Future works will continue this relationship between sexuality and other cultural and health fields, such as pornography, religion, creativity and medicine.

An academic and professional with a profound interest in mental and spiritual health, Drew has extensively explored differing cultural and historical perspectives of illness and health. This background has allowed him to see the dysfunctional perspective Western culture has toward sexuality and the void that exists in regards to its place in health, illness and disease.

Drew believes that we need to move beyond these cultural distortions and that medicine in the West needs a reintegration of sexuality from more than the objective, scientific and even demeaning position it has gained in recent generations. He further sees as fundamental and more than a coincidence that the spiritual bereftness of the West parallels the lack of integration of our sexuality.

www.ingramcontent.com/pod-product-compliance
Lightning Source LLC
Chambersburg PA
CBHW032050020426
42335CB00011B/275